STARS
AND
SCARS

About the Author

Jeff Jones was born in London's East End and has been part of the boxing scene there for decades. He has been researching the history of boxing for many years. He is the author of *East End Born and Bled: The Remarkable Story of London Boxing.*

STARS
AND
SCARS

THE STORY OF JEWISH BOXING IN LONDON

Jeff Jones

AMBERLEY

First published 2023

Amberley Publishing
The Hill, Stroud
Gloucestershire, GL5 4EP

www.amberley-books.com

Copyright © Jeff Jones, 2023

The right of Jeff Jones to be identified as
the Author of this work has been asserted in
accordance with the Copyright, Designs and
Patents Act 1988.

ISBN 978 1 3981 0956 8 (paperback)
ISBN 978 1 3981 0957 5 (ebook)

British Library Cataloguing in Publication Data.
A catalogue record for this book is available
from the British Library.

1 2 3 4 5 6 7 8 9 10

Typesetting by SJmagic DESIGN SERVICES, India.
Printed in the UK.

CONTENTS

KEY LONDON BOXING LOCATIONS

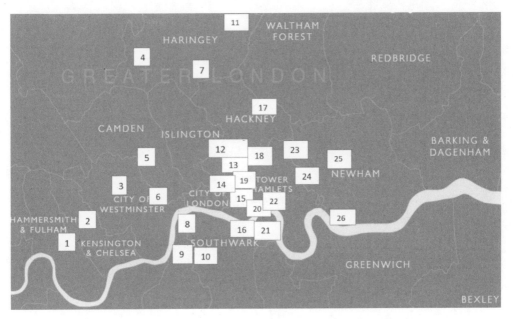

CURRENT WEIGHT DIVISIONS

Minimum weight	105 pounds (48 kg)
Light flyweight	108 pounds (49 kg)
Flyweight	112 pounds (51 kg)
Super flyweight	115 pounds (52 kg)
Bantamweight	118 pounds (53.5 kg)
Super bantamweight	122 pounds (55 kg)
Featherweight	126 pounds (57 kg)
Super featherweight	130 pounds (59 kg)
Lightweight	135 pounds (61 kg)
Super lightweight	140 pounds (63.5 kg)
Welterweight	147 pounds (67 kg)
Super welterweight	154 pounds (70 kg)
Middleweight	160 pounds (72.5 kg)
Super middleweight	168 pounds (76 kg)
Light heavyweight	175 pounds (79 kg)
Cruiserweight	200 pounds (91 kg)
Heavyweight	unlimited

There are now seventeen weight divisions in boxing; 150 years ago there were just two weight divisions, light and heavy. The National Sporting Club increased the number of divisions for professional boxers to eight from around 1908. References to the 'lighter weights' means the weight divisions from flyweight to featherweight. References to the 'middle weights' means the divisions from lightweight to middleweight. 'Heavier weights' obviously covers light heavyweight, cruiserweight and heavyweight.

INTRODUCTION

I'll hold my hands up straight away. As a gentile I am as guilty as many of my kind in believing that sport is one area in which Jews do not excel. I know all about the great Jewish names in the entertainment and business worlds. They produced not only the world's greatest physicist, but also some of its foremost philosophers as well as one of its greatest mathematicians. Jewish household names in sport though? No, not really, I thought. Why is that? Growing up in the East End of London just after the war, there were still Jewish families around in the area. I knew a couple of Jewish lads, I was friendly with one, but none of them were particularly sporty.

It was in 2016 that I first started researching the sport of boxing and the part it played in the development of London. That research led to the publication of my first book on the subject, *East End Born and Bled*. During my research on London boxing, it was impossible not to realise the significance of boxing to London's working classes and particularly to two of the immigrant communities that grew up in the capital from the eighteenth through to the twentieth century.

By the 1950s, much of the Jewish population that had inhabited the heart of the East End of London for the better part of 200 years had gradually prospered and moved on. In my time there in the 1950s, the Gants Hill area of Ilford in Essex along with Stamford Hill and Golders Green in North London became the new Whitechapel, Aldgate and Bethnal Green. I had very little knowledge of the large, close-knit inner-city Jewish communities that my father would have known when he was a young man living in East London. History shows that the Jews were a persecuted race and consequently, in part, a nomadic one. Jewish communities could be found scattered around the globe, going back hundreds of years. Much of the time they lived on the margins of mainstream society in many countries. They tended to keep themselves to themselves. It was no surprise, then, that I had not come across many great Jewish sportsmen and women – I had developed a blinkered view of Jewish sporting history.

In my younger years I had only come across a couple of Jewish footballers, a few boxers and a well-known swimmer, so it came as quite a surprise when I discovered just how many great Jewish athletes there have been down the years, from all around the world. To prove the point, answer me this. Have you ever heard of Agnes Keleti? Unlikely, I would think, but Agnes, a Hungarian Jew, is considered by most experts to be one of the greatest female gymnasts of all time. She won ten Olympic medals, including five golds, in the 1950s. Only Mark Spitz, the aforementioned swimmer, has won more Olympic gold medals as a Jewish Olympian.

I also suspect that very few would have heard of Richard Bergmann, but he was a multi-world champion table tennis player and is considered to be the greatest exponent of the sport in its history. Bergmann won seven world championships including four singles, two doubles and a team title, and dominated the sport either side of the war. He was Austrian, and in 1938 he moved to England in the face of the rise of fascism.

Alright, you may not have heard of Keleti or even Bergmann; and some may say of Mark Spitz that he was indeed a truly great swimmer but an amateur just the same. How about a giant global professional Jewish superstar? Do any come near to matching that particular description? Well, indeed they do. There are a few from this country, and three come from London – East London in fact. Two are boxers but the other is a footballer. David Beckham is Jewish in the maternal line and proudly considers himself half-Jewish. He is a global star and was born in Leytonstone E11. We will come to the boxers that carry that particular mantle a little later.

You may also be surprised to learn that another extremely well-known British Jewish sportsman was the gruff and belligerent Yorkshire cricketer Freddie Trueman. Freddie was one of the world's greatest fast bowlers and had a big personality to go with it. A typical gritty Yorkshireman through and through, he was half-Jewish as well. Athlete Harold Abrahams, on whom the film *Chariots of Fire* is based, is another great Jewish champion. There is no doubting their sporting prowess or competitiveness.

In fact, it is hard to believe that, despite Jesse Owens' remarkable exploits during the 1936 Berlin Olympics, the media in general still viewed great achievements by both black and Jewish competitors in many sports as something of a rarity for so long. In 1956, little-known Angela Buxton from Liverpool and Althea Gibson from America won the ladies' tennis doubles championship at Wimbledon. A British newspaper of the day carried the headline 'Minorities win famous tennis victory'. Althea Gibson was black and Angela Buxton was Jewish.

Although my earlier book included boxers from all backgrounds, it was clear to me that Jewish boxers, in terms of numbers, played a major part in the London boxing scene up until the mid-twentieth century. It is also clear that two countries have produced the greatest number of Jewish boxing champions: the United States and the United Kingdom. During the first part of the twentieth century, excellent Jewish boxers could be found all across the US, from coast to coast. Examples include world heavyweight champion Max Baer, middleweight world champ Al McCoy, lightweight champs Benny Leonard and Battling Levinsky, and featherweight Kid Kaplin.

Possibly the best of the earlier American Jewish boxers was Barney Ross (Rasofsky). A brilliant amateur who was an American Golden Gloves champion in the 1920s, Ross went on to become a professional world champion at three different weights and was considered the first Jewish boxer to use his fame to promote the Jewish cause stateside. Many years before America's entry into the Second World War, Ross was aware of what was going on in Germany. From the late 1930s he was vociferous in his support of the Jewish race and quick to denounce the Nazi regime in Germany as well as its supporters in America. He became a very popular figure with all Americans, galvanising the Jews to fight back against prejudice and leading by example both inside and outside the ring. After retiring from boxing, he enlisted in the US Marines and fought in the Pacific theatre of war. His actions during the Battle of Guadalcanal earned him a Silver Star, a Purple Heart and a Presidential Unit Citation.

In Britain, the start of the fightback against anti-Semitism started 150 years before the efforts of Ross. Again, it was the sport of boxing that led the way. During the late eighteenth and nineteenth centuries, London became the breeding ground for boxers of all faiths. For Jewish boxers it all started in Aldgate, Whitechapel, deep in London's East End, on 5 July 1764.

I

PRIDE AND PUGILISM

It is a truth universally acknowledged that a fit young man in possession of quick hands and feet, sound ringcraft and a will to win can achieve fame and fortune in the noble art of pugilism.

From biblical times, the history of the Jewish race has been beset by long periods of persecution. Driven away from the lands of their origin, they have settled in various parts of the world only to be persecuted again. Their plight in Europe is well documented, but to many it may come as a surprise that the first country in Europe to expel Jews en masse was England.

At the time of the Norman invasion, Jewish communities could be found all over Europe and England was no exception. Allowed to settle by William the Conqueror, from the late eleventh century onwards the Jewish community quickly became an essential part of the English economy. Jewish settlements in important towns such as London, Norwich and Lincoln prospered. In London, they settled in an area near to where the Bank of England now stands and the nearby thoroughfare, still called Old Jewry, is a reminder of those early Jewish settlers. England's Jews were skilled individuals who worked as doctors, goldsmiths and traders. Lending money was one of their primary sources of income, and Jewish people were fundamental to the working of the English economy for this reason; they were permitted to loan money at interest, something Christians were forbidden from doing. Jewish lenders provided loans for many of the most important figures at the royal court for the purchase of land, castles and payment of taxes and dues to the king. They were also exploited by rulers, who were often in dire need of funds.

Jewish communities in England were largely protected by the reigning monarch of the day until the time of the Crusades, when Catholic religious zealots began to question the power and position of the Jews in this country. Encouraged in some cases by priests, several attacks were made on Jewish communities. Around 1185 their situation worsened when Henry II tried to levy heavy taxes on the Jews to fund his military campaigns. Enforcing these new taxes resulted in worsening relationships between the Jews and the landowners and barons, who in turn were asked to pay back more money on the loans they had been given by the Jewish lenders. The situation came to a head with the 'York Massacre' of Jews in 1190 shortly after the death of Henry, when the country was in transition following the coronation of Richard I. The Crown did step in to control the situation but tensions between the common folk and the Jewish community continued.

During the following century, the Jewish communities continued to eke out a living under the devout Richard the Lionheart and then Edward I, but the financial position of most Jews deteriorated. In 1275, Edward curtailed the business activities of the Jews still further by introducing restrictions on their trading and by 1290 the relationship between the king and the English Jewry became untenable when their taxes went unpaid. Virtually all Jews, nearly 4,000 in all, were rounded up and expelled from England by the end of the year. No Jew openly set foot in the country again until Oliver Cromwell relaxed immigration restrictions in 1665.

The persecution of Jews in mainland Europe and the Middle East was still evident during Cromwell's time, so gradually a trickle of Jewish immigrants started to arrive in Britain. In London, a small Jewish community settled in the Whitechapel and Spitalfields area of the capital at the turn of the eighteenth century. These were the Marrano Jews, who originated from the Iberian area of south-western Europe. The Marranos were part of the larger set of Sephardic Jews, who had populated Spain and some parts of Portugal since the twelfth century and for many years enjoyed life there and were free to practise their religion. Gradually, though, in Spain particularly, pressures were applied to try to integrate these people into the wider Catholic society. Some converted – willingly or otherwise – but some stayed true to their original faith.

Things changed dramatically in 1492, when the Spanish Grand Inquisitor Torquemada ordered the Marranos to convert to Catholicism or risk expulsion or even death under the infamous Spanish Inquisition. Many did convert, but some carried on practising the Jewish faith secretly. By the late sixteenth century, the Marranos were generally regarded as 'Convertos' or 'Crypto-Jews'. Those who failed to conform to these ideals eventually moved on. One such example was the Mendoza family, who found their way to an increasingly liberal England.

Aaron De Mendoza, who was born in Portugal in 1708, arrived in Whitechapel in London with his family around 1720, settling there and prospering in the area. In July 1764, one of Aaron's many grandchildren was born. His name was **Daniel Aaron Mendoza**. Aaron himself died in 1751, so did not see his grandson Daniel grow up to become one of the greatest names in the history of boxing.

Daniel Mendoza was born in Aldgate, Whitechapel, in 1764, one of nine children of Abraham and Esther Mendoza. A bright lad, he found work reasonably easily. He was also acutely aware of the aggressive anti-Semitism that prevailed in the area, so in his early teenage years he approached Jack Broughton, one of the great exponents of the sport of bare-knuckle pugilism. Known as the 'Father of English Boxing', Broughton held boxing sessions in West London and the young Daniel was interested in being taught by the great man.

Broughton had developed some new techniques, and Mendoza thought he could develop them to help smaller men take on larger opponents. He introduced better footwork and movement around the ring. He also studied the human body to identify areas that could be targeted to greater effect. Whilst still young he worked and trained with other notable fighters of the day, including Richard Humphreys, with whom he was later to fight three epic matches. To fund his progress in the sport he worked hard, mainly in retail and other services in the East End of London. It was while working in a tea shop that he first put his skills to the test when he fought an aggressive youth who had insulted his Jewish employer and her faith.

Daniel Mendoza's family had continued to practise their faith after arriving in the East End, and they regularly attended the Bevis Marks Synagogue in the City of London, close to St Mary Axe. The synagogue, still active today, was built in 1701 to provide the Sephardic Jews with a place of worship. Attending frequently, Daniel Mendoza grew up with a strong Jewish faith. Athleticism, in particular heavy contact sports like boxing, was not a part of the Jewish tradition. Although some rabbis encouraged ball playing, calisthenics and moderate exercise to promote health, Jewish people were generally advised to avoid violence, preoccupation with the body, sensuality and physical force. Instead, they were encouraged to cultivate learning, intellect, and spiritual values.

In his early years in the sport, Mendoza would have probably found it difficult to reconcile his love of the sport with the

Jewish teachings. Fortunately, Daniel was practising what was termed the 'noble art' and was introducing a more scientific approach to the sport. He did not think that it was something particularly elevated that he was doing, but he certainly did not regard this early form of boxing as mere physical, thuggish aggression. He spent most of his adult life defending his faith to the hilt, and so it was that the poor unsuspecting youth who spat anti-Semitic vitriol at his employer was the first to witness, at first hand, Mendoza's version of the noble art.

Further unregulated fights for Daniel followed, mainly as a result of anti-Semitism. In 1798, after a bout against a local coal merchant, he fought his first organised and publicised prize-fight in Barnet, North London against Sam Martin, 'the Bath Butcher'. Martin was a loud-mouthed anti-Semite, making him a perfect opponent for the dangerous Mendoza. He was also a very experienced boxer, but Mendoza produced a masterclass of boxing to defeat the larger man. Watching was the Prince of Wales, who heartily congratulated Mendoza and praised his boxing skills. Young Daniel was on his way. For his first few organised prize-fights, the older Richard Humphreys acted as his 'second'. Mendoza's later fights against Humphreys were to define and cement his reputation in the sport.

As we have seen England was not a particularly comfortable place for Jews, who regularly faced discrimination. Like present-day minorities, young Jews turned to boxing as a way to gain respect and disprove stereotypes. Then, as now, boxing was a way out of the ghetto. As Jeffrey T. Sammons wrote in *Beyond the Ring*, 'Discriminated against at all levels of society and ridiculed for their appearance, language, and manner, some Jews turned to boxing as a way to earn respect, a sense of belonging, and, for a few, money.'

Mendoza fought at a time when the influential rabbi David Levi was gaining respect as a great orator and defender of the Jewish faith in Britain. After Mendoza's impressive defeat of Richard Humphreys in 1789, a published print of that prize-fight was footnoted with the caption: 'The Christian pugilist proving himself as inferior to the Jewish hero, as Dr Priestly, when opposed to the rabbi, David Levy' (a reference to that pair's debates). His third and final defeat of Richard ('Dicky') Humphreys inspired a drinking song that expresses the change in attitudes to the Jewish fighter:

My Dicky was all the delight of half the genteels in the town;
Their tables were scarcely compleat, unless my Dicky sat down;
So very polite, so genteel, such a soft complaisant modest face,
What a damnable shame to be spoil'd by a curst little Jew from
    Duke's Place!
O my Dicky, my Dicky, and O my Dicky my dear!

... He contemptuously viewed his opponent, as David was viewed
    by Goliath.
O my Dicky, my Dicky, and O my Dicky my dear!

... Now Fortune, the whimsical goddess, resolving to open men's
    eyes;
To draw from their senses the screen, and excite just contempt
    and surprise,
Produced to their view, this great hero, who promis'd Mendoza to
    beat,
When he proved but a boasting imposter, his promises
    all a mere cheat.
O my Dicky, my Dicky, and O my Dicky my dear!

For Dicky, he stopt with his head,
Was hit through his guard ev'ry round, Sir
Was fonder of falling than fighting,
And therefore gave out on the ground, Sir.

Mendoza officially became Britain's sixteenth heavyweight champion, and during both his boxing career and his lifetime he achieved a number of notable firsts. On becoming heavyweight champion, he became the first boxer of middleweight size to win the heavyweight title. He was the world's first Jewish champion. He was the first to use his foot movement in conjunction with his fists. And he was called the 'father of Scientific Boxing' because of the thought he put into which area of the body to attack to gain the best results. He had exceptional ringcraft.

Outside of the ring Mendoza was the first Jew to teach and write books and articles on the subject of boxing. He was also the first Jew and possibly the first sportsman to write an autobiography. Furthermore, he was the first of his race to mix with British royalty and talk at length to a reigning monarch. Without doubt, he elevated the status of the London Jewish community. The Jewish boxing story in London started with Daniel Mendoza.

Unfortunately, despite a glittering and ground-breaking career, Mendoza died in poverty. Indeed, the same fate beset most of his eleven offspring, a couple of whom fell foul of the law and ended up being transported to Australia. One of his more distant relations fared better, however, becoming a policeman of note and a French one at that – Inspector Clouseau! Peter Sellers is a direct descendant of Daniel Mendoza.

Apart from boxing, Jewish men excelled in gymnastics and fencing. The latter, a spectacle that at one time could be witnessed in a forest glade at dawn between two men as a way of settling an argument, had gradually disappeared by the early nineteenth century. It had, though, survived as a 'closed' sport, still fairly popular in London during the first part of the century. So called

'Sporting Booths' remained evident in London and featured fencing as well as boxing and cock-fighting.

In 1789, at the age of ten, Amsterdam-born **Isaac Bitton** moved with his parents to London. As a young teenager, Bitton started to fence and by his late teens was quite proficient. He would have entered competitions in these multi-event arenas. By the turn of the nineteenth century, boxing was becoming more popular as fencing started to wane somewhat in popularity. At the age of twenty-one Bitton decided to start boxing and in 1801, aged twenty-two, he had his first taste of prize-fighting.

Bitton's fights were notable for their length. In his first fight he took on Tom Jones from Paddington in a match that lasted forty-four rounds. Bitton came out as the victor. Several more lengthy fights followed over the next couple of years. He then fought George Maddox in 1804 in a much-anticipated match. They were hard to split and fought out a staggering seventy-four-round draw. His last fight was also shaping up to be a long-drawn-out affair until the thirty-sixth round, when several Bow Street Runners arrived to stop the fight and disperse the crowd.

The authorities were beginning to curb the excesses of bare-knuckle fighting and for a time it was made illegal to prize-fight in London. After this, Bitton fought some exhibition matches but retired from the sport to set up an athletics school in Whitechapel where he gave lessons in both fencing and boxing. London was starting to produce large numbers of prize-fighters, and East London gave rise to the next great Jewish champion heavyweight. By pure coincidence, this next champion had something in common with Isaac Bitton.

Samuel Elias was born in Aldgate in 1775, but both his parents were Dutch. As a result of this, he became known as 'Dutch Sam'. So, both Bitton and Sam had links to the Netherlands. They also both won their first prize-fight in 1801. Dutch Sam, though, went on to fight about a hundred matches. Sam Elias was one of several boxers who developed their technique under the tutelage of the great Daniel Mendoza, and he also developed new moves in the ring. Like Mendoza he was on the small side, and like him he was proud of his religion. He developed the use of the uppercut, enabling lighter and smaller boxers to compete more with the bigger pugilists of the day. At the peak of his career, he was known as 'the Terrible Jew' as a result of his fairly extensive use of this vicious uppercut blow. He readily accepted his nickname and promoted it with pride.

Elias had some very memorable fights during his career. His three fights against reigning champion Tom Belcher were described by many as some of the best-contested and most skilful battles ever witnessed. Elias was seconded by Daniel Mendoza in all these fights and under his watchful eye was to became another English champion boxer. He lost only two fights, including his final match against Bill Noseworthy in 1814. Toward the end of his fighting life, he started to drink heavily and died in 1816. Sam produced a son, **Young Sam Elias,** who also boxed and became an English champion. Young Sam was technically a fine boxer but he had some brutal fights that took their toll. His fight against Dick Davis in 1827 lasted over three and a half hours, one of the longest on record. The Eliases were one of two father/son national champions. However, like his father before him Young Sam also started to drink heavily. He fell in with some very dubious company and served a short sentence for assaulting a police officer. He too died at a fairly early age, in 1843.

As the popularity of boxing increased throughout the early part of the nineteenth century, boxers became more evenly matched when prize-fights were divided into lightweight and heavyweight bouts. The first great lightweight boxer was once again a Jewish boxer from London.

Barney Aaron (Snr) was born in Aldgate in November 1800. Aaron was another staunchly proud Jew, so much so that in

One of a series of satirical images featuring eighteenth- and nineteenth-century boxers. This one is a Dutch Sam fight. The 'seconds' in those days followed their fighters around the ring, issuing instructions.

his later life he was prepared to fight and die for his religion outside of the ring and became known as the 'Star of the East'. Details on his early life are sketchy, but it is thought that he had some unregulated street fights in his teenage years before his first recognised match in 1819 against William Connolly, whom he beat over sixteen rounds under the 'Broughton Rules'.[1]

His next match he lost to another good London Jewish boxer, Manny Lyons, after a gruelling seventy rounds. Aaron was one of the smaller lightweights and Manny was one of the heavier ones, and while Aaron boxed very well he had to retire after being unable to raise his bruised and battered arms due to sheer exhaustion. That fight underlined Aaron's grit and determination, and he went on to dominate the lightweight boxing scene for the next ten years. He fought some of the best around, including Ely Bendon and Ned Stockton, and he became the English lightweight champion. Other notable Jewish bare-knuckle fighters who boxed extensively during this period were Londoners Solomon Reubens, Aaron Moss and Izzy Lazarus.

Barney Aaron's victory over one of the leading contenders of the day, Peter Warren, on 6 April 1824 confirmed him as one of the best lightweight boxers of the era. In a gruelling fight, most of the first half was evenly contested but Warren was thrown down heavily in the thirteenth round. After leading the second half of the match, in the twenty-ninth round, Aaron sent Warren to the canvas from a blow to the head that resulted in a knockout. London's *Morning Chronicle* wrote that 'Barney has shown himself to be one of the best of his weight'.

During Aaron's career, bare-knuckle boxing was extremely popular around London and some of the bigger fights tended to be staged on the outskirts of London in an effort to keep clear of the Bow Street Runners. Just to the north of Barnet was an area known as 'No Man's Land'. It was a popular venue for prize-fighting. It is thought that it got its name through its association with the exploits of the infamous highwaywoman, Lady Katherine Ferrers, who was adept at relieving gentlemen travellers of their money as they were on their way north through that area. She was mortally wounded there in 1660.

Aaron was at the height of his abilities when he faced the experienced Dick Hare in No Man's Land in 1826. Even before the match, arguments had broken out between the two parties over the purse split and the number of supporters that each fighter had attending. The fight itself was a one-sided affair in favour of the younger Aaron, with Hare becoming very vocal and complaining that he had been hit with a low blow in the forty-first round. The referee did not agree and Hare left the ring. He did not return but still claimed the match. A war of words was entered into and it took several days before Aaron was officially declared the winner and the prize money was paid.

By 1830, Aaron's boxing was declining and he fought and lost his last fight to Tom Smith in 1834. Throughout his career Aaron championed not only the Jewish faith but also the working-class poor of the East End. During the early 1840s the growing Jewish community was joined by large numbers of Irish immigrants who were fleeing from Ireland in the wake of the Potato Famine. Although the two communities did not share the same religion, they did share a reduced social standing.

Aaron met many influential people and became quite friendly with Lionel de Rothschild, a philanthropist who took a special interest in the position of the nation's jewry and the capital's working-class inhabitants. Plans were hatched for Rothschild to stand for Parliament, representing the City of London, which in those days included some of the western areas of the East End. The 1847 election in London was marred by claims and counterclaims by the various candidates and feelings began to run high, with some violence breaking out. Aaron and fellow Jewish boxer Abraham Belasco led a lightly armed band of followers patrolling and protecting the streets of London's East End in support of Rothschild.

Rothschild won a resounding victory, but Parliamentarians had to commit to Christian ideals and the Jewish Rothschild refused to do so. His family was hugely wealthy and influential, and pressure was brought to bear on the government to amend the rules on non-Christians becoming Members of Parliament. This petition was originally rejected but later the rule was amended and eventually Rothschild, having been elected four times to Parliament but never previously attending, finally took his seat in Parliament in 1858. The first openly Jewish Member of Parliament, he worked alongside future Prime Minister Benjamin Disraeli, who earlier had to relinquish his Jewish faith in order to take a seat in Parliament.

Aaron lived all his fifty-eight years in East London and died in Whitechapel in 1868. In later life he worked as a police constable and also made a little money in the fish trade. Barney had a son, Barney Aaron Jnr, whom he taught to box. The young Barney started boxing as an amateur and became a decent prospect, but when he was eighteen he emigrated to America where he boxed in bare-knuckle prize-fights. He improved greatly in America and became a lightweight champion. Like his father, Barney junior was a proud Jew and never disguised that fact from his audience. He became quite a celebrity and helped raise the profile of American Jews. In recognition of this and as an acknowledgement of his father back in London, he was known as 'the Star of the West'. The Aarons are the only example of a father and son holding national championship titles in different countries.

Abraham Belasco, the aforementioned brother-in-arms to Barney Aaron, never reached the heights of his comrade but nevertheless had a very decent career. Aby, as he was known, was a protégé of fellow Sephardic Jew and near neighbour Daniel Mendoza, and the pair remained firm friends for many years. In their later years they also toured together in England and Scotland, giving boxing exhibitions and being matched against the local champions. Aby boxed at the heavier end of lightweight and was quite successful in his early bouts. In a much-publicised match, he defeated Jack 'the Butcher' Payne in sixteen rounds, but it was his next two matches against the tough Tom Reynolds and the great English champion Jack Randell in 1817 that brought him to the public's attention.

Tom Reynolds was sweeping all before him in his native Ireland and came over to England to match his skills against the country's best. The ring was set up on Molesey Heath in Surrey, a popular venue. There then followed an attritional sixty-six rounds of boxing that lasted for almost an hour and a half. Pierce Egan, the foremost observer of the sport in Georgian times, was present and wrote:

Rounds 30 to 33 were brutal to Belasco, and he received a mighty blow to his head, but after the 34th Belasco planted so many repeated blows to Reynold's face that it began to swell, and his opponent's chances of recovering seemed to be fading. In the 59th, Reynolds eyes had been badly closed and swollen, yet he continued to connect with the occasional blow. In the 61st round, Reynolds had his swollen eyes lanced and came from behind for the next five rounds, seeming to lead the match, despite having been badly punished throughout. Finally, in the 66th round, he landed a blow that sent Belasco down for the last time. Neither the Christian fans of Reynolds nor the Jewish fans of Belasco were entirely pleased with the outcome of the match, possibly due to its brutality, or by the manner in which the lead changed so unexpectedly in Reynolds' favour at the end.

The match against the very accomplished Jack Randell was an altogether more stylish affair. It was a much-anticipated fight and a huge number gathered to witness it. Knowledge of Belasco's durability preceded him and the match was set to be another lengthy bout. In the event it was not to be, but it is considered one of the finest exhibitions of the noble art of the period. The fight was matched at 50 guineas a side, a hefty sum, and took place near Shepperton in Surrey.

Randell was considered a stylish, almost artistic boxer whilst Belasco adopted his mentor Mendoza's more scientific approach. The match lasted just six rounds and demonstrated Belasco's ability to breach Randell's defence by cleverly manoeuvring inside his long-range leads. Randell, however, had excellent foot movement and counterpunching abilities and picked off Belasco frequently. Although Randell drew first blood in the second round, Belasco rallied strongly before being put down for the first time in the fourth. The fifth belonged to Belasco when his in-fighting prevailed. Egan wrote of the finish: 'The final blow was a powerful right to the eye of Belasco that rendered him senseless and ended the match. Belasco staggered, fainted, and fell from the pain, and though he was able to rise, his eye was closed completely shut.'

The publication *Pugilistica* wrote: 'The fight between Randall and Belasco may be pronounced one of the most perfect specimens of pugilism ever witnessed.' *Bell's Life in London* says of Randall: 'His hitting and getting away, his style of stopping and returning, with the excellent judgment he manifested, added to his activity and quickness on his legs, all tended to stamp him as one of the most finished boxers of his weight.'

Although Belasco lost both those fights, his abilities marked him out as one of the best lightweight boxers of the time. It was an era when promoters and matchmakers would, where possible, often match a Christian with a Jew in order to give the contest a touch of extra spice. The Jewish boxers more than held their own. Belasco retired from the ring in 1824 and split his time between acting as a second for other boxers and working as a food-and-drink merchant. He opened up 'night houses' (dosshouses) and 'supper clubs' for the poor of London and acquired an interest in politics, which resulted in his work with Barney Aaron in support of Lionel de Rothschild's parliamentary candidature.

At the time that bare-knuckle boxing had reached the peak of its popularity, John Sholto Douglas, the 9th Marquess of Queensberry, was about to publish his famous boxing rules. These were the third set of rules that had been published to help regulate the sport and increase the safety of its participants. It was obvious from the growth of the sport that greater controls and regulations had to be introduced. Since the days of Jack Broughton and James Figg, unregulated bare-knuckle boxing had been viewed by some in society as a dangerous, anti-social and irresponsible sport. The introduction of these rules went some way to placate the critics. It also helped that many supporters and backers of the sport were royals and people in high positions. It was often left to the local authorities to step in to curb any excesses, as and when they occurred. In London, the authorities mostly turned a blind eye to properly arranged prize-fights.

In the 1860s, around the time of the introduction of the Queensberry Rules, large numbers of fights were taking place all over the country. The big fights attracted such great audiences that appropriate spaces had to be found to accommodate the crowds. It was not uncommon for upwards of 5,000 spectators to attend these matches. However, the smaller fights that could be seen in London's inner-city public areas were beginning to be considered too unedifying for public viewing as young children were able to witness them. These 'back-street' events were steadily curtailed and were eventually outlawed by local authorities.

The sport of bare-knuckle prize-fighting was restricted to more discreet and private areas of the capital. Smaller events moved indoors to pubs, private clubs and halls. In the very early days of bare-knuckle boxing, London pubs like the Lamb and Flag in central London and the Prospect of Whitby in Wapping were famous for staging bouts. By the mid-nineteenth century several more London pubs featured boxing, with a couple even boasting training facilities.

One of the most famous pubs to allow training was the Blue Anchor in Shoreditch. Many boxers, including some champions, used its training facilities and many more used its bar! **Ben Bendoff** was one such boxer who used the pub extensively. It was run by Bill Richardson who, along with another publican, Ted Napper, helped get men's boxing off the inner London streets and into a more controlled environment. Richardson was a hard man.

He had to be to run a pub like that in such a tough area. In 1865, a nasty disagreement between him and Ben Bendoff had broken out at the pub one evening. The incident and the subsequent events were recorded by Fred Henning.

Henning was a keen follower of boxing and made copious notes for publication on the matches he witnessed. He produced a seminal work on bare-knuckle prize-fighting in *Recollections from the Prize Ring* (1888), which offers an excellent insight into the world of prize-fighting. Henning was one of a group of avid followers who immersed themselves into the sport throughout the early and mid-Victorian era, travelling all over England to do so. His work includes the comprehensive detailing of many important fights of the day and the way of life that surrounded the scene. His account of the Blue Anchor incident and aftermath is comprehensive but very loquacious, so I paraphrase in part:

> After the warm discussions at the house (Blue Anchor) that almost involved fists, Bill Richardson, not a boxer himself, forwarded the proposition that Bendoff should fight a man of his (Richardson's) choice for a wager and to settle the argument. The match for a purse of £25 a side was agreed to be boxed at catch weight. Richardson acquired the services of Jack Smith, known as the 'Brighton Doctor', for the contest. In truth, I feel the match should not have been made as Bendoff was in no financial position to fund the £25 wager, not having boxed for some time...
>
> The Lane (Petticoat) has a Jewish quarter in the midst of the metropolis that for many years has been the home of the Israelites and they stick to it. Sunday mornings are particularly interesting, with all sorts of weird and wonderful characters plying their trade there. We have often wandered down the Lane and spoken to one or two familiar faces. Old Levy, who keeps a second-hand furniture store and Joe Aaron who ran The Black Lion in Spitalfields and The Crown in Mile End. Joe and Levy frequently supplied the cold

fowls, sandwiches and cold fish on the field of battle. In early 1865 we dropped into the Lion by chance and were talking to Joe Aaron when the man himself walked in. Bendoff looked down in the dumps and not anything like prepared to enter the ring against a fit antagonist like The Doctor. He explained that he had gone without in order to raise the money and could not afford to employ a trainer or second. He had thrown himself on the generosity of others to raise some money, but it was not enough. It is proverbial with what tenacity Hebrews will cling together that on the very night we met with Joe Aaron, he agreed to advance the sum to Bendoff...

We travelled by train over to Woolwich on the day of the fight and caught the steamer down to the Kent shore by the marshes at Lower Hope point on the Thames where the ring was being readied. On reaching the spot it was to everyone's annoyance that some of the Royal Blues (police) had arrived. With no hope of the fight taking place, it was decided to re-locate nearer the city and a rush was made to board back onto the steamer for the journey to Thames Haven where the coast was clear. Several hundred from the East End braved the journey and weather, and a tremendous volley of applause went up as the two entered the ring.

Henning describes the contest in some detail. The early rounds were apparently well balanced but it became clear from about round ten that Bendoff had trained insufficiently for the match and began to tire. His nose was badly split and one eye had closed by the twelfth round, and on coming out for the sixteenth Jack Smith planted a fearsome drive into the face of the Petticoat Lane pugilist and Ben's second stepped in to retire his man. So, the contest was settled in favour of Richardson's man and Richardson would have made a fair bit in the betting markets. A line was drawn under the whole affair.[2]

Ben Bendoff was never a prolific boxer and his record is rather patchy. He started to prize-fight around 1853 and had some very lengthy matches in his early days. Two matches that had started in the late afternoon were long, attritional affairs both running to well over seventy rounds and both having to be called draws after the fading light prevented further action. After the fight against Jack Smith in 1865, there is no further record of Ben fighting again until one final contest in 1871 when he lost narrowly to Bat Mullins at the Camden Arms public house in Leicester Square. It must have been a fine effort as Mullins was to be widely recognised as one of the greatest middleweight exponents of gloved boxing in the country around that time.

By the late 1870s, outdoor bare-knuckle fights were disappearing fast from mainstream boxing. The police, acting with local authorities, had drastically limited these events. The viewing public had changed somewhat, too. Outdoor boxing had always been at the mercy of the weather and people now demanded more comfort when viewing the sport. The Marquess of Queensberry rules were well in place and indoor gloved boxing was becoming the dominant version of the sport. So, this earlier form of the sport was being consigned to history but during its time it was a most effective vehicle for the entry of Jewish people into mainstream British society.

The centuries-long struggle of the Jews to be accepted into society in most places in the world is well documented. Since Roman times they have experienced persecution on a huge scale, culminating in the anti-Jewish pogroms in the Russian Empire during the later nineteenth century and the Holocaust of the Second World War. Compared with those parts of the world in which these atrocities were carried out, Britain was a liberal and enlightened place for Jews to settle. The deeds of these early Jewish boxers most certainly helped to raise the profile of their kind. Acceptance did not come overnight; it was a slow and painful journey for both their religion and their boxers. Britain was not exempt from strong anti-Semitism. Well into the twentieth century many Jewish boxers still chose to use a westernised 'ring name', but gradually, roughly 150 years after Mendoza first fought, Jewish athletes – their boxers in particular – had helped the Jewish people to integrate, and people with anti-Semitic views were marginalised.

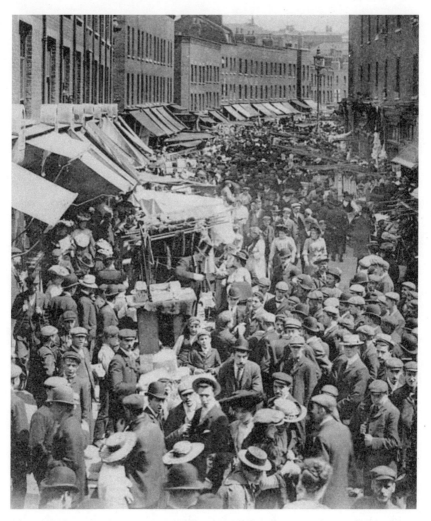

A thriving Sunday morning in Petticoat Lane (Wentworth Street), 1905. Petticoat Lane is an area of East London close to the City that features shops, market stalls and other commercial properties. It primarily incorporates Middlesex Street, Strype Street, Goulsdon Street, Bell Lane, Wentworth Street, Cobb Street and Old Castle Street.

2

STREET LIFE:
THE COBBLESTONE KIDS

There is no doubt that the vast majority of London's bare-knuckle boxers lived in grim circumstances. Petty crime was commonplace, but by and large the Jewish men who boxed for a living kept away from crime. Their noses may have been bloodied inside the ring but outside of it most stayed clean. That is not to say that one or two, as youngsters, didn't get into a few scrapes before they found boxing, of course.

From the 1870s, massive numbers of Russian Jews started to flee Russia in the wake of the infamous Russian pogroms. Thousands made it over to London. The Industrial Revolution and Britain's trade boom made the capital an attractive place to earn a living. But conditions in some areas were appalling. Already overcrowded, hastily built tenement buildings were constructed to house these new immigrants. Such areas of mass slum housing could be found almost all over London. These deprived areas became known as the rookeries.[1]

The Jewish boys who lived in these places could easily be drawn into crime. Some may well have dreamt of following in the footsteps of Barney Aaron, Dutch Sam or the famous Mendoza, but first they had to survive. This was the period of the 'Wild Boys' gangs, the sort of motley crews described by Charles Dickens in *Oliver Twist*. Dickens' Fagin was modelled on real-life East End villain Ikey Solomon, who recruited young lads from the rookeries to steal and pickpocket and used his shop in Bell Lane in the Petticoat Lane area of East London as a front to 'fence' the ill-gotten proceeds accumulated by his young protégés.

Two of the most notorious Jewish gangs during this time were the impressively named Bessarabian Tigers and the Odessians. The Yiddishers was another large gang that was very active. Later, the Whitechapel Gang would emerge. There were lots of them. The Irish immigrants had their gangs as well; the Watney Streeters were a well-connected Irish gang that made the most of the Dockland areas. Another well-known gang in the early part of the century was called the Darby Sabini Gang. This was a mixture of Jewish and Italian villains who operated in the Aldgate, Old Street and Clerkenwell areas but had strong influence around Soho in West London.

The gangs tended to control specific areas, so you had the likes of the Titanic Mob in Hoxton, the Brick Lane Boys in Bethnal Green and the Yiddishers in Whitechapel. The Elephant Boys controlled a large area south of the River Thames around the Elephant and Castle. Most of the street gangs had an older man, known as a captain or 'director', who controlled a number of boys, mostly young teenagers. These were his 'street soldiers' who carried out various crimes on his behalf. Many of the Jewish street urchins developed into what were termed 'star-glazers', on account of the shop windows they smashed to grab valuables. They also developed their fighting skills, some of them later becoming proficient boxers.

In London's criminal underworld, the most famous of the street soldiers to rise from the ranks was Alfie Solomon from Camden Town. Alfie Solomon had a fearful reputation. In his teenage years he indulged in unregulated backstreet bare-knuckle boxing. He quickly developed his criminal entrepreneurial skills and would often pick out young lads whom he could see had quick hands for pickpocketing purposes but were useful with their fists, too. By the end of the nineteenth century the London police forces had greatly reduced pickpocketing and other criminal acts on the streets of Central London. Solomon recognised this and turned his attentions to the dog tracks and racecourses in and around London. He fell in with the Darby Sabini gang and expanded his repertoire of criminal activities, adding debt collecting, prostitution and extortion.

As far as boxing is concerned, one of the first of the nineteenth-century gloveless boxers to come through the ranks of the street soldiers and into mainstream boxing was **Jem Smith.** Born in Shoreditch in 1863, the wits and fists that Smith used on the streets later served him well in an impressive boxing career. Smith's early life is rather vague and it is possible that he was born out of wedlock. He may also have been half-Jewish on his mother's side.

Smith's early fights were all fought without gloves, but as the introduction of boxing gloves became increasingly popular Smith fought a series of matches under both versions of the sport. Some of his matches were poorly recorded but a number of his more prestigious bouts were well documented. Jem Smith's earliest fights were fought around 1880 at middleweight and over the next few years he progressed well and increased his weight. His first officially recorded fight took place in 1884. More fights followed and he boxed reasonably well. This included a fight against Jim Kilrain, a title defence in 1887. The bout started late and the two fighters were well matched. With nothing to choose between them, the fight dragged on for 102 rounds and two and a half hours. Eventually, as night descended, the match was called a draw. Gradually he boxed in more gloved contests and started to fight at heavyweight. In 1895, he won the gloved version of the English title. Smith boxed on until 1902 when he retired. Amazingly there is a report of him making a comeback as late as 1918 in a match at Hoxton Baths. He retired to live in North London, dying in September 1931 aged sixty-eight.

Jewey Cook was a journeyman boxer at the end of the nineteenth century. Born in Whitechapel in 1875 as Abraham Cohen, Cook was a slightly built lad and was picked out for his wits and quick hands by those who conscripted the street urchins into the ranks of the street soldiers. He would probably have been put to work pickpocketing. The smaller lads had an advantage at this craft while the older, bigger lads were used for more physical activities! Cook must have been quite good at his trade as records show only one police caution for aiding and abetting. He must have also developed his boxing prowess during his later years. By the age of nineteen he had left his life on the cobblestones and swapped it for the ring, fighting all over London from 1894 to 1902 with some very good results at featherweight before he progressed to welterweight.

In 1903, Cook travelled to South Africa to box a number of bouts including three British Empire title fights, winning two and losing one at middleweight during a stay of just over three years there. After returning to England in 1905, he fought a few more times, including two excellent fights against Charlie Knock, before he stepped out of the ring. By this time, he was living in Bloomsbury. He returned in 1912 to fight fellow Jewish boxer and future British light heavyweight champion Harry Reeve, the bout ending in a draw. His final fight came in December that same year.

Around the time that **Jewey Smith** was born in January 1884, the housing conditions in a number of areas of London had become untenable. Some politicians of the day and many powerful individuals outside of Parliament were beginning to speak out about the dreadful conditions in the capital. The government was accused of being slow to act to remedy the conditions. Following on from the work that his father had started to relieve the suffering of the working classes of London during the mid-nineteenth century, in 1885 Nathaniel Rothschild founded the Four Per Cent Industrial Dwellings Company. The company was established to provide what were described as 'commodious and healthy dwellings at minimum rent for the industrial classes'.

This scheme was primarily aimed at serving the Jewish population of inner-city London, who were most affected by the overcrowding situation. The company was a commercial business but in reality it was never intended to be run at much more than break-even. At a return of just 4 per cent on their investment, the board, which consisted mainly of Jewish philanthropists, was motivated by the desire to generate greater social benefits through higher quality accommodation at affordable rents. By 1905, eight areas in East London, Camberwell in South London and Stoke Newington in North London had been redeveloped to provide large blocks of living space, known as 'Rothschild Housing'. Around 1,500 two- and three-bedroom flats were built.

Jewey Smith's childhood life is hazy. He is recorded as being born in Spitalfields, but it is possible that he was actually born in Hull. His father may have arrived in Hull, via Holland, from Poland around 1880 and lived there for a short while. His family must have moved south to London as it is known that Jewey did grow up in the East End. The family moved around the Spitalfields area a bit, from one cheap rented slum to another. An address in Dean Street is given at one point. Dean Street and Flower Street were the two areas that saw the first Rothschild's buildings, so it is possible that Smith's family took advantage of the philanthropy of the Rothschilds. The family name was Goldblum, so Jewey Smith was actually Joseph Goldblum. He was also rumoured to have been a Yiddishers street gang member, but there are no records of any arrests. Having started his boxing on the London streets, he joined the Navy for a while and further honed his skills there.

Although his official documented professional records do not start until 1908, there is little doubt he was boxing for several years before this in organised matches for money. In the navy he fought a number of top amateur fights in several countries. Like some of his early unlicensed professional fights, his amateur matches in other countries were not always detailed. Jewry boxed his first two officially recorded fights at the Wonderland arena in Whitechapel before being matched against Tommy Burns, the reigning heavyweight world champion. It took place in Paris and was billed as the world heavyweight title. Coming into the match, Jewey was advertised as the heavyweight champion of France and South Africa, but it is thought those titles were referring to amateur titles. The promoters probably had little idea at what standard Jewey Smith fought as a professional heavyweight. They had no doubt about the champ, Tommy Burns. His impressive record was there in black and white and his ability was self-evident.

Burns was on a world tour and had arranged both title and non-title fights in several countries. He was a seriously good heavyweight boxer. Tommy Burns was a big man with a big character. In fact, if it was a personality contest, the two fighters would have been evenly matched. Unfortunately for Jewey it was a boxing match and he was knocked out in the fifth round, having hung on quite well for the previous four. The reporters sat ringside were not impressed. They only had Jewey's two recorded matches to go on so they would have suspected that the outcome would have been a foregone conclusion.

The press was somewhat scathing of the match promoters. One paper wrote:

> Although billed as a world title defence for Burns (176¼), this was really scraping the barrel as Smith (187½) was little more than a novice fighting only his third traced pro fight. What is more, the Englishman received just £25 plus expenses for two. Although Smith started reasonably well, sending in some lusty hits to the body, he was soon being taken apart by Burns who had him down with a left to the head in the third. Knocked down twice in the fourth Smith rallied gamely in the fifth, but had no answer to the agile champion before being put down and out following a terrific right to the jaw.

It was a little harsh on Jewey. He was a reasonable boxer at this stage with dozens of good solid fights under his belt, but he was not in the same class as Burns. Jewey's boxing improved and it took him all over the world. In December 1910, he fought 'Iron' Mike Hague in Sheffield for what was billed as the British heavyweight crown. Jewey won over twenty rounds, but this title was not officially recognised in some quarters. Fighting in Europe, America and Africa, he enjoyed a decent career for one who had escaped the street life. He could have spent years looking at four grey walls of a prison cell; instead, Jewey's escape from his East London surroundings and the street gangs meant he certainly broadened his horizons before retiring in 1915.

We come now to the amazing, **Jack 'Kid' Berg**. He was the most famous graduate of the 'Wild Boys Gangs'. Jack's older brother, who also boxed professionally, ran with the gangs as well. Both were graduates of the 'Whitechapel Gang'. Jack Kid Berg emerged from the cobblestoned back streets of the East End and the shadows of London's underworld to conquer the world.

Jack's impressive stats are there for everyone to see. Not only was Jack one of this country's greatest ever boxers, outside the ring he was also one of its most colourful characters. Born in abject poverty in 1909 he would become a world champion and global star of the game. Jack was one of the last Jewish young boxers to run with the street gangs. By the time Jack was active on the streets, around 1920, names like Ikey Solomon were long gone and Alfie Solomon's influence was beginning to wane due in no small part to the increasing time he was spending in prison. A new breed of gangster was arriving on the scene. Pickpocketing was still around but in Central and West London the police had gradually got a grip on the problem. It was gambling, protection, black marketing and prostitution that were to replace street crime.

Jack Berg certainly was not averse to a bit of pickpocketing, but his street life was relatively short lived. That being said, the buzz of flirting with crime did not leave him. In his boxing years, in America it was heavily rumoured that he had some dealings on the fringes of Mafia circles. Back in England, in his teenage years he was to witness the rise of the notorious Jewish gangster, Jack Spot, The Jewish Godfather. Spot and Berg were born a stone's throw from each other and Spot became an influential force in the area.

Jack Berg and Spot knew each other from a young age. Spot found crime; Berg found boxing. Berg said he received no formal boxing training as a lad and was largely self-taught. There are, however, records of him at a couple of boxing clubs in his teenage years. Jack was fairly prominent in the Whitechapel Gang. An anonymous acquaintance of Berg wrote in the *Topical Times*:

We always knew him as "Yiddle" and we called him the kid's champion because he always had a following of smaller boys wherever he went. We always used to go to the Cambridge Music Hall in Commercial Road. There were rival gangs there. Yiddle was always getting the best of the scraps, even with older lads twice his size. We gave him every encouragement because he usually started things in defence of smaller members of the gang.

So Berg was useful with his fists before he stepped inside any club for training. He was a natural. He was spotted by influential promoter Victor Berliner who booked him to appear regularly at the East London venue, 'Premierland' on the Whitechapel/Stepney border.

After a couple of early unrecorded fights in 1923, Berg started his professional boxing in earnest in June 1924, fighting almost fifty matches at Premierland before showcasing his talents in America. Jack's rise to fame was guided by Harry Levene who had the ability to pick the right fights at the right time for him. His last bout came as late as 1945. What happened in between is a well-documented story of a truly astonishing and successful boxing career. Berg won the world championship at the Royal Albert Hall in February 1930, roared on by a large and vociferous mass of London supporters. Berg reached his pinnacle that night, but how long would he stay there?

The answer came five months later in New York. One Eligio Sardinãs Montalvo walked purposely from his dressing room at the Polo Grounds venue, continuing on his path to fame and fortune. Kid Chocolate, as he was known, came with a solid reputation. The formidable American-based Cuban fighter entered the ring at the Polo Grounds venue unbeaten in fifty-six fights and was considered to be, by far, the best 'pound for pound' boxer in the world.

Kid Chocolate was a firm favourite given the way he had despatched his previous opponents and his eyes were firmly fixed on the $66,000 purse that was up for grabs – an absolute fortune, one of the largest purses for a non-title fight to date. Sitting quietly in the opposite corner was Jack kid Berg. A win for Kid Chocolate against Berg would set up a world title fight later in the year. Neither boxer had fought for such a huge sum. Chocolate was there for both the win and the money. Berg knew he had his work cut out for him that day and over ten blistering rounds of boxing his all-action style and speed of punch was never more in evidence. Against such an accomplished fighter, East End grit and determination produced a narrow win for Jack; one of the greatest, if not *the* greatest win by a British boxer on American soil.

Wilbur Wood of the *New York Sun* wrote about Berg after the match: 'British Bulldog courage, remarkable stamina and being slightly heavier proved too much for Chocolate. Berg made war for three minutes every round, whilst Chocolate boxed only in snatches.' According to Wood, Berg threw almost 2,500 punches over the ten round, thirty-minute contest. Do the math...

Between then and 1939, he spent his time boxing regularly both sides of the Atlantic. In September, after beating American contender Joey Greb, Jack returned home to Britain and the papers were speculating on what he may do. Some suggested he was possibly ready to retire and was going back to Britain to hunt down a British heavyweight that could take on the mighty Joe Louis. Jack himself said he was looking to fight top British boxer Eric Boon, the recently crowned lightweight champion. Neither happened and a few weeks later Jack enlisted in the RAF to play his part in the war. He never boxed in America again.

Jack Kid Berg's last fight in the States had been against Joey Greb, who was a relation of Harry Greb's, the famous middleweight world champion and American Hall of Famer who dominated the middleweights prior to, during and after the First World War. Harry Greb was known as the 'Pittsburgh Windmill'. Jack's nickname was 'The Whitechapel Windmill'. And they both share their surname, in a way. Berg is Greb in reverse!

After his demob in 1945, Jack only boxed a couple of times. Already very wealthy and long since moved out of inner London, Berg settled down to live out his retirement in the affluent environs of St John's Wood in North West London with his wife Morya and daughter Stephanie.

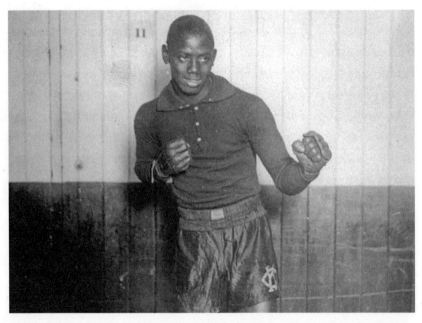

Kid Chocolate (above) and Jack Kid Berg (below) – the wily old campaigner Berg had just too much guile and work-rate for the up-and-coming, gifted young star from Cuba.

3

WELCOME TO THE CLUB

Between 1840 and 1905, England was a magnet for all sorts of people from ethnic backgrounds who were fleeing from their homelands for varying reasons. The large cities in England like Liverpool, Manchester, Leeds, Birmingham and Bristol all experienced a growth in their population during these times, but it was London that saw the greatest influx.[1]

A huge number of Irish arrived in London escaping the horrors of the Potato Famine in the 1840s. Some could not settle and moved to America. Many, though, settled in the dockland area of London and even more found their way to the Angel Islington and the Kilburn area of North London. Around 15,000 Germans arrived in both East and West London in the 1850s. Large numbers of Chinese found work in the more central parts of the capital, where 'China Town' can now be found and there was also a largish community of Chinese settled in the Lime House district of East London. Afro-Caribbean people found work in West London and around the docks either side of the Thames.

Most of these were escaping harsh economic and political conditions in their homelands, including Italian immigrants, who arrived around the mid-1850s. They were fleeing the turmoil that was Italy before its unification in 1861. Around

8,000 arrived, mostly in the Holborn and Clerkenwell districts near to the capital's city centre. Several decent boxers came from this stock.

It was though, the Jewish immigrants, fleeing persecution and economic deprivation, who descended on London in really large numbers that had the most impact on London life. Following on from the Sephardic Jews that settled in the Spitalfields area earlier, a small group of Dutch Jews had moved into the area in the 1830s. They brought the trade of diamond cutting and created a few small workshops and factories manufacturing and distributing cigars. They were then joined by the mainly Ashkenazy Jews from Central Europe.

It was forty years or so later that the Russian Jews started to arrive in the capital in really large numbers. They mainly settled in East London but a few found homes in some areas of North London. It is estimated that by the end of the nineteenth century the population of London had been swelled by the settlement of these immigrants by well over a quarter of a million. It would define London as a truly cosmopolitan capital city. Around half this total, about 140,000, would have been Jewish immigrants. East London had a reputation for cheap living and available work, due in most part to the shipping trade passing through the wharves and docks. It is estimated that by 1900 90% of the population of the Spitalfields, Petticoat Lane and the Aldgate areas of London was Jewish.

Even earlier than the European Jewish migration, the mainly French protestant Huguenots had come to this area and had built some elegant houses around the end of the seventeenth century before they moved on. The European Jews were far greater in number and most of these former Huguenots' houses were subdivided to accommodate the numbers. The overcrowding was awful and soon the sanitation started to fail. Disease quickly followed.

Mostly, people found employment and paid their way, but the living conditions they had to endure were desperate. For the children that were born into these conditions, it was a lottery as to whether they survived or not. Those that did would be looking to escape the hardships of their impoverished lives. Crime was rife and many young men 'worked the streets' as part of the street gangs described earlier.

As a way for parents to get their kids off the streets, many boys' clubs were set up in the inner-city areas. A few were secular but most catered for the various religions of the immigrant communities. Boys' clubs, or youth clubs as they were later known, first appeared in the country during the middle of the nineteenth century. Virtually all of them were set up by the Church of England for the benefit of the poor young of the indigenous population. Ostensibly, they were there to give both aid and hope to young kids. In truth though, most were just an extension of the Church, which used the facility to spread the word and help keep these young people within the fold.[2]

By the later nineteenth century, clubs were starting to be formed by the works of philanthropic individuals or groups. By this time, London had become a thriving city but there still existed several areas of crippling poverty. It was in these places that clubs proved to be a godsend to the local population. As far as Jewish youth clubs were concerned, the first records actually show a couple of young girls' clubs being set up. Records show a popular girls' club being established in Leman Street in Stepney during 1883, but this was simply a meeting house with few other facilities.

London's first couple of properly organised Jewish youth clubs were the Brady Boys' Club and the Jewish Lads' Brigade. They were both formed around the same time in 1885. The Brady Boys' Club was located in Brady Street, Whitechapel. The club was founded by three women philanthropists, Lady Charlotte Rothschild, Mrs Arthur Franklin and Mrs N. S. Joseph. Unlike some of the earlier C of E clubs, the Brady Boys' Club provided both educational opportunities and recreational activities. Summer camps were arranged to get kids out of the slums and rookeries of inner London and into the countryside for a few days. Both boxing and gymnastics were catered for and a couple of reasonable boxers first pulled on a pair of gloves at Brady's. Harry Levene, the well- known boxing manager and promoter, attended the club as a lad and boxed a fair bit.

That same year the first boys' club that focused a little more on physical activities was established. It was set up by Colonel E. W. Goldsmid, a retired Jewish British army officer. It was known as The Jewish Lads' Brigade. They, too, arranged for summer camps but soon a social club and sports club were added. The JLB, as it was soon known, gradually expanded and by the end of the nineteenth century, these clubs began to appear around Britain. It became, by far, the largest Jewish youth club association in the country. Branches were set up in America, Canada and South Africa. Shortly before the First World War, a purpose-built headquarters, Camperdown House, was established in Aldgate by Viscount Milner and the JLB became an integral part of the British youth movement in the twentieth century.

The club attracted a lot of young lads who wanted to try their hand at boxing and several very good amateur boxers came through the ranks. Between 1921 and 1939 the JLB won the Prince of Wales Shield (The preeminent tournament for British youth clubs) no fewer than twelve times. In London it produced three or four very useful professional boxers. Possibly the most well-known of these was **Sid Nathan**. Although Sid was best remembered as being an outstanding boxing referee after the Second World War, before it he was a decent southpaw flyweight and featherweight boxer.

Sid was born in Aldgate in 1922 and boxed professionally for almost 18 months from March 1939, winning fourteen out of sixteen bouts before he joined the RAF to serve in the war. Sid started to referee in the fifties and officiated at some of boxing's greatest matches. The two Lazar brothers, featured later, also boxed for the Lads' brigade. Aschel Joseph was probably the best boxer who was coached at the JLB as an amateur and he went on to carve out a very impressive professional career. He was also known as Young Joseph and his name will crop up again later. A great British and European champion.

Another great club was the Victoria club. It operated in the area from 1901 to 1956. The Victoria Club was a Jewish youth club that later developed into a community centre. The youth club was first established in Whitechapel in 1901, as a means of coping with Jewish delinquency in the East End of London. Before it moved to Stamford Hill in 1956, following the migratory pattern of London Jewry, it produced a couple of very good boxers. The most well-known of the ex-Victorian Club boys was **Jack Hyams** who carved out an impressive career fighting under the name of Kid Froggy. An interesting character, there will also be a little more about 'The Frog' later. The club was re-located in Egerton Road, Stamford Hill, beside the New Synagogue, on land leased from the United Synagogue. By 1976 the activities of the club were so diverse that it became the Victoria Community Centre, until its closure in December 1991.

It is fair to say that most Jewish youth clubs encouraged their members to embrace the Jewish religion and hopefully practise it through their local synagogue, but the evidence is strong that this was all it was, just encouragement. By and large the kids tried to decide themselves how much or how little they followed the edicts of their religion. Another quite large and very popular Jewish club was the Stepney Jewish Lads' Club in Stepney Green. It was founded in 1901 with physical education and sport high on its agenda. A tell-tale report on the club emphasises the point about the ratio of sporting leisure time to religious studies. The following appeared in the *East London Advertiser* in 1907:

> Among the many Jewish agencies at work in London none is more successful than the Jewish Lads' Club in Stepney Green. The annual prize giving for the club was given on Sunday and the Rev. J. F. Stern spoke to the members and said he joined the club not with the sole purpose of encouraging football and cricket and other games but to bring the club more in touch with the Synagogue. He deplored the fact that so few members attended the Synagogue. He said actions had been taken to remedy this but had failed so had to be abandoned due to the small number attending from the club.

I think it is an indication that this first generation of Jewish children growing up in the capital and attending these clubs were to some extent moving away from their previous generation's strict orthodox Jewish upbringing. They had found sport and other activities in a liberal environment and realised that although they were free to keep their faith, they could also expand their horizons.

As far as boxing is concerned, probably the two greatest Jewish clubs that produced the best boxers were the Oxford and St George's Club and the Judean Athletic and Social Club. Basil Henriques founded the Oxford and St George's Club in Cannon Street Road in 1914, a few months before the start of the First World War. Its name came from Henriques's university, Oxford, and from the area in the East End where it was situated, the parish of St George's. Henriques, a charismatic and ardent supporter of the youth movement, managed to secure backing from one of this country's greatest philanthropist, Bernhard Baron, who donated the huge sum of £65,000 to secure the club a base and equip it. The Oxford & St George's began as a club for boys but Rose Loewe, one of the club helpers, soon became director of a new club for girls.

In 1917 Rose married Basil Henriques, and in 1919 they founded the St George's Jewish Settlement. The Settlement, in Betts Street, housed both the boys' and girls' clubs, and Basil and Rose Henriques lived on the premises. They were affectionately known as 'The Gaffer' and 'The Missus'. In 1929, the Oxford and St George's Club moved to a former school building in Berner Street (now Henriques Street), Whitechapel. The move was funded by Bernhard Baron, a cigarette manufacturer. The new institution formally opened as the Bernhard Baron Settlement. Apart from the sports set up, it catered for other Jewish needs providing amongst other things a clinic for expectant mothers, a kindergarten, general youth development, religious classes, adult activities and free legal aid.

The Judean Club first opened in 1902. It was founded by two Jewish brothers, Dave and Barney Stitcher and focused on physical activities more than most clubs in the area, noticeably gymnastics and boxing. Situated just off Cable Street. it attracted

Boys sparring at Oxford and St George's.

some very good up-and-coming boxers. The most famous of all was the truly great Ted Kid Lewis but many other excellent boxers used the club's facilities and entered the boxing matches that were staged there. Young Joseph(s) also trained and fought there. So too did British champion Johnny Brown. Harry Reeve, a future British light heavyweight champion learnt his craft at the club.

It was clubs like these that were pivotal to the development of both the Jewish youth of the day and the sports they took up, of which boxing was the most popular. They produced the conveyer belt of professional boxers that dominated London's boxing scene through the first half or so of the twentieth century. Many hundreds of them in fact, first pulled a pair of boxing gloves on at these clubs. Several achieved fame and fortune, but the vast majority who stuck with it were content with just making a living from the game. These were the names you would see on the undercards of boxing events, not just in London but all around the country and occasionally abroad. Although it was the stars of this era that could grab the back page headlines for just a few minutes work in the ring, it was the rest that stretched out an evening's entertainment and ensured that the paying public got their money's worth. So yes, it may well have been a case of quantity over quality, but at a lot of events these 'also rans' were just as important to the sport as their more illustrious colleagues.

Although there was a concentration of clubs in the East of London, several other Jewish clubs were set up in other parts of the capital around the turn of the century. Most were in North London but one of the biggest was the West Central Jewish Club and Settlement that began life in one large room in Bloomsbury, close to the City of London. It was originally an all-girls' club and proved very popular. Within a couple of years, it moved into larger premises in Soho and a few years later, boys were accepted. Sports were available and it housed a very well-equipped gym;

but more than most, it concentrated more on academic interests. By 1940 it had grown significantly and had almost 1,000 members. It had become fairly influential over the years and the women's section were heavily involved in the Suffragette Movement and women's suffrage generally. In July 1940, at the height of the London Blitz, the building took a direct hit and was completely destroyed and twenty- seven people in the club at the time lost their lives.

One of the last Jewish boxing clubs that was set up in London was the Wingate Boxing club. It was an off-shoot of the Wingate football club that was an excellent amateur football outfit. The club was set up in North-West London in 1953, with the ethos of promoting further understanding between Jewish and non-Jewish amateur boxers. Ex-army instructor and multiple army boxing champion Len Fowler was brought in as head coach.

Apart from the many Jewish clubs that sprang up around the capital, the Jewish communities also set up a number of Jewish Social and Working Men's clubs. Two were set up as early as the early 1890s. One was situated in Central Finchley but as you would expect, the largest of these was situated in the East End in Mansfield Street, Aldgate. The clubs hosted the occasional boxing events. Some were standard boxing bills under normal regulations and others were fundraising events for the community. Both Jewish and Gentile boxers appeared there.

4

THE AMATEUR SCENE

Unlike the earlier nineteenth century Church of England clubs, the youth club movement of the twentieth century were more secular. To a certain extent, they helped to promote racial and religious integration and harmony. Although a few popular boxing clubs tended to attract boys from the same ethnic backgrounds, some were formed that were more open to all of London's youth. The top Jewish boxing clubs like the Judean and the Oxford and St George's were not exclusively Jewish. Other London clubs like the Stepney Institute and St. John's Bosco, that were largely looked upon as Catholic, welcomed all comers. In the years leading up to the First World War, the big secular boxing clubs began to emerge. Most of these were set up by philanthropists who had limited or no religious agendas.

This period saw the rise of five or six extremely successful clubs, led by Lynn AC in South London and the impressive Repton Boys Club in East London. These did initially offer other sports but gradually the sport of boxing took centre stage. The Eton Manor Boys' Club in Hackney was an excellent all-round sports club and this, too, developed a really strong boxing section. The West Ham Boys Boxing Club was founded to be just that, and despite the recent participation of girls in the sport it still retains its name. Girls were not excluded from the club and

West Ham have produced a couple of female champions. In these clubs you could see black and white. Jews and gentiles sharing the same club facilities.

Lynn AC Boxing Club, prior to Repton, was this country's foremost amateur boxing club. It was founded in 1892 in South London and dominated the amateur boxing scene for the next forty years. It boasted multiple amateur champions, three of whom had Jewish ancestry and were brilliant amateur boxers. Harry Moy won championships at two different weights and Ruben (Rube) Warnes became the first amateur boxer to win five middleweight ABA titles, a feat he achieved between 1899 and 1910. The third and most famous was Matt Wells. Matt Wells of Lynn and a bit later, Harry Mizler from the St George's Club, were probably two of the greatest Jewish amateur champions produced in this country. Over the course of each of their seven or eight years fighting on the amateur circuit, from Schoolboy to senior ABA boxers, they won numerous amateur titles.

Mizler's three senior ABA titles between 1930 and 1933 at three different weights were impressive. Harry's first title in 1930 came in the bantamweight division before moving up to featherweight to compete in the 1931 championships. That year's championships produced some outstanding amateur boxing. Harry Mizler got through to the semi-final where he met the reigning champion J. W. Duffield and knocked him out. He went through to the final where he faced another young Jewish boxer, Phil Caplan. Phil had also boxed extremely well and the two well matched youngsters produced a great bout. A report in the *Jewish Word* praised both boxers: 'Both lads gave a great display. Mizler is a rising star and it was a shame he should have met and been defeated by a fellow Jew in the featherweight final.'

So, Phil Caplan defeated the future great professional British champion and was the standout performer that year. Mizler was

Rube Warnes (above) and Matt Wells (left), two great amateur champions from the Lynn AC Boxing Club in South London.

still fighting for the Oxford and St George's Club, the club that Caplan had originally joined. On the night though, Caplan picked up the trophy as a member of the Polytechnic Boxing Club. Mizler went on to pick up the featherweight title the following year before completing his hat trick of ABA championship titles, winning the lightweight division in 1933.

Matt Wells won four consecutive lightweight titles between 1904 and 1907 before going off to box for Britain in the 1908 Olympic Games. Wells and Fred Grace were the two outstanding amateur lightweights of the day and they boxed against each other on several occasions. Matt had beaten Fred in the ABA finals in 1907 before they both went to the London Olympics the following year. Their paths met again in the competition but this time Matt lost a close match to Fred, who went on to claim the gold medal. Fred was a London lad from Edmonton and boxed out of the Eton Manor Club in Hackney. On returning home Matt decided to turn professional but Fred remained an amateur until he retired in 1919. Both Harry Mizler and Matt Wells always had their eyes on professional purses. Benny Caplan and Joseph Freeman were another couple of Jewish amateur boxers who also picked up national titles and turned professional.

Although amateur boxing at local level was extremely popular with Jewish boys, in reality, apart from the couple of national amateur boxers I have mentioned, Jewish boxers had nowhere near the impact on the amateur boxing scene as they had on the professional side of the sport. The same could be said of their Catholic counterparts. For these two groups of boxers the majority had their hearts set on boxing for a living. In contrast, the amateur ranks tended to be dominated by white, Protestant young men from slightly more middle-class backgrounds, until the Afro-Caribbean boxers started to emerge later in the twentieth century.

The 'Ragged Schools Movement' began in the early nineteenth century and was formalised in the capital as the London Ragged School Union in 1844. Its aim was to provide basic schooling for some of the country's most destitute children. The movement targeted inner-city areas of great poverty and London was obviously one. It was a charitable organisation with volunteers that gave their time free of charge. Over 200 schools were set up to help educate the very poorest in society. In London alone, hundreds of thousands of children of all faiths passed through the system between 1850 and 1900. The Union also worked alongside the various boys' and girls' clubs. Eventually, the government acted on education and between 1880 and 1897, legislation was bought in and funds made available to supply free education to all children up until the age of fourteen.

In London, with this huge improvement in education, together with the multiplication of both girls' and boys' clubs, the Ragged School Movement turned its attention more toward this and started to operate as the 'Federation of London Youth clubs'. It became the overarching body that co-ordinated the London Youth movement. Soon after the turn of the century the F.L.Y.C. was organising inter-club competitions. Along with the Amateur Boxing Association (ABA) and the London Schoolboys Association, the F.L.Y.C. helped turn London into one of the most competitive amateur boxing areas in the world.

Lots of Jewish boxers competed in all the various competitions but as I have said, most of the Jewish boxers saw this period of their career as a stepping stone onto the professional road. If not, they tended to drift off onto another career path altogether. For example, father and son boxers Alf and Cecil Bright both boxed for The St George's Club. Alf turned professional and fought about twenty bouts during the 1920s. Cecil though, did not take up the professional reins. Instead, he went into business and married Irene Goodman, who herself came from a sporting family. Her father, Bert Goodman, was an accomplished inside forward footballer and played 136 games for Charlton. He also played for Tottenham and Leyton Orient.

Apart from domestic amateur competitions, a few London Jewish boxers represented Britain in both the Empire (Commonwealth) Games and the Olympics. Frank Brooman, who boxed out of St Pancras, won the ABA welterweight title in 1930 before picking up a bronze medal in that year's Empire Games. The other significant sporting occasion that attracted Jewish boxers was the World Maccabiah Games, first held in 1932. The games are a sort of Jewish Olympics. They attract the elite of Jewish men and women from a whole host of sporting events, including boxing. Held every four years they now regularly hosts around 10,000 competitors, making them the third largest multi-sport competition after the Olympics and the Pan-Am Games.

A number of very good Jewish London boxers fought at the games. Laurie Gold, who boxed for Eton Manor, won the lightweight boxing title in 1950, and Dave Levy won a heavyweight gold medal at the 1965 games. The games themselves were first staged in 1932. Initially they attracted mainly Jewish competitors from Central Europe, Britain and America but now they are truly global.

One of the big boxing stars of the early Maccabiah games was **Jakab Malz**. Malz competed in two games and won medals at both of them, boxing at lightweight. Malz wasn't from London when he competed in the games. He actually competed for Germany between 1924 and 1934. He was born in The Ukraine in 1902 into a middle-class Jewish family. In 1912 his father was offered a chance to work in Switzerland and so the family moved to Basel. A couple of years later, through his father's work, he moved once again, this time to Berlin, and Malz completed his education there and indulged his passion for sport.

Malz was extremely fit and enjoyed athletics, hockey and football. After the First World War he took up boxing and moved steadily up the amateur ranks in Germany and was winning prestigious club competitions. By the early 1920s, Berlin was becoming second only to London as a hub for European amateur boxing. The future German world heavyweight champion Max Schmeling boxed for one of the Berlin clubs and Jakob and Max new each other. Max was not Jewish, and in those days, comradeship between Jewish and Gentile sportsmen was unexceptional. That was to change within a few years.

Jakob Malz went on to represent Germany and was in the Jewish team that went to compete in the first Maccabiah Games in 1932. By this time though, things had started to change significantly in his country. Hitler had come to power and was promoting the Aryan race and its ideals. Sport, particularly amateur sport, was at the heart of German youth and young manhood. Jewish amateur boxing still continued but under some restrictions,. In 1933, measures were put in place to ensure that Jewish professional boxers were not allowed to compete against gentiles. Eric Seelig, another excellent Jewish boxer, who was the German middleweight and light heavyweight champion between 1931 and 1933, was stripped of his titles under the Nazi regime and was forced to flee the country.

By this time Max Schmeling was an established global professional star who held the world heavyweight title between 1931 and 1932. Outside of Germany, Schmeling could box who he wished. His manager, Joe Jacobs, was Jewish and in America he sparred with Jewish boxers and displayed no anti-Semitic tendencies at all. Pre-war, Hitler did all he could to persuade Schmeling to join the Nazi Party and denounce the Jewish race, but Max never did. In fact, after Schmeling's loss to the legendary black boxer, Joe Louis, in 1938, Max was shunned by the Nazi party in his home country.[1]

Meanwhile, Jakob Malz was continuing along the amateur path, winning numerous events and competing in the second Maccabiah games in 1935. Under the Nazis, his days of competing for his country were over so he was not present to see the infamous 1936 Berlin Olympics and the headline-making Jesse Owens, who ruined Hitler's showpiece event.

Malz had built up a number of contacts, both inside and outside Germany, during his earlier international career so the following year he started making plans to leave Germany. By 1939 several of his family had moved on, some to Palestine, but Jakob moved to London. On 15 August 1939, Malz arrived in London and took up residence in Aldgate. His wife and children arrived shortly after. Malz, like most German immigrants during wartime, had to spend three months in a British internment camp. All German Jews had been stripped of any wealth they had and Malz was no exception. Once he was released from internment, he joined the British army as a fitness trainer and rose to the rank of sergeant before leaving in 1945.

His competitive boxing days were long over. His family had moved out of the East End and after a short stay in Stoke Newington, they settled in Maida Vale. Now aged forty-six, Malz was still supremely fit and he found work as a personal fitness and gym instructor and masseur. He also found time to work as a trainer with some young and up-and-coming amateur boxers. His wife made up jewellery items, which was quite successful and the pair prospered. They moved to the very expensive Bishops Avenue in North London. Jakob Matz died in 1982.

Jacob Malz was fortunate to escape the Nazi regime. Countless others in Germany and other European countries did not. 1939 Britain was, for the most part, unaware of the horrors that were beginning to take place across the Channel. But much of British Jewry knew by this stage that for their race in Europe, this could well mean extinction at the hands of the German fascists.

In the summer of 1939, Leon Greenman from Whitechapel was a thirty-year-old barber living in Rotterdam. Leon was British-born but he had friends and family in the Netherlands and for the previous thirty years had spent his time between London and Rotterdam. As well as hairdressing he was also a bookseller and this meant he had business interests in both countries. Leon enjoyed boxing and had a passion for the sport. As a lad in London, he had joined a boxing club, primarily as a way to keep fit but he boxed in some low-level events. In his later teenage years, he joined the mainly Jewish Bram Saunder's boxing school in Rotterdam. He also met the professional boxer Theo Kourimsky in Rotterdam and they became friends. Greenman and Kourimsky would sometimes train together, although Greenman limited his boxing to the occasional amateur event. Nevertheless, he was very fit.

At the outbreak of war, Leon was still working in The Netherlands. He was a British citizen and at that point the German blitzkrieg had yet to start and the Netherlands was going about its business as usual. Leon considered himself and his wife and son, who were living with him, perfectly safe. For months nothing really happened. That all changed. In May 1940, the German war machine rolled across the Dutch border. Even then, Leon felt reasonably secure. Greenman held a British passport and had expected that he and his family would be evacuated, but the staff at the British consulate in Rotterdam disappeared and he could not escape. Even so, he expected to remain safe, as the Geneva Convention protected enemy civilians. He gave his money and passport to a non-Jewish friend to keep them safe but fearing that Germans may find out that he had helped a Jew, the friend destroyed the passport. Greenman and his family were sent to the Westerbork transit camp on 8 October 1942 to be deported. Despite Greenman's protestations that he was British and should be released, he and his family joined 700 others on a train out of the Netherlands in January 1943. Proof of his nationality arrived soon after they left. It was too late.

Greenman travelled for thirty-six hours across Europe with no food or water, to Auschwitz where his wife and son were taken to one side and were murdered in the gas chambers almost immediately. Greenman was sent in a different direction. Although not a big man, his boxing had given him an impressive physique. He was one of fifty men selected to be slave labourers. Many were worked to death but the strength of Leon saw him through for almost two years, until he was transferred to the Monowitz industrial complex inside Auschwitz, also known as Auschwitz III, in September 1943, where he was subjected to medical experiments. He became the camp barber.

When the camp was evacuated in early 1945, Greenman was sent on one of the notorious death marches in freezing weather. First, he went to Gleiwitz, and was then taken in open cattle trucks to the Buchenwald camp. Not long after, Greenman awoke from his bunk at the camp to find that the camp guards had fled and the camp was liberated by General Patton's American Third Army. Of the 700 on the train from Westerbork in 1942, only Greenman and one other man survived. He, too, was a boxer, Leen Sanders, whom he knew from his boxing days in Rotterdam. Leen was a Dutch amateur and professional champion before the war and the younger brother of Bram Sanders who ran the boxing school that Greenman used in his amateur days.

After the war Leon Greenman returned to London and moved to Gants Hill in Ilford. He worked in Petticoat Lane and also earned some money performing in the odd stage show where he sang and acted under the name Leon Maure. After hearing Colin

Jordan, the leader of the National Socialist Movement, addressing a rally in Trafalgar Square in 1962, Greenman determined to tell his story to anyone who would listen. Late into his life, he would visit schools to bear witness to the Holocaust, showing them his concentration camp tattoo and telling them his remarkable story.

Leon Greenman OBE, an Englishman who was in Auschwitz. He was an active anti-fascist until the end, pictured here speaking at a protest rally in 1993.

5

STAR QUALITY

By the 1950s, the appalling social conditions that existed in London in the previous century had improved greatly. The slums and rookeries of the Victorian era, from which young Jewish men fought their way out, had mainly disappeared. Twentieth-century slum clearance, aided by the Luftwaffe during the war, cleared areas ready for post-war urban redevelopment.

During the earlier part of the century the Jewish communities established themselves as strong and resourceful people and boxing played a big part in this development. The Jewish bare-knuckle boxers of the previous centuries set the standard for the twentieth-century boys and many boxing venues and gyms were set up in London to promote the sport. Following the publication of the Marquess of Queensberry rules in 1867, greater boxing safety was gradually introduced. Although there were some old school boxers that were uncomfortable using gloves, eventually they became commonplace and gloves in the sport were officially recognised from 1890 onward and became the accepted version of mainstream amateur and professional boxing.

One of the first recognised London Jewish gloved national champion was **Jack Scales**. Jack wasn't London-born. He hailed from just outside the capital in Buckinghamshire. There is little known about his early life. It is possible he left school to work on the various farms in the area. He was born in 1874 and in those days, agriculture still employed millions, but wages were pitifully low for agricultural labourers. The next time we pick him up he is living in Bethnal Green and the Aldgate area around 1896. He may have moved to the area to earn better money.

He is shown as having his first professional fight later that year, but around this time he is reported to have had a few fights that were not officially recorded. Scales boxed at heavyweight around London initially but soon began to pick up fights all around the country. The days of grafting away on the land meant he was extremely fit. He was quite an imposing individual standing at around six feet and weighing just under fourteen stone; quite sizable for a heavyweight in those times.

In April 1900, Jack was apparently pitted against fellow Jewish heavyweight Woolf Bendoff[1] for the vacant English championship, although this has been disputed. We know he put on a good show to win against a poor opponent at the Wonderland Arena. For the next few years Jack's form was consistent and he managed to defend his title a few times.

He fought the talented Jack Palmer from Newcastle in 1901 and knocked him out to secure the undisputed British title. Later he fought the tough, uncompromising, up-and-coming future British heavyweight champion, Mike 'Iron' Teague to an honourable draw in 1907. A rematch was arranged in early 1908 and big Iron Mike knocked out Jack in the second round.

Over the next few years, Scales found wins scarce to come by. In one last effort he was pitched in against Matthew Curran for the British and Empire title in 1911 and was again knocked out, this time in the fourth round. Jack boxed once more a few months later. After losing, he called it a day and retired.

A young Gershon Mendeloff appeared from the slums of Aldgate on the amateur boxing scene around 1906, a time when teenage London lads were already passing through the amateur ranks and onto the professional circuit with some success at national level. Gershon was a tough street scrapper and pulled on a pair of amateur gloves for the first time aged thirteen, purely to settle an argument with another Jewish tearaway kid. Gershon dispatched his slightly older and bigger opponent one afternoon at a novice amateur session at the famous Judean boxing Club.

Gershon enjoyed the experience and took up the sport. He worked hard and long as an amateur and for the fights he had at this level he would have boxed under his birth name. As he progressed, he would be entered into minor boxing matches at his club. If he won, he would be rewarded with a sixpence. He won quite a few but those early amateur fights, although quite impressive, told nothing about what was to follow. Gershon would elevate Jewish boxing onto the world stage and become its biggest star since Daniel Mendoza over 100 years earlier. He was about to re-write the record books – but the name that appeared on those pages was not Gershon Mendelhoff.

Ted 'Kid' Lewis was the name Mendelhoff used when he fought his first professional fight. Lewis, as we will now call him from now on, was born at Aldgate Pump, on the boundary of East London and the City of London, in 1893. He came from a fairly large family and he had an older brother who boxed a bit and who first used the name Lewis as a ring name. He helped guide Ted throughout his first few years in the sport. Ted had that first professional fight in August 1909, the first of around 300 bouts of boxing that spanned the next twenty years. Fighting at six different weight divisions and winning numerous British, Empire, European and World titles, Lewis was this country's greatest Jewish boxing star. One of Britain's greatest ever boxers, he still regularly appears in most boxing expert's top fifty boxers of all time, worldwide.

By the start of the first World War Lewis was a British and European champion and becoming a household name. He was about to surpass Britain's other big star, fellow East Londoner Bombardier Billy Wells in that respect. Wells went off to fight in the trenches, Lewis went off to fight in America. Glory awaited. Although Wells and the Kid both grew up in the same tough, uncompromising area, their approach and attitude to boxing were complete opposites. Wells just fell short of world glory due mainly to the fact that he did not possess what is regarded in boxing parlance as 'the Killer instinct'.

In comparison, as a boxer, Lewis was a clinically cold and calculating assassin. He was utterly ruthless once inside the ropes. Outside of them he was an extremely pleasant, warm-hearted and gregarious man. He was instantly recognisable. As intimidating to behold as he was to fight. His large, almost sad looking eyes were permanently fixed on his opponent from the time the pair touched gloves before the opening bell. His nose, flattened by his opponent's fists, was part of an oversized chunky head. Unmistakably a boxer. He carried a quite terrifying impassive expression around the ring. His eyes were like that of a shark, deep, dark and cold with very little movement. Dead almost to the onlooker, but they missed nothing. Looking back, perhaps he could have become known as the 'Great White Shark' but instead, he became known as the Aldgate Sphinx after the tough area he came from – and that extraordinary head.

Of all the boxers that appear on these pages, Ted Kid Lewis probably demands more space than most. His achievements were astonishing. Notwithstanding his excellent amateur record over four years, Lewis fought 299 recorded professional matches and several more that may have slipped past the recorders of the day. For most of his career, Ted was conceding significant weight to a great many of his opponents and also going into their back yards to do so. Aside from his native Britain, he fought in America,

Australia, Canada, South Africa, France, Italy and Germany. In one incredible week of boxing in America, he fought six times in seven nights in five different cities.

The Lewis style was noticeably different from most of that era. In fact, it was more akin to many of today's fighters. If you look at the old pictures of boxers in those days and their earlier bare-knuckle colleagues, you will often see them posed with hands held high and somewhat forward. This high style was the accepted norm of the day. Ted carried his hands lower. You would often see his left hand resting on his hip before he delivered it. His right was only slightly higher, positioned into its firing position, half-cocked but never telegraphing the volley of vicious hooks that would spearhead the next attack.

Ted Kid Lewis was considered an aggressive attacking fighter as opposed to those that favoured a more defensive counter punching basis to their boxing style. Ted was never a 'slugger' and he possessed great patience during his matches. He stalked his opponents relentlessly. Never better was his style illustrated than in the second of his two fights against Johnny Basham, the excellent Welsh welterweight. In 1920 Lewis fought a twenty-round re-match against Basham for the British/Empire and European titles. The first fight, five months earlier, had resulted in a win for Lewis via an unfortunate ninth-round retirement by Basham. Basham upped his game for this re-match. With youth on his side, he tried to out-manoeuvre Lewis and counter-punch. Things went more or less to plan for Johnny and he was boxing cleverly. The longer it went on, the greater Basham's chances were of wearing down the older man. Lewis however, was a different animal.

From the many reports I studied of the match, it was an evenly balanced game of cat and mouse that was seen from ringside that night. Lewis stalked his man throughout the first eighteen rounds, unable to land a decisive blow. Never once though, did Lewis betray his frustration at failing to catch the elusive Welshman. Quick and skilful, full of artful feints, subtle shifts and pin-point counters, Basham boxed beautifully and had fashioned a reasonable points lead after eighteen rounds, but Ted kept shadowing him with the patience of a big cat that knows the best meals can take a long time coming. There never seemed a moment when Ted was idle in the ring, even when he was having to make the most of a bad job. Basham was a shrewd mechanic, a thinking man's boxer using the ring space to its fullest extent and it was essential for Lewis to make the most of the rare chances that came his way. The Kid was a mean operator in the clinches, all the time ripping punches to Basham's body to slow him down and tire him out, but Johnny held on gamely.

Johnny was so close to getting over the line and securing a points decision when the violent end to his efforts came in the nineteenth round. Having skilfully manoeuvred his way around the tornado that was Lewis for the best part of an hour, he was suddenly sucked into its eye and sent sprawling by a vicious two-fisted combination that culminated in a big left hook to the jaw. Clearly dazed, Basham was up at the count of nine but now had nowhere to hide and no more cards to play. Trapped on the ropes, he was caught by a fusillade of punches and was trying desperately to escape when a big left hook swept him into oblivion.

The referee that evening was one of Britain's foremost officials, Eugene Corri. Twelve years later Corri wrote about Ted Kid Lewis, someone he got to know quite well, in one of a series of articles about London boxing that appeared in the *Sunday Pictorial*. Firstly, describing the fight as one of the best he had the pleasure to handle, he made this telling comment about Lewis:

I suppose the chief boxing characteristics of Lewis is what American sports writers, with their gift for picturesque exaggeration, call the Killer-instinct. That is not to say that he went out to slay his opponents but merely that his tactics were more merciless than those of the average boxer. He was, too, adept at all the tricks of his trade. Any opponent of his who tried what we euphemistically term 'unorthodox' methods usually had cause to regret it, for almost always Lewis knew a better trick.

It was armed with these qualities and expertly trained by Charlie Harvey that Ted Kid Lewis's adventures in America cemented his reputation. The crowds there loved him. They supported aggressive fighters more in America. Paradoxically, some American referees did not. They were still looking for pure technical abilities. Experts today look back on Lewis's boxing records and the various fight reports and can confidently claim that if those fights happened under today's perception of what constitutes a winning round, then Lewis's record would be even better. For all of his fateful misfortunes on those close points decisions, Lewis scooped nine official championships in his long and illustrious career, starting out as a featherweight and working his way through the divisions. At one point during his career, despite rarely hitting the scales at more than 140lbs, he held the British welterweight, middleweight and light heavyweight titles simultaneously.[2]

Ted's work Stateside was hugely impressive. Not just for his results but for the pure number of fights and the distance he travelled to appear at so many venues. In 1917 alone, he fought thirty times all over America, from New York in the east to San Francisco in the west. Without doubt his time in America would be most remembered for his legendary series of fights against the equally tough and durable Jack Britton. This was the period that he boxed at welterweight. It was probably the golden period for Lewis. Indeed, it was a golden period for welterweights generally. The division was packed with some seriously fine boxers in both

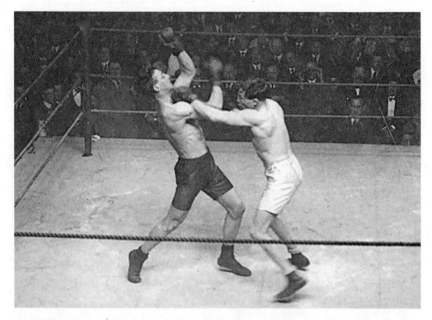

Ted Kid Lewis (right) v Roland Todd. Todd, who had sparred with Ted Kid Lewis as a young pro, lost this title fight but won the return match held three months later.

America and Europe. It would take a separate book to detail just half of Lewis's matches and achievements so I will just finish off with some brief points about his famed series of twenty fights against American Jack Britton.

The growth of sport world-wide grew exponentially from the turn of the twentieth century thanks to the advances of transport. Most sports have become inter-continental with an enormous number of sportsmen being able to travel long distances to pursue their activities. Rivalries in sport have long been around but over the past 100 years or more a number of high-profile sporting rivalries have captured the public's imagination. Borg v McEnroe, Alain Prost v Senna, Seb Coe and Steve Ovett. Even the Ashes Cricket Tests have enthralled spectators since Harold Larwood tried to decapitate Don Bradman. Countries too can be great sporting rivals, even if they have to travel halfway around the globe to meet. Boxing is no exception. Some experts view the two Evander Holyfield/Mike Tyson fights as a great boxing rivalry, and the Ali and Joe Frazer battles, but these do not compare with the six gruelling fights that took place between Jake La Motta and Sugar Ray Robinson. All great fights undoubtedly, but even the latter pale into insignificance when compared to the Lewis/ Britton series of fights.

Quite a few words have been written by boxing experts on the Lewis v Britton series of fights. Yes, those series of matches were of an age. Yes, those fights were fought by boxers whose power and speed may not be that of the top modern-day professionals and yes, today's training techniques and dietary regimes were not around then. Little footage remains to accurately assess the standards. The modern fan poring over all those fights between Lewis and Britton might easily misconstrue their rivalry as being something of an old pal's act. Nothing could be further from the truth. The competition between the two men burnt with fierce intensity throughout its six-year duration that began in August 1915, when Ted dethroned Jack on a 12-rounds decision at the Boston Armory.

For those who labour under the sweet delusion that the fighters of the past were too gentlemanly to trade insults or ignore today's traditional pre-fight customs, let it be said that Lewis and Britton didn't behave like boy scouts prior to that first fight. The two parties argued intensely over the weigh-in. Acrimony was present in subsequent fights too. The two men exchanged threats, refused to shake hands and tried their best to take each other's heads off once in the ring. Both boxers and their accompanying corner men often hurled insults at each other. Even the early use of a gumshield by Lewis was hotly argued over.

They would need a further nineteen arguments before they got the bad blood out of their system. Many of the rematches were no-decision affairs, but they were never dull. Jack Britton finally put the lid on the long-running feud with a unanimous decision over The Kid at Madison Square Garden on 8 February 1921. Even this match was marred by controversy. Charles F Matherson, the acclaimed *New York Times* boxing reporter who was at ringside that night wrote:

> After the bell sounded to end the second round, Britton walked over to Lewis's corner to complain about unfair tactics and the way Lewis was delivering his punches. One of the seconds made some remark to Britton who then hooked him in the face, knocking him through the ropes. Britton's seconds, and some police who had stepped in, finally induced Britton to go to his corner.

So, controversy was present to the very end of a series of boxing matches that everyone agrees the likes of which will never be witnessed again.

Two great adversaries, Johnny Basham and Ted Lewis ahead of their 1920 championship fight.

When Ted Kid Lewis fought his first professional bout of boxing in 1909, lots of good Jewish boxers were already parading their talents around the capital. From the turn of the twentieth century, several specialist boxing venues started to appear around London. One of the first, The Wonderland, in Whitechapel highlighted several of this new breed of Jewish boxers.

Aschel Joseph, otherwise known as 'Young' Joseph(s), boxed at the Wonderland soon after it opened in 1900 and fought continuously at the venue until 1905, losing just once. In May that year Joseph fought out a draw for the British lightweight title before going on to take the British welterweight title against Corporal Bill Baker in 1909 and followed that up with winning the European title in Paris the following year. In 1911, he was due to fight the next rising star of the East, Johnny Summers, but the match was postponed. A couple of losses followed and when he lost the re-arranged match against Summers in 1912, and then his European title against Albert Badoud in 1914, he was rapidly approaching the end of the road. After a dispute with the National Sporting Club over a title defence against Arthur Everdon later that year, he was stripped of his title and called it a day on a very good career. He fell into poor health in his middle age and died in 1952 aged 67.

During the first half of the twentieth century, Britain failed to produce a great heavyweight boxer. In fact, with the exception of possibly Henry Cooper, only Frank Bruno and then the great Lennox Lewis were to immerge as approaching world class during the latter part of the century. In London, none of the Jewish lads that took up the sport would make a serious impact in the heavyweight division. The incomparable Ted Lewis, who fought at many weights, had a couple of light heavyweight fights at the tail end of his career but all his great work was done at the middle weights. At the start of the century, Jewish boxers were coming through in force at the lighter weights. One of the first very lighter weight boxer to have a big impact was Sid Smith.

Sid Smith was born in Bermondsey in 1889, not far from the notorious Jacob's Island rookery, on the Thames. Smith is listed as a Jewish boxer but from my research it would seem he was half Jewish. It looks like his father was possibly a Catholic and a keen boxing fan. One day his dad took him along to the Oxford Medical Mission Boxing Club in Bermondsey. This was a Christian club and produced a couple of very good Catholic boxers. Smith was to join the well-known Catholic organisation, The Knights of Columbus, in America in his later life. What is beyond dispute was that he was a superb boxer, with great ringcraft and at the peak of his career, he was a world-class act.

Sid started professional boxing in 1907 and became Britain's first official flyweight champion in 1911. In 1912 he travelled to America to fight a couple of bouts with the hope of challenging for a world title. At that particular time there was not a flyweight division in operation in the States. Sid was good enough to fight 'light' at bantamweight and challenged the American bantamweight world champion, Johnny Coulon, but Coulon's connections were not interested.

Sid returned to Britain to fight in defence of his title against Curly Walker at the 'Ring' boxing arena in Blackfriars, which he won in a close twenty-round contest. This set up a match against the impressive French flyweight European champion, Eugene Criqui, in Paris on 11 April 1913. It was billed as a joint European and World 100lb title (flyweight) championship match, under the International Boxing Union. Criqui is regarded alongside the acclaimed George Carpentier as one of France's two greatest boxers.

Sid duly won a great fight against this exceptional opponent over twenty rounds. That win made Sid Smith the first British boxer of Jewish heritage to hold a world crown. Criqui went on to take the featherweight world title a few years later. Sid was now universally regarded as the best flyweight around, but it was to last just two months. In a defence of his British title in June, he surprisingly lost to Bill Ladbury. In October that same year, he also lost his European crown. Sid boxed on with mixed success for another year until he got matched against the world's greatest flyweight boxer of all time, the brilliant and legendary Jimmy Wilde. He fought the phenomenal Wilde three times between 1914 and 1916, losing all three.

Although Sid Smith fought on until 1919, he was rapidly approaching the end of a fine career. In his final bout, appropriately on Boxing Day in 1919, he beat Johnny Marshall inside eleven rounds to turn back the clock. Sid realised that his time was up though, and he climbed out through the ropes and into retirement.

Welshman Jimmy Wilde, the Mighty Atom as he was often called, totally dominated the world flyweight division for almost ten years. Including Sid Smith, he fought several other very good London boxers. Many Jewish boxers fought at the lighter weights so Wilde was matched against quite a few. Such was Wilde's power and skill he was often pitched in against heavier boxers, although he always climbed into the ring at minimum weight, around 40kgs or 100lbs (seven stones) He was a tiny but powerful man.

Joseph Cohen from Bow was a better than average featherweight journeyman boxer. By 1918 the unbelievably gifted flyweight, Jimmy Wilde had run out of opponents at flyweight and had already fought and won against bantamweight fighters. Joe Cohen, who fought under the name Conn, was progressing well at featherweight and he answered the call to fight Wilde at that weight. The bout took place at Chelsea's Stamford Bridge football stadium. The promoters wanted to see just how far Wilde could go against bigger men. Joe put up great resistance to the amazing force of nature that was Wilde and boxed with skill and determination. He had Wilde in trouble a couple of times but eventually Wilde gained the upper hand and stopped Joe in the twelfth round. One of the great fights. Joe came out of the fight with an enhanced reputation.

Joe Conn was another Jewish boxer that came through the ranks of the many East End boys boxing clubs. Unlike his nemesis, Jimmy Wilde, his early career was fairly unimpressive. However, in 1915 he started boxing at the Premierland Arena and his results started to improve. He also fought at the more prestigious Ring arena at Blackfriars and his results there improved still further. His run of twelve winning fights is what brought him to the attention of the promoters for the Wilde fight.

He was promised a title fight at featherweight if he performed well against the world beating Wilde. We know now that he did. So, eight weeks after the Wilde fight, Joe got his crack at the British title. It couldn't have been a tougher ask. Sitting in the opposite corner was Tancy Lee. Lee, a canny Scot, was another excellent boxer from the period. Lee was the first boxer ever to defeat Jimmy Wilde at flyweight and furthermore, he did so in a title fight against Wilde when the small man was approaching the peak of his powers. Tancy originally boxed as a borderline fly but with the emergence of Wilde he had sensibly moved on to bantam and then featherweight. Coming just eight weeks after the Wilde fight, Conn was not at his sharpest and was knocked out well inside the distance. Conn had a tilt at the European crown in 1920 without success and in his later career he became a steady, journeyman type boxer who fought both here and in America with mixed results. He retired in 1925 after 125 bouts.

The two 'kids', Lewis and Berg, are by far the most well-known of the great Jewish boxers of the twentieth century. They both won multiple championships and were both world champions.

They were both larger than life characters who carved out astonishing results at the middleweights. They were also born within a mile of each other in London's East End. There was however, another great but lesser-known Jewish boxer that could also lay claim to be counted alongside these Jewish greats.

Matthew Wells was not born in the East End but came from south of the River Thames. He was born in December 1884 in Walworth, yet another young Jewish lad started his career at the turn of the century. Wells had a very impressive amateur career. As indicated earlier, he boxed at the famous Lynn AC Boxing Club in South London and held the British amateur lightweight title between 1904 and 1907. Matt Wells's early fights were a series of close-fought affairs, but he managed to come through them all undefeated. He then went over to fight a series of matches against some very good American lightweights, losing just once. He was becoming a serious contender and in February 1911 he returned to London to fight the talented Welsh boxer Freddie Welsh (real name Thomas) at the National Sporting Club, Covent Garden, for the British and European lightweight title. Welsh came into the fight on the back of some impressive results and was a more experienced boxer than Wells. The fight was a fiercely fought twenty-rounder, a humdinger of a match that Wells won on a points decision. He was awarded the Lonsdale Belt, the first Jewish boxer to win one.

Later in the year he returned to America and fought well until running up against the extremely useful Packey McFarland and was well beaten. He left the ring blooded to lick his wounds. Back in Britain at the end of that year he fought a re-match against Freddie Welsh but this time he lost. It was again a closely fought match. Welsh was later to claim the world lightweight title. In 1912 Wells tried his luck in Australia with some success, but he decided to move up to fight at welterweight in 1913 and easily won his first bout before taking on Tom McCormick for the British Empire and World welterweight crowns. Wells just did enough in a packed-out Sidney Stadium in front of a vociferous Aussie crowd to secure the win in another of his trademark close matches. Wells was officially the world welterweight champion.

He was not to know it then, but that was to be the pinnacle of his career. Back home he boxed a few more bouts with reasonable results, and in March 1915 he took on the rising star Johnny Basham in a non-title fight. Basham you will recall was the fighter that Ted Lewis had stalked so relentlessly in that pair's later 1920 epic contest. Matt Wells had beaten Johnny in his earlier days but this time the very improved Welshman just got the better of Wells over fifteen rounds. Wells headed back stateside for a title defence of his world crown against Mike Glover and lost a tight match on points.

Matt fought a few more contests with some mixed results until he came up against the future world feather and junior lightweight, American Johnny Dundee, in a twelve-round contest in Boston on 16 May 1916. In the one-sided affair Wells was soundly defeated. Worse was to follow. Wells succumbed to his only knockout on 11 July 1916, from British-born but American-based lightweight, Charlie White, in the fifth round. White had a renowned left hook and that is what did for Wells.

Matt Wells boxed on until 1922 and had some more tough fights against world champions Jimmy Duffy and Ted Kid Lewis. He retired on a record he could be rightfully proud of as one of Britain's greater lightweight boxers. His career should have stayed in the memory of most boxing fans of the day but if it did, it soon faded. Unlike his namesake of that era, Bombardier Billy Wells, Matt did not go on to pursue other lines of work after leaving the ring. Instead, he became a time-keeper and sometime referee and it was for his refereeing that he may be better remembered: but for all the wrong reasons.

In March 1933, Wells was retained to referee a non-title heavyweight match between German champion Walter Neusel and the South African Don McCorkindale at The Royal Albert Hall. The fight went the distance, but the in-form German champion dominated throughout most of the rounds and at the final bell all Wells had to do was to raise the German's arm. You could hear the audible gasp in the audience when Wells called the match a draw. Not one person there that night, not even the boxers themselves, could believe the decision. The German's corner went mad and calls were made in its aftermath to investigate the fight.

The British Boxing Board of Control (BBBofC) hauled Wells in front of them and asked for an explanation but Wells merely stated that as an 'old school' boxer, he thought it was too close a contest to call. He was later asked to produce his score card for the match but said he had shown it to a ringside reporter on the night and not got it back. The authorities refused to agree with Wells and did not believe his story about his score card. His licence was suspended. Rumours were now rife that the fight had been 'fixed'. Match fixing in this country, unlike some other countries, has been virtually non-existent. Matt Wells took the matter to court. It was suggested that he was being backed by some shadowy underworld figures who wanted to ensure their man carried on in the sport. Unfortunately, after a week-long hearing, Wells lost his case and if his underworld 'friends' were around, they faded back into the shadows and left Wells to foot the legal costs, which bankrupted him. A sad end to a very good career.

I referred earlier to the fact that many Jewish boxers would adopt an anglicised ring name under which they fought. The great

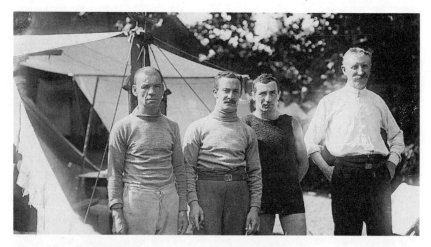

Matt Wells, a great lightweight boxer, third right, seen here at a training camp in America in June 1911 with (left to right) an unknown sparring partner, an unidentified trainer and manager George McDonald.

Ted Kid Lewis did so, and the popular Jack Kid Berg shortened his surname from Bergman but both were proudly Jewish. Berg always boxed in a pair of trunks that displayed the Star of David. I am not sure whether it was a promoter or one of his coaches who persuaded this next gifted Jewish boxer to change his name but I suspect most people who saw this young man box could not care a jot under which name he fought. His ringcraft and flashing fists is what they came to see.

Johnny Brown is known as one of the world's greatest bantamweight boxers of the 1920s but as with so many, Brown was not his real name. Depending on what genealogy or early history you read, Johnny's real surname was either Hickman, Heckman or Eckman. From family history research, I believe he was an Eckman. He came from a sporting family and was by far and away the best bantamweight boxer in Europe for several years. He changed his name when he turned professional in 1919. Starting his career as a flyweight, he also occasionally fought at featherweight and lightweight. Brown was born in Spitalfields in 1902 and fought as an amateur out of the Oxford and St George's Boxing Club and was their main star of the day. He showed promise from an early age and fought most of his early professional fights at The Ring, the prestigious boxing venue at Blackfriars. By late 1921 he had established himself and was offered a series of fights in North America. He was put up against some of America and Canada's best bantamweights and he produced some very decent results.

In the summer of 1923, he settled back in Britain in preparation for a tilt at the British title. In November 1923, he stepped into the ring at the National Sporting Club, Covent Garden, to fight for the British, Empire and European titles against Bugler Harry Lake. Lake was a vastly experienced boxer with almost 100 fights under his belt, losing only six times up to that point. It was an extremely close contest and it must have been a tough decision to split them but Brown's ringcraft probably just shaded it over twenty rounds and the judges awarded the bout to him.

Brown boxed regularly for the next two years, mainly at the Premierland venue, losing just once and successfully defended his titles a further two times. Brown became the first Jewish boxer to hold a Lonsdale Belt outright. By the end of 1925 Johnny sat at the top of the tree in Europe and was looking to step up a weight and maybe fight in the States once more, with a view to having a crack at the world featherweight title. At the start of 1926, Johnny had achieved everything possible this side of the Atlantic and was undoubtedly looking forward to taking that extra step to the very top. He had a few fights lined up in Canada and America over the next couple of months and crossed the Atlantic in great anticipation. Fate and form can be fickle and nobody on this side of the pond would ever have imagined what was going to happen in those North American fights.

Johnny Brown arrived in Toronto in early February in tremendous shape for what was supposed to be a straightforward warm-up fight against Carl Tremaine, a decent but journeyman Canadian boxer. In an extraordinary bout of boxing Brown was put down over ten times in a very one-sided affair. Things then went from bad to worse and Johnny lost his next seven fights in a huge turn around in his form. Any thoughts of challenging for a world title disappeared.

Brown returned home in early 1927 to reflect on his performances and have his ego massaged. After a few months rest, he stepped into the ring again and won. Things seemed to be improving slightly and he won a couple more fights before he was sent into face the prodigious talent that was the young Teddy Baldock, the 'Pride of Poplar', for a title clash. It was to be a fight too far for Johnny. On a hot August day at Clapton Orient's football ground in 1928, Johnny was comprehensively out-boxed for two rounds and offered little in defence. His corner had seen enough and threw in the towel. Johnny Brown walked away from that encounter and into retirement. For Baldock it was another step on the road to becoming Britain's youngest ever world champion.

Johnny Brown was followed into the ring by his younger brother who, unsurprisingly, went by the name **Young Johnny Brown.** Young Johnny, as we shall call him was almost three years younger than his brother and as an amateur, equally as good. Young Johnny was soon chasing his brother up the rankings. His early fights were at flyweight but he soon went to bantamweight, the same weight at which his elder brother boxed. Young Johnny was good and won his first seventeen matches. With two good boxing brothers the promoters cottoned on quickly that they could use this as a marketing ploy. In 1922, the bantamweight division was dominated by three boxers. One was the elder Brown brother and the other two were Frankie Ash and Bugler Harry Lake, both of whom were from the West Country. Harry Lake came from a boxing family, and he too had a precocious younger brother who had just started on the professional trail after being an impressive boxer in the amateur ranks. It was an opportunity not to be missed by the promoters.

On 25 August 1922 Young Johnny and his elder brother travelled down to the Cosmopolitan Gymnasium in Plymouth. The two younger siblings, followed by the two vastly more experienced elder siblings, were to face off against each other. 'The Battle of the Brothers' was how it was advertised. Young Johnny Brown was thought to have the edge on young Percy Lake but the non-title fight between the two older men was, on paper, too close to call. As it happened, on the night both fights were very close. The younger brothers from each family were first up and fought a reasonably decent contest, which young Percy Lake just won over fifteen rounds. The elder two brothers fought out a really close match over fifteen rounds of excellent boxing before Bugler got the decision. So, unfortunately, both the Browns were swamped by the Lakes that night and returned to London defeated, although the elder sibling was to take his revenge the following year.

Young Johnny's record, in terms of the number of fights, was very similar to his brother's and he did fight some top-ranked British fighters. Unlike his elder brother though, Young Johnny never quite made it to the very top of British boxing. He fought twice for the title but lost both times. He fought on until 1932 but his form that year started to fall off. By coincidence, both the brother's careers ended fighting East London boxers at football ground venues. Elder Johnny lost to Poplar's Teddy Baldock at Clapton Orient's ground in 1928 and the end for Young Johnny came at Southend Football Ground in 1932 at the hands of Bethnal Green's Dick Corbett.

Initially, Young Johnny thought he might box on but decided to take a break and consider his future. Early the following year he was driving a group of friends, including boxing champion

Harry Mason, when his car was involved in a bad collision with a coach near Colchester. The coach driver was seriously injured but fortunately the car passengers escaped with just cuts and bruises, apart from Johnny who had his wrist badly crushed. As a result, he decided to retire.

A little later we will deal with the journeyman boxers who were so important to the sport. Their names would be unknown to most people. **Mike Honeyman** was a boxer whose status falls somewhere between a Jewish star and a Jewish journeyman. His record mainly has the look of a journeyman about it, but it is a record that throws up some tremendous results. Mike was a great servant to the sport and after his boxing finished, he worked tirelessly within the sport and for several years was a physical education instructor in the RAF.

Honeyman was born in Woolwich in 1896 and had his first professional fight in January 1914. His first couple of years were notable for the number of boxers he faced multiple times. In his first seven fights he fought fellow Jewish boxer Sid Cohen from nearby Greenwich four times, winning them all. His eighth fight was against Alf Reed who was a really terrific and tough fighter from the East End Docks. Alf was already a veteran of almost 100 fights and Mike knocked Alf out in the second round.

His talent was beginning to be noticed. Most of his fights took place at the Pavilion in Manor Park, a short trip across the Thames on the Woolwich Ferry, but by the end of the year he was boxing at the more illustrious Ring venue in Blackfriars. During 1916 and 1917 he fought Fred Housego and Young Joe Brooks seven times. He was to fight Brooks six times during his career. By the end of the War, he was reaching his peak and in January 1920 he defeated Manchester's Billy Marchant to claim the British featherweight crown. He lost and then regained that title later the same year before losing it once again, the following year, to Joe Fox from Leeds. He never boxed again for a championship but carried on fighting regularly until 1926. He fought the Welsh featherweight Rossi brothers Walter and Francis Rossi six times and the great journeyman, Billy Bird, three times.

After retirement he was approached by his old manager, Joe Morris, to help prepare his young boxing prodigy, Teddy Baldock, for his bid to take the British bantamweight title. Mike instilled the ringcraft that he had acquired in over 150 professional bouts into the young Teddy and it added to his undoubted skills. They worked well together and Baldock not only took the British crown, he also went on to claim the world title in May 1927.

Although born in the heart of London, **Albert (Al) Foreman** could easily be referred to as being Canadian or American or British. Al was orphaned at an early age, and for ten years lived in an orphanage, the Hayes School for Jewish Boys in Middlesex. He moved to North London and learnt to box there. Foreman began boxing professionally in England in 1920 under the name of Bert (Kid) Harris. He fought over fifty fights in this country before moving to Canada in the summer of 1923 to try his luck over there. He also toured the United States Eastern Seaboard extensively. Now here is where it gets interesting. Although a resident of Canada he spent many months in America, and it appears that he joined the American army. There are several cases of Canadians serving in America but at this point Foreman was still a British citizen. Regardless of how this could happen he spent almost three years serving in the army and boxed both professionally and also for the army in their regimental competitions.

Al Forman finished his stint serving Uncle Sam by holding three of their service championships! Al returned to Canada and continued his boxing there and in October 1928, fought for the Canadian lightweight title and won. In May 1930, Foreman was back in Britain fighting at the Premierland against Fred Webster for the British and Empire lightweight title. By knocking out Webster in the first round, it meant that Al Foreman held a British and British Empire title, a Canadian title and a joint American Service championship title. Foreman was considered a late starter in his professional career, but he was now making up for lost time. Fights were coming thick and fast. He retained his British title in October that year. His win ratio was exceptional when he headed over to Australia to fight Bobby Kelso in early 1933, for the Empire title, and in a shock result, he lost narrowly on points to the Aussie. A month later though, the rematch took place and Foreman regained the title.

Al Foreman was in his fourteenth year as a professional boxer when he returned to his old haunt, Montreal, to fight Tommy Bland. Al was defending his British Empire title against Bland and Bland was defending his Canadian title against Foreman. Bland was almost ten years younger than Foreman but Al defied the odds to gain a hard-fought point win over the Canadian champ. The following month he contested a non-title fight, also in Montreal, against the big-hitting American Joe Ghnouly. In the second round Ghnouly smashed the bridge of Foreman's nose, which partially closed his eye and such was the impact that Foreman boxed blind in that eye for the next three rounds until his corner thought it too dangerous to continue and threw in the towel.

Although Al recovered from his injury, he must have realised that time was catching up with him. He fought just two more fights, one in Canada and one in the States and struggled in both. He brought the curtain down on his career in June 1934. Was it to be quiet retirement for the great Al Foreman now? No, it never entered his head! Instead, he embarked on another stage of his life that was just as dramatic and successful as his time in the ring. That is a very long story and one for another day I am afraid. Let's just say one of his later achievements was to be awarded the Distinguished Flying Cross (DFC). For now, you will have to make do with the ring achievements of this poor Jewish orphan boy from London. Sadly, he never got the chance to fight for the world championship crown. He travelled round the world and fought almost 150 bouts of boxing. A great champion.

Moe Mizler may not feature in the pantheon of the greatest London Jewish boxers but his place in these pages is assured. Moe Mizler and his brother Judah were among the first Jewish London boxers to make a name for themselves who were direct Eastern European immigrants, fleeing from their country at the turn of the twentieth century. They arrived with their parents around 1906. Moe was still a baby. Both lads joined Jewish youth clubs and fought at a very good standard at amateur level.

Moe fought at flyweight with his first recorded professional fight in 1926 at Premierland. His opponent that day was Nipper Pat Daly, the child boxing prodigy. Nipper was fighting his twenty fifth professional fight and when they faced each other Daly was just 13, about four years younger than Moe. (Daly would fight his first 15-round contest in October 1927, still aged just 14!) Daly was a huge rising star in the game, tipped in some quarters to be the next Jimmy Wilde, and despite Moe being a lot older and bigger, he lacked Daley's professional experience. Moe had his work cut out for him that day. Daley swarmed all over Moe at the start and it looked like being a very one-sided affair. To his credit, Mizler put up a stout defence and a very good contest developed. Luck though, was on Moe's side and an accidental clash of heads opened up a bad cut above Nipper's eye. The referee halted the fight and awarded it to Mizler. With that piece of good fortune, Mizler was off to a winning start. Moe won his next seven fights before drawing against the very experienced 'Kid' Rich.

By the end of 1927, he was fighting over fifteen rounds against some useful boxers. Taking on and beating the likes of Dod Oldfield, Young Siki and the durable Sheffield journeyman boxer, Dickie Inkles. He did lose the odd fight but Moe could be a dangerous fighter who could upset the odds and produce some excellent results. No more so than his series of fights against Frenchman, Praxille Gyde. On his day, Gyde was a world-class act. He was a multiple French and European champion when he fought Moe in three non-title fights in 1930 and 1931. After being somewhat controversially disqualified in his first match, Moe produced two stunning performances to beat Gyde, both over fifteen rounds in London. Mizler eventually got to within one fight of having a crack at the British Flyweight title. Sadly, he lost his final eliminator match in January 1931. It was probably at this point that Moe realised that the top spot was going to elude him. That was one reason he retired from the ring a year later. The other reason was his younger brother.

Harry Mizler was the younger brother of Moe Mizler and was another Jewish star in waiting. Harry was born a couple of years after his parents arrived in London so he was London born and bled. He is sometimes compared to Jack Berg, although they were different types of boxers. Harry was born four years after Jack, in Wicket Street, St George's and within a few hundred yards of Berg. By the time Berg was beginning to sweep all before him in the professional fight game, especially in America, Mizler was beginning to do the same in the amateur ranks.

By the late 1920s Harry Mizler had joined the Oxford and St George's Boxing Club and started to produce some impressive performances. Not too much of a surprise, as this boxing club was already established as a leading London club and his elder brothers were also spending time developing his boxing and ringcraft skills. Both Moe and Judah could see the potential star the family had in front of them. In 1930, Harry Mizler won the

British ABA bantamweight championship. In 1931 following Moe's defeat in his eliminator, young brother Harry was storming through the amateur ranks. It was just a matter of time before Harry would follow big brother Moe into the professional ring.

Moe was spending more and more time working with his brother, but Harry elected to spend a few more years in the amateur ranks with outstanding success. So, Moe was instrumental in nurturing young Harry and guiding him through his career. Harry Mizler won three amateur titles. Mizler's success as an amateur came at a price, but he would not realise just what that price was until a couple of years later. On his run to the 1933 ABA title, Harry noticed that his hands would swell up occasionally after a fight. In his ABA semi-final win, he displaced two bones in his right hand and he fought the final only after receiving some temporary treatment from a leading osteopath. It did the trick and Harry went out and won his third and final British amateur championship. Harry's hand healed up and he signed professional forms later that year.

He made the transition from amateur to professional seamlessly and his brother Moe was there to mentor him through the early years as he started to chase Jack Kid Berg up the rankings. It was a rapid rise, with sixteen straightforward wins. His hands held up well, but in most of his fights he stopped his opponents well inside the distance. Those short affairs meant he wasn't exposing his hands by banging away for round after round. In late 1933, he fought the tough Welsh lightweight champion, Evan Dale, over ten hard rounds. Mizler won, but once again his right hand swelled up after the fight. With a shot at the British title not far away, Mizler changed his more aggressive style and worked on his footwork, speed of movement and counter-punching, using his right hand more sparingly. Berg and Mizler fought at around the same weights as each other but as I said, they had quite differing styles. Berg was the all-action fighter whereas Mizler had now become a more circumspect and somewhat stylish operator. Mizler met veteran boxer Johnny Cuthbert for the British title later the following year at the Royal Albert Hall and he outboxed the older champion over fifteen rounds. A further rest was needed for his hands but his winning ways continued.

The 1930s were probably the golden period for Jewish boxing, with dozens of British area champions, and several British and European champs. Although Mizler failed to reach the very top of world boxing he did secure both the British and European crowns at lightweight. The Jewish boxers around at that time knew each other well. They were foes inside the ring but friends outside of it. Harry Mizler eventually fought Jack Kid Berg twice, but they were always firm friends. The first of these two fights between the two leading Jewish lightweights was a British title fight in late October 1934 and it was during this match that Harry realised the price he had to pay for his earlier success. He broke both hands inside the first four rounds of that match. Harry left the ring distraught that evening after losing his title, but he was determined to fight on. More work was required on his hand injuries, but he came back and boxed at very high levels for several more years. His astonishing win against Gustave Humery in late 1935 was a testimony to his will to produce tremendous results despite fighting with the handicap of delicate fists.

Boxing in London in the 1930s was big business and the London gladiators of the ring were the superstars of the day, with huge followings. Jewish boxers like Harry and Jack Berg grabbed the back page headlines along with the likes of the Corbett brothers, Johnny Quill, Eddie Phillips, Archie Sexton, Alby Day, Kid Froggy and Dave Crowley. It was more likely that the young London boy's sporting heroes of the day were the ones that climbed into the ring rather than those that kicked a ball. In an amusing interview given by eighty-year-old Jack White back in 2004 about him growing up as a Jewish lad in the 1930s, he recalls singing in the Shul choirs at the Philpot Street Great Synagogue. In 1939, Harry Mizler married Betty Greenfield in the Synagogue and young Jack was in the choir. At the end of the ceremony, Harry walked over to the choir and thanked them. Jack recounts:

> Harry Mizler came over to thank us lads, most of us knew who he was. One of the older boys at the back shouted out, "'Arry, make sure you give Drescher a good ol' tonkin' next time you meet."[3] Quick as a flash, Harry pulls out his left hand from behind him and there is a boxing glove on it! "I certainly will," Harry says. The boys all laugh but his gloved hand was spotted by the choir master who looked very displeased with what was going on, not to mention the officiating rabbi. Harry then sweeps up his new bride with his right arm and walks to the exit of the Synagogue where almost a dozen well known boxers of the day, including Jack Berg, Ted Lewis and Benny Caplan, had prepared a ceremonial 'arch of honour' for Harry. Each of them with a glove on the end of a stick to form the arch. Harry walked through with his arm raised high, turned with a big mischievous grin on his face and gave one last wave before he went on his way.

The story shows the camaraderie of the boxers in those days. No matter how hard the fight game was or how brightly their star shone, they always had the common touch. They never forgot their past and expected nothing from their future. Indeed, Harry Mizler continued to work long hours, helping out with his family's fish business throughout his boxing days. It beggars belief today, but at 6.00 am on the freezing cold morning of 19 January 1934, and just 9 hours after defeating Johnny Cuthbert to win the British lightweight title, Harry was pushing a stall-load of fish from Billingsgate Fish Market to Watney Street Market for the family business there; a distance of well over a mile!

Four days after he k.o.'d Norman Snow, Mizler took on Newcastle boxer Norman Dale and won on points. Mizler looks calm enough in this picture taken during the fight at the Ring. It was Christmas Day, 1933, and the referee was former British lightweight champion Johnny Summers.

The great Harry Mizler proudly displaying the Star of David on his shorts, with London-based ex-champion Johnny Summers officiating.

In the few years before the Second World War, the lightweight and welterweight divisions in British boxing were really strong. Of the many world-class boxers that were around then, most commentators on the sport agreed that Harry Mizler was the pick of that very good bunch. Harry possessed it all. The fact that he never made it to a world championship fight was, according to many that knew him, down to his commitment to his family and the hours he spent working in their business. Harry fought eighty of his eighty-one professional matches in this country. He probably needed to showcase his talents Stateside, but he never did and once his hands began to prove a problem, the chance passed him by. Mizler's career included a number of tremendous feats of courage and endurance that backed up his undoubted skills. None more so than his fight against the superb Frenchman and fellow Jew, Gustave Humery, at the Royal Albert Hall in October 1935. It probably goes down as one of the greatest lightweight fights seen in this country ever.

Both *The Courier* and *The Times* comments were telling:

An absolutely tremendous fight – Mizler, floored four times for 9 counts and once for 8 was saved by the bell. Battered at least half a dozen times along the ropes, Mizler suddenly landed a left-right on Humery's jaw, Mizler still could have lost but he kept his head and with a series of upper-cuts and hooks gave Humery no chance to recover.

Humery was iron-barked enough to stay on his feet, but he was now dazed by the rain of blows and blinded by their effects. To all intents he was "out" on his feet and the only course was the throwing in of the towel.

Harry's eldest brother, Judah, accompanied him to many of his fights and kept a diary of all his contests. He, too, thought the Humery fight was the best of Harry's career. Judah kept the diaries from his earliest days in boxing and they give a great insight into Harry's life in the ring.

Finally, we come to the last of the great Jewish champions. The Aldgate Tiger, **Al Phillips**. Al had an excellent amateur career, boxing for the Jewish Lads' Brigade and was tipped for great things. They were right. Signing pro forms in 1938, he had his first professional fight in September that year and a year later he had completed sixteen matches, winning every one with relative ease. He was well on his way to a championship, which was why it came as a surprise when, in his next fight, he was caught cold in the first round and was knocked out. That defeat to Red McDonald who, on paper, was never going to be in Phillips' league, was a bit of a shock but every dog has his day and that particular day belonged to Red.

The fight almost did not happen as Britain had just declared war on Germany three weeks before. Red had enlisted and was waiting for his papers to come through. Red just got the fight in before he went off to war the following week on the back of that win. Al however, dusted himself down, put that defeat behind him and continued his climb to the top. Al Phillips also served with great distinction during the war and saw a lot of action as part of the British special forces. He boxed a bit in the army in various service matches but continued boxing professionally when he could. Boxing was curtailed during hostilities but over those war years he went on a twenty-five-match unbeaten run until he met the very experienced Neil Tarleton for the British and Commonwealth featherweight title, at Belle Vue in Manchester in February 1945.

What was about to occur was that classic battle, a boxer versus a fighter. Not just that but it was also a match-up of the 'old master' v the young pretender. Phillips was a young powerhouse all-action fighter with lightning quick fists and reactions to match and a powerful punch. Tarleton was a hugely experienced boxer with great ringcraft and fight management skills. He had an impeccable defence and was technically one of the best boxers this country had produced. Tarleton was giving Phillips fourteen years in age and he was fighting his 148th bout. Al was fighting his 58th. It had all the hallmarks of being a very good match indeed. It was more than that. It was a breathtaking encounter of two different styles by two men at the top of their game. During the course of the match the different styles ebbed and flowed in terms of domination over fifteen pulsating rounds of non-stop attack, defence and counter-attack. Just when Al thought he was getting on top, Tarleton seemed to produce the perfect last-ditch defence and then follow it up with some impressive counter punching.

As the aggressor, by the later rounds Phillips must have thought he was just doing enough but over the last two rounds, Tarleton avoided nearly every punch thrown and replied with interest. In the last round Phillips launched one last attack and although he got through with a couple of punches, the sting had gone out of them. Neil carried on picking off Al with some sharp jabs and that proved just enough to gain Tarleton the win. A couple of dozen journalists and commentators were privileged to be ringside that night. Some had been reporting on the sport since the turn of the century, so had seen a lot of boxing. Most went on record as saying that the fight was the greatest championship boxing match they had witnessed in this country. High praise indeed, but little comfort to Al Phillips. For Neil Tarleton it was a super effort that ultimately was his last. Shortly after the fight he started to suffer from some ill health (Tarleton only had one lung) and with no prospect of fighting again for some while, he had to relinquish the title.

The way was left open for Al to try again and this time he defeated the hard hitting, powerfully built Guyanese-born Cliff Anderson in March 1947, to gain the British featherweight crown. It was another good fifteen-round match that was held at the Royal Albert Hall in front of a large crowd and with noisy Jewish support. He followed this up by winning the European title against Frenchman Ray Famechon. It was a very messy match and although Al started reasonably well, he had a nightmare of a seventh round against the Frenchman when he was put down five times. Al just hung on and recovered slightly at the break and went out to face Famechon, who must have thought the title was his. He waded in all guns blazing, but in his urgency, he head-butted Phillips forcefully, although it appeared accidental to many of the ringside reporters there. Al's forehead was cut quite badly. The ref ruled that it was Famechon's fault and he was disqualified. It was a fortunate result for Phillips, but you sometimes need some luck along with your talents and Al had the scar to prove it.

He defended his British title successfully two months later. His reign was short-lived though, fighting Ronnie Clayton later in September that year and losing. Al boxed on for a few more years but was in decline. He lost his European crown but kept boxing. In 1951, he had one further attempt to regain his title but he lost on points. He announced his retirement with immediate effect, making him effectively the last of the really great London Jewish boxing stars. He kept in the game and became a manager and matchmaker. He managed British heavyweight champion Brian London and was working well into his sixties.

6

'NEVER MIND THE QUALITY –
FEEL THE WIDTH!'

Amongst the older readers, some may remember a TV comedy series of the sixties with this title. It was a Thames Television production featuring John Bluthal and Joe Lynch that told the story of an Irish Catholic and a Jewish tailor who went into business together in London during the late 1950s. The two had differing religious, political and business views, which was often the prompt for comical events. The Irish tailor produces trousers and considers himself a real master craftsman and uses the description 'Trouser Maker to the Gentry'. His Jewish, less pretentious partner makes jackets to go with the trews. It was very popular and ran for almost five years. Very irreverent and with obviously stereotypical characters, it would probably never get aired on today's television.

The premise of the show was that the Irish tailor wants to produce high-quality trousers cut from the finest material and the Jewish tailor wants to get as many jackets out of a single cheap width of cloth as possible. The result: incompatibility in both their working lives and the products they produce. On the religious front, the parish priest and the local rabbi also get in on the act. It's all pretty obvious.

Around the time this was set, the fight game in London was coming to the end of an era that very much echoed the sentiment of that TV title. From the start of the century, the demand for boxing both nationwide and abroad grew enormously. Londoners loved the sport and all over the capital boxing venues started to appear. Jewish boxers stepped up to fill the demand during this period. Their names appeared regularly on the billboards and posters that advertised the fights. There were hundreds of Jewish fighters boxing at venues up and down the country and beyond. There were some great champions as well as durable journeymen boxers in their ranks during this period, especially in the earlier times – the 'width'.

This was also true for the many Irish boxers that also found their way out of the slums through boxing. These boxers were realists and they fought to feed their families. As long as the public flocked to the boxing halls and arenas, it was a case of the more the merrier for most of these men.

A couple of the early purpose-built boxing arenas were the Wonderland Arena in Whitechapel Road, which started life in 1900, and the more prestigious Ring boxing arena in Blackfriars, south of the Thames. The Ring in particular was a magnet for any decent boxer in these early days, but it was at the Wonderland that a huge number of Jewish boxers climbed into the ring for the start of their journey. For many, it was a long and painful one.

One of the first Jewish characters to ply his trade at the Wonderland was **Cockney Cohen**. He was actually born in Leeds in 1882. His parents had made the journey north to escape the London Victorian slums although I would have thought that the heavy industrialised Leeds was probably not much better. Nevertheless, the lad obviously felt a tie to the East End because after starting his professional career in the North East he moved south in the summer of 1902. He was also married around this time.

Cockney's first name was actually Morris and after bedding down in London, he fought almost exclusively at the Wonderland until 1909. He often made a trip back up north for a fight or two and to meet up with his wife and other family members. He started well at the Wonderland and enjoyed seven straight wins in that year, but after that his form became more inconsistent. In 1905 he was back in the North East for the birth of his son. Fighting mainly at featherweight, Cockney persisted and went on to rack up over eighty fights, finishing his career at London's other well-known boxing venue, Premierland. Morris (Cockney) Cohen is sometimes confused with another colourful East London character with the same name. Morris 'Two Gun' Cohen will appear later and has an extraordinary tale to tell. In some cases, Jewish boxers fought under three, four or sometimes five different names during their time in the ring. It can get quite confusing. When this happened though, it generally denoted a long career and that is certainly true of Freddie Jacks.

Freddie Jacks was born with the name of Jacob Koppleman but during an interesting career he fought under various aliases including Fred Jacques, Stoker Jacobs, Eddie Welsh and Sailor Jacks. Freddie had his first pro fight at the Judean Club in 1910 but soon gravitated to the Premierland Arena and then The Ring venue in Blackfriars. Freddie boxed at featherweight and lightweight. He was born in Aldgate in 1893 and he grew up with the great Ted Kid Lewis. They were born within a few weeks and a few yards of each other. Their boxing careers, however, were nowhere near as close.

In December 1913 Jacks went over to France to fight French Champion Paul Til. He fought quite well but lost on points. They had similar styles, so when Til and Ted Lewis were matched to fight for the European title the following year, Lewis called on his old childhood friend to act as his sparring partner. It paid off as Lewis duly won his match against the Frenchman. Jack's career was unusual. Up until 1920 he fought the most of his matches in and around London but in that year, after a few disappointing results, he decided to try his luck further afield. For the next eight years he fought almost continuously in America and Australia. Unlike his childhood friend Lewis, who successfully travelled the world during a glittering career; for Freddie there were only meagre pickings to be had in these places. His form deteriorated still further and after twenty straight defeats, he called time on his career.

Throughout **Sid Burns'** time in the ring, the term quantity rather than quality was often used in describing Sid's career. Initially, his matches were typical of a young professional boxer starting out. He began in 1910 with fifteen bouts and had duly won ten of them. There followed no shortage of matches for Burns, twenty-six in fact, during that year, but the men that he faced in the ring were distinctly average. Burns made the point that he could only beat what was put in front of him and beat them he did, losing just once that year. He even intimated that it was possible that some of the higher ranked boxers were deliberately avoiding him.

Burns was getting a bit of a reputation for arrogance and word was getting out from his sparring sessions that he took pleasure in humiliating some of the young lads that were brought in to work with him during training. It was not until later in 1911 that Burns started to be matched against better opponents. Still, his form remained very good until he met Jack Goldswain, a previous holder of the British and Empire lightweight title and still a very good boxer. Sam put up a decent show but lost on a points decision. Rumours were still around about his attitude when he pushed to be matched against the brilliant up-and-coming French star, George Carpentier. Carpentier was being tipped to reach the very top in boxing. Burns obviously thought a win against such a brilliant fighter would silence his critics. For Carpentier it was just another fight on the way up and despite a brave attempt by Burns, the Frenchman proved too good.

It seemed that Sid Burn's detractors were being proved correct. Another loss to the durable Bermondsey boxer, Young Nipper, cemented their views that Burns was a good but not a great fighter and that a title would prove too much for him. That was not quite the case. In January 1912, against all odds, he fought and defeated British champion Johnny Summers in Liverpool. It was billed as a championship fight to claim the British welterweight title. Occasionally when British title contests did not take place at boxing's HQ, the National Sporting Club in London, the result was not officially ratified by the sport's governing body, but in most circles Sid Burns was the true champion. Sid had gone some way to disproving his critics' claims.

Buoyed by success, Sid reeled off a few more wins before accepting a rematch against Summers. This time it was to take place at the National Sporting Club. An excellent twenty-round fight resulted in a narrow win for Summers. In 1913, Sid travelled to Australia for a series of arranged fights. He was matched to face two of his old rivals, Johnny Summers for a third fight and a second match against Young Nipper. Although he beat Nipper in a non-title fight, he lost again to Summers for the British Empire championship. Sid's career petered out and soon after retiring from the ring, he was forced to pick up some money by sparring with some future champions. Unfortunately for Sid, a couple of them were the youngsters he had treated with disdain in previous years. They had progressed well and were rising through the ranks. Young, fit, dangerous and with a long memory, including future World champion Ted Kid Lewis, they gave old Sid a taste of his own medicine during those sessions.

Unlike Sid Burns, **Lew Pinkus** was a very popular figure on the circuit, but he was not too successful. He fought 107 fights between 1926 and 1933 but never really got close to challenging for a title. Lew was a home-loving lad, that's why I think it safe to say that, like a fine wine or a decent cask ale, Lew did not travel too well. In fact, of the 107 bouts of boxing, he only fought outside London eighteen times. He lost fifteen of them! Lew was born in 1908 in Bethnal Green, into a very poor household. Of slight build and rather sickly as a child, he did well to survive his formative years. His parents thought that joining the local boys' club would toughen him up. It did indeed. He picked up boxing, turning professional on his eighteenth birthday. His first fights were at flyweight but he gradually started to fill out and within a couple of years was boxing at featherweight. It would be only too easy to dismiss Lew as a poor 'also ran' but his record of won 35, drawn 15 and lost 59 fails to tell the story of the man.

The 1920s and 30s were the golden age of British boxing and Lew fought right in the middle of it. In 1927 he fought and drew a great match against a very good Fred Housego, before taking on Billy Hindley two months later. Hindley was the opposite of Lew as he travelled all over the world practising his art and fought some good boxers from many other countries. Hindley was a very experienced boxer and although Lew lost the bout, he fought well. Over the next six years he fought the likes of Dick Corbett, Alf Kid Pattenden, Al Forman and Nel Tarleton, all of whom held British titles and had a decent fight against the great world champion Teddy Baldock. He also fought Nipper Pat Daly, the amazing 'Boy Boxer'.

Pinkus can be rightly proud of his career. So too his parents, as they were the ones that helped get him into boxing as a youngster when they sent him off to the local boxing club to toughen him up. They would probably also have been surprised that their somewhat frail son not only completed 107 matches but also lived to the ripe old age of ninety. Some feat, given his background.

Con Lewis, like Lew Pinkus, lived in Bethnal Green. They were almost the same age and fought on the same amateur and professional circuits together. Con also boxed mainly at featherweight. Con and Lew fought each other professionally just twice, which is quite surprising. In those days, boxers of the same weight and similar standards often fought each other fairly regularly, especially if they lived in the same area. They were easy matches to set up and promote.

Lewis was probably the pick of the two. Con was even more content to fight close to home. In fact, Con never boxed outside London during his entire career, which spanned eight years and almost sixty fights. Well over half of these were at the Premierland in Whitechapel and the furthest he ever got was boxing at the Vale Hall in Kilburn, North London. He lost that fight and quipped, tongue in cheek, after the match, that he had come so far north he got a nosebleed and that was why the ref stopped the fight. In actual fact, he also faced the superb boy boxer, Nipper Pat Daly and was well beaten before the ref stopped the fight in the seventh round. The blood from the Lewis nose caused by leather rather than altitude.

Many boxers often changed their name to anglicise it for promotional purposes or in some cases to enhance their style and image. By the outbreak of war in 1939, the various communities had more or less integrated into the wider demographics of a developing cosmopolitan capital. They were becoming increasingly comfortable with their place in London society and proud of their religion. Several Jewish boxers wore the Star of David. Jack Kid Berg, Harry Mizler and Young Johnny Brown proudly displayed the star on their trunks in their fights in front of some big crowds all around the country, but even around the smaller events, the reputation of teak-tough Jewish boxers enabled them to carry this emblem of their faith into the ring with them.

Phil Lolosky was born in Aldgate. Phil was a proud Sephardic Jew and boxed under his family name rather than use an alias. The question of boxing under an alias was once put to Phil. In an interview he gave to *Sports Weekly* in December 1926, he made his point of view clear:

> I was born in the city of London on 17 May 1905 and my parents are born Londoners. I state this because my name might be thought foreign, as it were. When I was fighting in the West End (I will not mention the precise occasion for obvious reasons) not so long ago, a friend of mine heard someone remark 'Lolosky? Another of those blooming foreigners.' As a matter of fact, my opponent who bore a borrowed English name was the foreigner, yet he was passed without question. I am English and proud of it, why, my forefathers, for goodness knows how many generations, have been born either in or within a stone's throw of the city boundary.

Phil, a lighter weight boxer, had a shorter career in the ring which started in 1925 and was initially quite successful. Having lost in his debut contest, he then won his next thirteen matches including beating the Belgium European champion, Nicolas Petit-Biquet, in a non-title fight at the Royal Albert Hall in November 1926. Phil was short and while he was boxing at flyweight and bantamweight, he was quite competitive. Lolosky fought some good fighters but never quite got to the top of the British rankings and by the time he met and married the beautiful model and Palladium Tiller Girl, Isabel Da Costa in 1930, his best fights were behind him.

Phil loved his food and he started to put on the pounds. He began to be known as Phil 'Tubby' Lolosky and as his weight increased, he had to move up to featherweight where he faced taller and better men. He then ran into some really talented boxers in the shape of the brilliant Teddy Baldock and Young Johnny Brown. Possibly at the urging of his young wife, Phil fought less and eventually retired in 1934.

Jack Hyams knew Phil Lolosky well during his time as a boxer, but unlike Phil he never made any reference to using aliases so it's a mystery why he started fighting under a very strange one indeed. He boxed professionally as 'Kid Froggy'. It is said that he may have picked up the nickname of froggy growing up as a lad in the Whitechapel/Stepney area of London, but nobody seems to know for sure. Hyams, or Kid Froggy as we shall call him, said little about his faith or background. He let his fists do the talking and they never stopped chatting. Froggy was to become a prolific fighter. He attended school in Myrdle Street with Jack Kid Berg and learnt to box at the Victoria Boys' Club in Commercial Road, Stepney.

He turned pro in 1924 – which was against his parents' wishes – and started to box professionally under the pseudonym of Kid Froggy from the outset. In almost nineteen years as a pro, he fought at every weight class from bantamweight to light heavyweight, taking on almost every reigning champion of the day. The men he beat include such top-notchers as Harry Corbett, Dave McCleave, Len Fowler, Young Johnny Brown, Archie Sexton, Alf Mancini and Eddie Maguire. Despite his decent fight record, Froggy never got that close to fighting for the really top honours.

Ever-present on the circuit, he racked up 150-plus fights. Froggy was very well known and very popular around the London boxing halls and arenas. He also had a few fights in America as well as the occasional bouts in France. He was more than your average journeyman boxer. He retired in 1943. Looking back on his career though, he was the sort of character who would fully accept his life in the ring was as much about quantity than quality. To him it mattered not, as long as his longevity inside the ropes meant he had a comfortable retirement outside of them.

Jimmy Lester could be forgiven for thinking that he would not be one of the 'also rans' of Jewish boxing after reeling off twenty-three straight wins once turning professional in 1934. In fact, when he dispatched the vastly experienced Nottingham featherweight George Marsden in two pulsating matches in 1936, he may even have had hopes of fighting for a British title. Jimmy was born Ronnie Cohen in Clerkenwell around 1914 but moved to Dagenham after the First World War. After the Marsden fights, he took on and beat the very useful Welsh bantamweight and featherweight champion, Len Beynon, inside six rounds in October 1936. He started fighting on some decent bills and at some premier venues.

In January 1937, Jimmy was matched to box Benny Caplan at Jack Solomons' Devonshire Club. Benny, if you remember, was a big mate of Harry Mizler and was part of the 'Guard of Honour' at Harry's wedding. Benny was a formidable amateur and an ABA national champion. By 1937 Jimmy was beginning to make a name for himself in the professional ring and this bout looked like being a really good match-up between two stars of the future. The pair of them were being tipped for bigger and better things. For the first time, Jimmy's name appeared at the top of the advertising posters and he must have thought that a shot at the title was getting very close. That night the two climbed into the ring with almost identical records. The contest was predicted to be a tight one and so it proved. The fight went the full ten rounds and swung from one boxer to the other. At the end it was unlikely anyone ringside knew who had done enough to win. It was obviously a very close call, but the decision just went Caplan's way.

After that fight, Jimmy Lester's form started to dip slightly and although he picked up the odd win against some useful opponents, he was also losing just as many. In 1940, shortly after war broke out, both Jimmy Lester and Benny Caplan joined the army. Both saw action and both rose to the rank of sergeant. Professional boxers in the forces were still allowed to fight occasional matches when on leave. By pure coincidence, both Caplan and Lester were given leave for Christmas in 1941 and a match was made between them at the Alexandra Palace, Stoke Newington.

The two sergeants squared up to each other for a second time. In a repeat of the 1937 match, Sergeant Caplan just nicked the verdict over Sergeant Lester in eight excellent rounds of boxing. The two boxers got a standing ovation from the crowd and both left the ring smiling. Each boxer had one more fight the following year. They both won and then they both promptly retired. Though they did carry on fighting for their country.

Wartime boxing in Britain continued, albeit slightly reduced in terms of the number of events that were put on. London was no different from other large cities in the country. Most of them were bombed by Germany's air force at one time or another. London was especially targeted in the early years of the war and by the end of the war it was being hit by the V1 and V2 rockets. Several big, well known boxing venues were hit during the blitz. The Ring, The Alcazar, The Devonshire Club and the Holborn Stadium Club were all completely destroyed by the Luftwaffe. One venue though, proudly opened in the spring of 1942, at the height of the blitz and operated continually through to December 1945, defying the missiles that were thrown at it: The Queensbury Club.

The club was established in what was originally the Prince Edward Theatre in Berwick Street, Soho, primarily as a forces social club, but it started to run boxing matches with four or five events every month. Most evenings it featured anywhere between five and ten matches. The quality of boxing on show there possibly was not of the best but it was reasonable entertainment given the times. It never held a championship, but it did host a couple of Southern Area fights and title eliminators. Occasionally, it was used to showcase one or two of the services finals. Al Phillips boxed there eighteen times during his distinguished career. After the war the club reverted to its original name and became one of the great West End musical theatres.

In terms of the numbers of spectators, London boxing had reached its peak by the late 1930s. TV coverage of the sport was still some years off and venues, hundreds of them all over London, were packing in the boxing fans. The Jewish conveyor belt of boxers was still working. After the war, with the gradual relocation of a great number of inner-city families into the outer suburbs and to the various 'new towns' that were being built, the face of London boxing started to change. Greater TV coverage of sport in general started in the late 50s and once boxing hit the small screen in the sixties, this era of huge numbers of paying punters arriving at a multitude of venues around London was over.

7

BROTHERS IN ARMS

For the Jewish immigrants that flooded into the country around the turn of the century, it would seem they hardly had time to come to terms with their new environment before they were faced with the outbreak of World War One. It was therefore impressive that so many joined up to fight in the Great War, many of them still only with a basic grasp of the English language. They served and died with distinction. A big commitment to and sacrifice for a country that had been home to them for relatively few years.

It is estimated that around 50,000 British Jews served in the armed forces during the Great War. 2,500 were killed and a further 6,000 seriously wounded. Several London Jewish boxers were among the casualties. Over 500 past and present members of the JLB joined the cause. Some members of the Judean and St George's Clubs also hung up their gloves and enlisted for the duration.

Most fought throughout the war in the various army regiments on the Western Front. Many of the London Jews enlisted in the local regiments like The London Infantry, the Surrey Rifles and the Middlesex Regiment. A few found their way into the only all-Jewish 'Zion Mule Corps'. This was a name given to some battalions of the Royal Fusiliers that were set up to fight the Ottoman Empire at the start of the Gallipoli Campaign in Turkey.

The company becoming affectionally known as the 'Judeans'. The Mule Corps was initially a mixed nationality division but by the beginning of 1918, virtually all of the 39th Battalion of the Royal Fusiliers was made up from London Jewry.

Nat Young Brooks and Young Johnny Cohen, two talented London boxers, both served in the fusiliers toward the end of the war. Young Johnny Cohen fought his last two professional fights in Europe whilst stationed with the army in Cologne in 1918 and 1919. **Jack Marks** was an ex-Judean Club lad who fought almost seventy recorded matches from around 1909. Jack was a career soldier, joining the army at fifteen in 1908. He used his army rank on the boxing bills so he fought under the name Private Marks for well over ten years. His rise up the army ranks was similar to his rise up the boxing ranks. Not that far! He fought the young Ted Kid Lewis three times but lost on each occasion. He fought at flyweight and bantamweight professionally and for the army in many inter-service matches. A lot of his fights were recorded but briefly and it is reported he could have had over 150 fights.

As an experienced soldier, Jack saw a fair bit of action during the early months of the First World War. He managed to keep boxing a little through the first year or so of the conflict, but 1915 saw him in the trenches on the Western Front and he was wounded on a couple of occasions. This curtailed his boxing and he only fought once more whilst in uniform, in 1917. He had his last fight as a professional in December 1918. After the war, Jack took up dentistry and worked with his old opponent, Ted Kid Lewis to develop the first proper boxing gum shield that was later to become universally used by all boxers. Jack may not have made much of an impact in gloves – but he saved a few boxer's teeth over the years.

Another young boxer who boxed at the Judean that served with distinction was **Joe Shear.** Joe though, did not join any of the British forces. After turning pro in April 1909, flyweight Joe progressed very well indeed and he was already a veteran of twenty fights when he won the English flyweight championship in December that year. There were some very good flyweights plying their trade in the years running up to the First World War and Joe fought several of them. In 1911, Joe was offered a number of fights in North America. He boxed in both America and Canada between 1911 and 1914. He fought future five-time featherweight and lightweight world champion Johnny Dundee twice in two very close matches, which they split, one win each.

At the outbreak of the war, he enlisted in the Canadian Expeditionary Force as a driver. In later fights he often boxed under the alias of Driver Shear. Shear boxed off and on in Britain throughout the war whilst serving at the front. He often took part in inter-services matches as well. In fact, as a driver, up until 1918, the only real threat of being wounded was probably whilst fighting in the ring. Alas for Joe, in one of the last big pushes for victory in August 1918, the Canadians were involved in some very heavy fighting at Amiens and it was a matter of all hands to the pump. Shear picked up his rifle and went over the top. He was badly injured. Fortunately, he recovered and carried on boxing from early 1919 until he retired in 1920.

The Old Nichol area of western Bethnal Green was an unimaginably grim place. The most notorious of all the London Victorian rookeries. The survival rate of infants reaching their fourth birthday was put at about 65%. The conditions for kids growing up in these surroundings were horrendous and required huge amounts of grit and determination as well as a degree of luck just to live each day. If a young lad managed to get to his teenage years growing up here, he would be tough as old boots and quick with both his wits and his fists.

Kid Morris was born into these grim surroundings. His family was destitute. They probably had periods of moving from one doss house to another before resigning themselves to a stay or two in one of the local workhouses. The Kid survived childhood and like many of his ilk, he would have to make a choice. He could eke out a meagre living by grafting away for long hours, look for more easier, but illegal ways to survive – or use his abilities and any natural talent he may have to make a living between the ropes. He was small, compact, fleet-footed and had acquired the necessary toughness to make a reasonable fighter. Like so many both before and after him, he headed for the ring. His toughness more than his boxing skills would see him through.

Those men that take up the sport know that, at the very least, hardship and pain would be a constant companion on their journey. Of all the many injuries sustained by boxers, by far the most common are eye injuries. A bad eye injury can easily cut a boxer's career short. Most young boxers starting out would put these thoughts out of their minds. They would always fancy themselves to overcome any injury setbacks. Kid Morris debuted in December 1910 and looked forward to having an injury-free and successful life as a boxer. He had a reasonable start by winning six of his first seven fights before he ran into the unstoppable flyweight world champion, Jimmy Wilde, on Wilde's home patch in Wales. Morris put up a really good show and Jimmy never had him in any serious trouble over six rounds. Jimmy Wilde shaved it on points. A year later, he fought Wilde again, but by this time Jimmy was at his imperious best and Kid Morris was forced to retire in the fifth round with a badly cut eye. This was only the second time the Kid had not made it to the full distance.

Morris's eye healed fairly quickly and he fought a few more matches with mixed results until he was offered a chance to go over to the States to fight a pretty ordinary American featherweight.

Morris was knocked out in the second round. He woke up the next day with another black eye. It was now July 1916 and the Great War was raging in Europe. Morris decided to leave the boxing on the back burner and go off to fight for his country. He was still a fit young man with his senses intact. By 1917, he was in the trenches during The Third Battle of Ypres when the Germans launched a new gas over the British lines, mustard gas, the invisible killer. In the panic to rush and don his mask, he was late getting it on and was badly exposed to this awful substance. His eyes, that were mostly quick enough to have avoided the threat of thunderous fists, were now damaged beyond all repair by something that floated in on the breeze and could barely be seen.

That was the end of his career and he fell on hard times. His childhood poverty had returned. However, boxing rallied round and a couple of big gala and fundraising nights were held for him. Premierland raised almost £500 in an evening's entertainment for the benefit of a brave man. A very decent sum in those days.

There is a very long list of sportsmen who served during the First World War. Some were household names, but many were not. The press was quick to recount the actions of those well-known athletes. For a few it was their acts of courage that were reported but sadly it was more often their deaths that were highlighted. Boxers were no exception. Though they tended to make the transition from a civilian to a uniformed serviceman a lot easier than most.

There were several well-known London boxers who served in the army. Probably the most well-known was Bombardier Billy Wells, but British champions Pat O'Keeffe and Dick Burge also served. The press was always keen to print the occasional story of their time in uniform. Joining them was another Jewish London boxer of note. He was the reigning British light heavyweight champion, but he had very few column inches written about his army life.

Harry Reeve was equally accomplished as his boxing brothers in arms. Reeve knew Wells and O'Keefe well. During his time in the ring, he would fight them both. Reeve was also well acquainted with Dick Burge, the famous owner and promoter from the Ring boxing venue. Burge had arranged many boxing nights at the Ring in support of the war effort. O'Keefe and The Bombardier were, at the time, often used by the Army to bolster morale by giving boxing exhibitions around the various army camps both here and in France. They were both larger than life and their names regularly appeared in the mainstream newspapers of the day.

Harry Reeve's army days went largely unreported during the war but the part he played in it was to become the subject of much speculation afterwards. Reeves was born in Stepney in late 1894 to Jewish parents of German extraction. His father, Louis Isaacs, had moved from Norfolk to London some years previously and changed the family name to Reeve. By the outbreak of war, Harry had established himself as a formidable middleweight boxer and narrowly lost a middleweight championship fight in 1914. By early 1915, he had moved up to box at light heavyweight and in 1916 he won the British light heavyweight title.

Reeve was, by now, a leading name in the sport but soon after his win he chose to enlist in the army's Military Police. Why he chose them is unknown, although it probably meant it would be unlikely that he would end up fighting in the front-line trenches. In early 1918 he was assigned to the miliary police at the giant Étaples military camp on the Northern French coast. The camp operated as a sort of 'halfway house'. Its main role was to process troops moving up to and back from the front line. It also ran a brutal so-called training regime. Shortly after arriving there, he was heavily involved in a disturbance which quickly turned ugly and then into a riot, after he shot and killed a Scottish soldier.

A mutiny by soldiers in the camp ensued, the infamous Étaples Mutiny. It was the subject of Alan Bleasdale's acclaimed TV series, '*The Monocled Mutineer*'. Very recent research has uncovered some fresh information on the affair, as well as on Reeve in particular. Unfortunately, it tends not to clarify how the incident occurred but adds more intrigue.

Thirty years earlier, East London and more specifically Whitechapel, was in the grip of Jack the Ripper. Running up to his brief reign of terror, the population had been complaining that the police were doing very little to halt crime and violence in the area. It was around this time that socialism, and indeed communism, began to take root in the East End. The poor working class in London were beginning to voice their disgust at the government's refusal to improve their lot.

In Jubilee Street, Whitechapel, stood the Jubilee Club, which was gaining a reputation as a hot bed of communists and anarchists. Lenin made his first speech in Britain at the club. A short distance from the club lived Charles Reeve (Samuel Isaacs) and his family. Charles was Harry Reeve's uncle. He was a member of the club and he was also the founder of the Whitechapel Vigilance Committee. In 1888, two of The Ripper's victim's bodies were found in close proximity to Charles Reeves' home and it was these events that prompted Reeve to form his committee to help protect the local community. The group intended to do what the local police force could not do and that is to protect its citizens. According to statements made to the press, they were following their own lines of enquiries about the Ripper murders and were bringing in private detectives to work on the case. The group became very pro-active and attracted the attention of local political figures.[1]

Charles Reeve started to move into some more elevated political circles and became friends with the liberal and political activist Horatio Bottomley. Reeve was said to have had some sympathy for some of the anarchist views if they meant getting something done by the government to alleviate the problems in the area. Charles Reeve died in 1901 but his ideology passed on to his daughter, Ada, and his nephew, Harry Reeve. Ada's role during the war has been well documented. A fairly famous music hall performer and later film actress, she toured Australia and New Zealand during 1915/1916 and after arriving home she exhibited a particular interest in the conditions of the troops from those countries that fought on the Western Front. She kept her father's connection with Bottomley and labour leader, Ben Tillett. She also knew Dick Burge and his famous wife, Bella.

It is though, the part that Lady Angela Forbes played in the Étaples riots and mutiny that is most interesting. An aristocratic socialite turned philanthropist, Forbes started to harbour pacifist views in the light of the huge loss of life she was witnessing close up. Forbes was hugely sympathetic to the plight of the ordinary soldiers fighting at the front. She set up canteens in many of the big military bases during hostilities. The huge Étaples base camp was no exception, with several of her soldier canteens on site. She was a fine sports woman and had no problems with the sport of boxing. So much so that she built an outdoor boxing ring at the Étaples camp and it was very popular with the men. She became the non-singing version of Vera Lynn, a forces sweetheart.

Both Forbes and Vera Brittain, the mother of the late politician, Shirley Williams, witnessed the brutal regime under which the camp operated. Brittain was a voluntary aid nurse on the base and wrote her *Testament of Youth* about her experiences there. Forbes gained a reputation for criticising the officers and NCOs that ran the camp. It is thought that Forbes and her lover, Hugh Charteris, who worked alongside her, had some contact with both Bottomley and Ben Tillett. Bottomley, by now the MP for Hackney, was known as a trusted friend of British and Empire troops. Forbes relayed her concerns about the camp to him. Those two women were not the only ones to highlight the Étaples camp. The Great War poet, Siegfried Sassoon passed through the camp. His satirical poem, *Base Details,* underlines its uncaring approach to the ordinary troops there:

> If I were fierce, and bald, and short of breath,
> I'd live with scarlet Majors at the Base,
> And speed glum heroes up the line to death.
> You'd see me with my puffy petulant face,
> Guzzling and gulping in the best hotel,
> Reading the Roll of Honour. 'Poor young chap,'
> I'd say—'I used to know his father well;
> Yes, we've lost heavily in this last scrap'
> And when the war is done and youth stone dead,
> I'd toddle safely home and die—in bed.

(Taken from Sassoon's war diary entry
17 March 1917)

A few weeks before the Mutiny started, Harry Reeves was transferred to the Étaples camp at the request of Forbes, ostensibly to help with the morale of the troops by undertaking some boxing exhibition matches. By some extraordinary coincidence, or maybe not, both Bottomley and Victor Grayson, a close friend of the influential Union leader and political activist, Ben Tillett, had arrived at the camp shortly before the riots and were able to report back on the events. It is this that now leads some to conclude that it is quite possible that Harry Reeve was brought into the camp to deliberately stir up trouble, a sort of agent provocateur, in order to get the authorities to take action to change the camp regime or possibly even close it down. It would not have taken much as feelings towards the camp's regime had been running high for some time. The shooting of a soldier by a camp policemen would easily be enough and so it proved. Although it was thought that Reeve was never convicted of any wrongdoing, recently released camp diaries show that Reeve was found guilty of involuntary manslaughter and sentenced to one year's hard labour.

No further record has been found that showed he served his time for this. He is reported to have been hospitalised with some

Harry Reeve, British light heavyweight champion during the First World War. He was to become embroiled in a notorious wartime event.

minor wounds he received a few months later. The camp was never shut down but the Lady Forbes canteens were. General Haig considered them as talking shops building up the unrest in the camp. Reeves saw out the remaining months of the war and continued to box professionally again. He also began to make money in the new film industry, taking small parts in early silent movies. Reeve's first film, *The Door that Has no Key*, featured a boxing match between Reeve and the famous Irish boxer and film star Victor Mclaglen. Reeve fought his last professional fight in 1934.

After the horrors of the First World War, politics in many countries began to polarise. Both wings of the political spectrum began to grow in popularity. The dust had barely settled after the guns fell silent on the Western Front than the spectre of fascism began to cast its long shadow over Europe. Mussolini came to power in Italy in 1923 and that created the spark which ignited the fascist movements in Germany, Austria, Spain and Portugal.

Mussolini's brand of National Socialism appealed to the British Member of Parliament, Oswald Mosley. In 1932, Mosley formed the BUF (British Union of Fascists) and saw what was happening in Spain under Franco and in Germany under Hitler and was confident that his party would become a major force in British politics. Like Hitler, he targeted the Jews and set his sights on London's East End and its Jewish community. It was a grave misjudgement.

Apart from the European Jews who had started to arrive in the area fifty years earlier, thousands of Irish immigrants also settled in the East End during the mid-nineteenth century. By and large the two communities lived in peaceful harmony. They were both fundamentally working class, independent people with mutual respect and support for each. The working classes of London were, at best, ambivalent about extreme brands of politics. Most saw Mosley for what he was, a titled upper-class toff with an appetite for power. His black-shirted private army were perceived as bullies and thugs.

In some places in London, after the First World War, it was socialism and communism rather than fascism that gained a foothold. The doctrines offered hope to the working-class poor. The left-wing activists on the ground in 1936 were confident that Mosley would struggle to garner much support in East London. London's working class came together. For some time, a sort of unspoken bond between the various communities existed. Oswald Mosley was either unaware of this or chose to ignore it. Mosley went ahead with his intention of marching through London's mainly Jewish East End areas. He had made little secret of it. Opposition to the march started some days before the events. Labour's most eminent politician George Lansbury as well as leading rabbis, priests and the various borough mayor, all opposed Mosley's actions and encouraged local people to stay away.

On Sunday 4 October, crowds started assembling around Aldgate and Whitechapel. Loudspeaker vans toured the adjacent streets of Stepney and the band of the Young Communist League, headed by Harry Gross, led a counter demonstration. The Jewish Ex-Serviceman's Legion, near Aldgate, organised a march around Stepney as well. They planned to march towards the City to Gardener's Corner, which was on the route of Mosley's march. The police, who had given consent to Mosley and his black shirts to march, hurriedly threw up a cordon just to the East of this junction, to stop Gross and his supporters as well as the ex-servicemen confronting Mosley. This is where the first of the day's actions took place.

The police sent in horse-mounted officers to break up the crowd. Mosley's marchers arrived in the area shortly after.

Estimates of almost 10,000 people, including those from both sides of the political divide and a large number of the immediate local population, most of whom were Anti-fascists, spilled out over the area. With a couple of the main roads leading into the East End blocked by either police clashes or just sheer numbers of people, Mosley's men moved south to the junction of Cable Street, which is where the famous stand-off was to take place. The street was a narrow and cobblestoned thoroughfare.

Cable Street was a mix of Jewish traders and workmen as well as Irish dockers. Anything large that came to hand was flung into the road and behind this barricade stood the immovable force that were tough East Enders. The police tried to unblock the path for Mosley's men but failed, with objects being rained down on them from upstairs windows in the street. The police horses often reared and then slipped on the cobblestones. The Irish and the Jews had stood together before, during an earlier bitter dock strike in 1910. The left-wing unions had also supported the anti BUF action. It was a formidable defence and one that prevailed on the day.

After a couple of hours, the police called off the march. The Battle of Cable Street never was some sort of huge military style victory. It was though, a small but significant stand against anti-Semitism. There is little doubt that a few Irish and Jewish boxers were at the barricades that day. There were half a dozen popular boxing clubs in that area of Stepney but no well-known boxer would risk losing their licence by taking part in a public disturbance and risk arrest.[2]

Left wing influences had been permeating through London opposing the march of fascism both in this country and on mainland Europe. The activists that stood alongside the Jewish population in Cable Street in 1936 were instrumental in forming the International Brigade that went over to Spain that same year to oppose General Franco's attempt to introduce a fascist state there. Harry Gross, who led the communist counter demonstration in the East End that day, was to give his life to the cause in July the following year, fighting Franco's fascists in the Spanish Civil War.

Phil Richards was born as Phil Caplan, very close to Cable Street, in 1902. He took his boxing name from the street on which he lived, Richard Street. Phil had a younger brother Benny, who also boxed professionally. Benny Caplan, whose name crops up occasionally in these pages, kept his original family name. Phil fought at the middleweights and in his early years he developed into a more than reasonable journeyman boxer. Between his debut in 1922 through to 1924 he boxed all over the capital winning the vast majority of his fights. In early 1924 he fought Ted Lewis from Manchester four times in 30 days at the Premierland and won three. Although Lewis was coming to the end of his career, those victories for Richards were impressive. Buoyed by this, he started to box abroad. He had a series of fights in America and Canada during 1925 and 1926 against a better class of opponent where victories were more difficult to come by. Phil went on to complete well over 150 matches, but by 1930 his form had deteriorated and wins were beginning to become hard to achieve. He had two impressive wins in 1931 against the former British featherweight champion, Johnny Curley from Lambeth, but after that Phil really struggled and he retired in April 1934.

Richards was a bright man and his boxing travels brought him into contact with people from all walks of life and he turned his attention to the class and political struggles of the day. He was one of the archetypal working-class Jewish socialists. He became very active. He knew Harry Gross, the local young communist leader. Although Phil was probably not a 'card carrying' communist, he was very sympathetic with the views of Gross and his colleagues. It is possible that he may have been one of the

The International Brigade, which included a couple of Jewish boxers, launching an assault on General Franco's forces in the 1937 Battle of Jarama, part of the Spanish Civil War. Sadly one of them, Phil Richards, died fighting fascism.

boxers who stood firm against the tide of fascism as it swept into Cable Street on that cold October day in 1936.

Along with Gross, he decided to join the newly formed International Brigade and he went over to Spain to fight for the incumbent Spanish Republic government against Franco. He arrived in Spain and joined up with the International Brigade on 28 December 1936. On 13 February 1937, whilst fighting at Jarama, close to Madrid, he was killed.[3]

At the outbreak of World War two, even greater numbers of Jewish men and women were available to fight the German Nazi regime. Many knew of the horrors that were being inflicted on their race in that country. There was no shortage of volunteers for all three of Britain's military services. Around 75,000 served in the forces, with several thousand more older ex boxers volunteering for Home Guard duties. We have heard about the battle of the Sergeants earlier. Top boxing champions Jack Berg, Harry Mizler and Al Phillips also served. Jack Hyams, aka Kid Froggy, made it to the rank of Sergeant and served with the RAF. Several other notable London Jewish boxers also fought.

In London, even at the height of the Blitz, sport and entertainment still continued. It was government policy that they should do so. They were of major benefit in keeping up civilian morale. The capital endured night after night of bombings, but the beleaguered population was entertained. During one period in 1941 London was bombed fifty-seven nights in a row. But 'The show must go on' and it did.

By the end of 1941, Britain was giving as much as taking and the German threat of razing London began to disappear. Although gradually, as the country began to fight back and the bombings subsided somewhat, the number of boxing shows in and around the capital reduced as more and more men were called up to serve. In December 1941, *The Jewish Chronicle* had reported on a number of London Jewish boxers in action in the ring:

This week saw a number of high-quality bouts of boxing. At the Seymour Hall, Marylebone, on Monday, clear cut wins were registered for East London favourites, Harry Lazar and Jack Hyams (Kid Froggy). Lazar's meeting with Dave Crowley was a "rubber" match, each having a verdict to his credit. Lazar had never boxed better. He was Crowley's master in every department and at the end was well ahead on points. Jack Hyams came out full of pep to meet Al Marsden and plugged steadily away, round after round. One of the wickedest barrages of punches ever handed out by Hyam ensued. At the end of the eight-round contest Mickey Fox, refereeing, held up Hyam's hand. At Leeds the following Monday, Jack Berg beat Joe Conolly, the towel being thrown in during the eighth round. At the Alexander Theatre Sunday Boxing Club this week, Dave Finn was narrowly outpointed by Jim McGrory in a very closely fought contest. At High Wycombe the following day, Johnny Cunningham clearly outpointed Mick Carney. We now look forward to the all-Jewish match when Benny Caplan meets Jimmy Lester at the Alexander Theatre.

Of the twelve boxers mentioned in that report, eleven of them would go on to serve in the war. Two more well-known boxers were Sid Nathan who served with the RAF and Harry Silver (Kid Silver) who saw front line action in the army.

Dave Finn was one of the twelve boxers mentioned in that earlier press report, boxing at his peak during the war years. Dave was born in Stepney and turned professional in September 1930. It would be a long road he would walk and looking at his record, the first half of that road was all uphill. 1931 saw him fight thirty matches, most of which were underwhelming at best. By 1935, he was a veteran of almost ninety fights and had barely won half of them. Dave decided to try his luck further afield and at the end of that year, he moved to the US and spent the next year or more fighting on American bills. His name on the bills appeared as Dave Fine. The promoters thought his name wasn't Jewish enough, so it was tweaked slightly, goodness knows why. Dave Fine adorned his trunks with the Star of David so it was plain for all to see. If Finn (or Fine) thought he could have better luck Stateside, he was mistaken. Fifteen months of fighting up and down American's East Coast resulted in no change to his fortunes. He won about half of his bouts there.

He returned to Britain and picked up where he left off, losing fights mainly. Then, in late 1937, things improved. He knocked out a reasonable boxer, Jim Anderson, and then went on a run of eleven matches, losing just once. He was boxing well and beating some good opponents. Suddenly, after nine years the road he was treading became less rocky. In April 1940, he fought the aforementioned Dave Crowley, the former British featherweight boxer who had fought and lost a somewhat controversial world featherweight title fight a few years earlier. Crowley was a seasoned performer and was hot favourite to win that night. Finn upset the form books and completed a comfortable points victory over Crowley.

Soon after this, Dave joined the RAF. Finn carried on boxing as much as he could and, spurred on by the Crowley result, he fought some other notable championship contenders. Crowley was also still boxing through these war years and in April 1942 their paths crossed again. Finn won again and became a real thorn in the side of Crowley. They fought five times against each other during the war years and Dave Finn won each time. Finn's war record both in and out of uniform was impressive. Post-war was a different matter though and Dave Finn's career ended after three bad defeats in 1946. Dave competed in 171 bouts and stayed in the game for a few years as a trainer and manager.

Not only professional boxers served in the armed forces during the war. Far more amateur boxers enlisted. Eighteen was the official minimum age for conscription. Some of the older youth club boxers, although by this age, at work, were keeping up the sport. Thousands of Jewish club old boys and girls served the country, many seeing some serious action.

Operation Market Garden was the allied plan, in part devised by Field Marshal Bernard Montgomery, to foreshorten the Second World War by seizing a number of bridges over the Rhine, specifically the one at Arnhem. Limited success would be an overstatement. It was more of a military failure. The Parachute Regiment was a big part of the operation. Private Gerald Flamberg was a serving member of 156 battalion, part of the regiment. He was also the Parachute Regiment's middleweight boxing champion. Flamberg was born in Holborn

Jack Herskovitch (left) and Myer Segal compete in an exhibition match at the Bernhard Baron Settlement club on Berner Street, April 1942. Both boys were twenty years old and had been stokers in the Merchant Navy for a year. They had already been torpedoed once.

to poor Jewish immigrants. He grew up to be a very good amateur boxer who learned to box in one of North London's boxing clubs before the war.

On 19 September 1944, thirty-six hours after his battalion was parachuted into Arnhem, Flamberg was attacking German defences. He was slightly wounded as the attack failed. His battalion regrouped and Flamberg agreed, despite his wound, to advance into an open area for reconnaissance. He was met by a German tank whose machine gun opened fire and put a bullet through his shoulder and proceeded to pin his company down. Flamberg crawled back to his lines and concealing his badly wounded shoulder obtained permission to attack the tank with a gammon bomb. He tracked the tank and threw the bomb with his good arm under its tracks, badly damaging it. The tank withdrew and that left the way open for another and more successful attack.

It was one of very few successful actions and the whole operation stalled badly. Private Flamberg along with hundreds of other soldiers were captured and he saw out the war in a prisoner of war camp. He was awarded the Military Cross for his gallantry. His commanding officer wrote to Gerry's mother shortly after he was taken to the German PoW camp: 'Truly a son to be proud of. You can always say without fear, he is a great fighter in battle and in the ring.'

Gerry Flamberg returned home post-war to North London. Flamberg was a charismatic socialist and politically active from his youth. He once led a strike about working conditions. He became a committed anti-fascist. Within a few months of the war ending, Oswald Mosley, who had been imprisoned as a German sympathiser, was released and with another fascist, Jeffrey Hamm, had formed new right-wing neo fascist parties.

In February 1946, Flamberg and a few ex-military colleagues broke up a Hamm meeting in London. Several other Jewish ex-servicemen joined up with Flamberg to form the 43 Group. (The room number that the group met in.) The young and future famous hair stylist, Vidal Sassoon, joined the group along with several other decorated war heroes.

The group grew in strength to around 300. They harassed the right-wing movement and broke up the various meetings, street rallies and marches in the capital by these groups. They were very effective in thwarting any further rise in extreme right-wing politics in Britain immediately after the war.

Gerry Flamberg (front left), a Group 43 activist, seen after his acquittal on the trumped-up charge of attempted murder of a neo-fascist organiser.

Flamberg's 43 Group was set up to challenge Oswald Mosley in the immediate post-war period and it succeeded. Mosley's force in Britain faded and it was another ten or eleven years before the far-right once again tried to gain a political presence. Mosley, who had been in semi-exile in Paris for several years, still showed up occasionally but this time the far right's push for power was led by Colin Jordan who campaigned under the slogan 'Free Britain from Jewish Control'. Once again, another Jewish backed anti-fascist group was formed to counter the threat; the 62 Group. The 62 Group were the subject of the BBC's political drama, *Ridley Road*, that was broadcast in 2021.[4]

As with the 43 Group, the 62 Group included one or two boxers. Ex-Jewish boxer Barry Sulkin was a prominent member and the 62 Group's intelligence officer, Dave Freedman, a real street fighter, could handle himself in tough situations. Just as well, because Mosley and Jordan could also call on one or two ex-boxers as minders. North London's ex-heavyweight boxer, Danny Harmston's services were retained by Mosley. Perhaps he made a better minder than boxer, as he lost every fight he had in the ring...

On a personal note, I had some insight into these times when the far right was trying to make inroads again into British politics. In January 1965, I attended a Labour Party Rally that was held at Leyton Baths. The baths had just stopped being used for boxing events and were often used to stage music concerts, dances and meetings during the winter months.

Ex-cabinet minister Patrick Gordon Walker was standing for the Leyton parliamentary seat and a labour rally was held to help promote his campaign. George Brown, the then deputy Prime Minister and the Defence Secretary Denis Healey were there. In those days political rallies were not the over-orchestrated and formal events they are now. Back then, anything could happen and often did. Raucous heckling was commonplace and rallies could get out of hand. That night I attended with my father. The rumours had got round that Colin Jordan would turn up and try to disrupt the proceedings.

Just before the meeting started, a large group of men entered the hall and sat at the back. Sitting with them was Colin Jordan, my father pointed him out to me. A few minutes later he pointed out another group of men that had appeared at the side of the hall. He called them the Jewish mafia and told me they were Jewish black cab drivers from Gants Hill. I asked him what they were there for and he said, 'unofficial security'. He was right. Shortly after George Brown started speaking, Colin Jordan walked down to the front and climbed onto the stage. Spurred on by his cohorts, he launched a verbal barrage against the platform, calling them Jew lovers, communist sympathisers and traitors. His supporters were now on their feet, urging him on. His speech was short-lived. The 'Jewish mafia' waded into Jordan's men and on stage a punch was thrown that nearly knocked Jordan off the stage. I could not be sure who threw the punch but it came out later that it was Denis Healey. Some 'official security' then arrived and between them and the cabbies they hauled Jordan and his supporters out of the building and locked them out.

It was incidents like these that followed the British right-wing movements around. It shocked me at the time that the Jewish community, who gave so much in the First World War as well as the later struggles against European fascism running up to and during the Second World War, still had to endure the threats of right-wing activists. The Holocaust was still fresh in people's minds, yet Mosley, Hann and Jordan could still incite anti-Jewish feelings. My concerns for the Jewish population though would be short-lived. By the end of the 1960s, Jordan and his contemporaries eventually realised that London Jews were an accepted part of the British way of life. The focus of their hate switched to the Afro-Caribbean and Indian sub-Continent immigrants.

The Jewish boxing brothers were a rare breed. Some fought on three fronts. In the ring for their livelihood, at the front for their country and on the streets for their faith.

8

THE JOURNEYMAN

'Little do ye know your own blessedness; for to travel hopefully is a better thing than to arrive, and the true success is to labour.'

Robert Louis Stevenson,
Virginibus Puerisque (1881)

London, January 1960. The dawn of a new and unique decade for the capital. Three years earlier, British Prime Minister Harold MacMillan declared, 'You've never had it so good.' He was correct, relatively speaking that is. Compared with the Dickensian conditions of the previous century, the two world wars and the depression years of the 1920s and 1930s, he was right. The austerity of the post-war years of the late forties and early fifties had been replaced with consumer growth and society was entering a more scientific age. Unemployment was low and for the working class, living was getting easier.

In the 'Swinging Sixties' London was the place to be, and to be seen. 'In this century, every decade has its city. Today it is London, a city steeped in tradition, seized by change' (*Time* magazine, 1966). Boxing was no exception. Television mainly saw to that. During this decade many of the smaller boxing venues started to close. It was to spell the end of a band of boxers that were, for half a century or more, the cornerstone of the development of the popularity of the sport. The journeyman boxers.

The term journeyman boxer was first used in the early 1920s to describe those fighters that travelled up and down the country filling the boxing undercards. They were making up the numbers. Journeymen boxers, by definition, tended to fight more regularly and over a longer period than those better-known champion boxers. The development of transport in the early part of the twentieth century meant that boxers could more easily travel round the country than before. One or two of the better ones even managed to fight abroad where the money on offer could be very attractive.

Many boxers from the last years of the nineteenth century and the early part of the twentieth managed to rack up plenty of fights as well as miles in pursuit of the money. Nat Young Brooks and Young Johnny Cohen, the two boxers mentioned in the previous chapter who had fought together in the fusiliers were both prolific journeymen boxers. Although they boxed around the same weight and around the same time, their paths to the ring never crossed. They knew each other well from their army days. They were both Aldgate lads and used the Judean Club together.

Cohen's boxing career was approaching its end when they were discharged from the army in early 1919. Cohen had two further fights before finally stepping out of the ring for good in 1921. By this time, he had already amassed over 100 boxing matches and had fought extensively on both sides of the Atlantic and also in France, Germany and Poland. Nat Brooks, whose boxing career was even longer, fought 180 matches over twenty years. He also travelled extensively, retiring in 1929.

Sam Kellar was another such well-travelled journeyman boxer but he was a cut above those many 'also rans.' Sam was born in September 1885 in Aldgate, turning professional in 1902 aged just seventeen. He was small, boxing at the lowest weights. Initially, he would struggle to push the needle round to seven stone! In fact, his first couple of fights were at the Whitechapel's Wonderland Arena in a novice's competition in which he first boxed in the 6stone 10lbs class.

Later he put on a little weight and went on to win a prestigious novice's competition for young boxers under eight stone. Boxing light, he comprehensively defeated a couple of useful up-and-coming boxers. He mainly fought at the Wonderland at flyweight until 1905 and was fighting well. He went undefeated in fourteen matches before losing to fellow Aldgate boxer Barnett Soloman, aka Bob Kendrick, in a very close match. That defeat only spurred him on and he started to box all over London and further away in places like Cardiff and Coventry. Fights and wins were coming thick and fast and in October 1906, he was matched to face Mark Verrall from Tottenham in what was billed as the English 108lb Championship at the National Sporting Club, Covent Garden. In some quarters this was viewed as the British flyweight title. Sam knocked out Verrall in the ninth round to claim the title.

So far, his route towards the top of his profession in Britain had been reasonably straightforward, but in 1907 he was offered a chance to box in America. The money available in the States was far more than the prize money that Sam would be able to pick up in Britain. He took up the offer. The opposition Stateside was tougher, but he fought reasonably well over the next eighteen months in New York and Philadelphia, racking up a further twenty fights.

He returned to Britain in May 1908 a reasonably wealthy man. Sam barely drew breath before he was on his travels again. For over eight years he boxed in venues all over the UK. On a warm August night in 1916, Sam took a trip to the coast. To all intents and purposes, he was to fight one last match before hanging up the gloves. He stepped into the ring at the Kursaal Amusement Park at Southend -on-Sea for his 108th fight. His form had deteriorated, losing his last two fights, and this one was to be no different. Unsurprisingly, he lost a points decision to Tommy Noble, the former British and European bantamweight champion.

At that point, Sam Kellar prepared for retirement from the ring. He was still a reasonably wealthy man with no need to punish his body further. That was the case for the next three years until, out of the blue, he was offered a chance to climb back through the ropes to face the truly excellent French featherweight boxer, Eugene Criqui, in Paris. Criqui had already taken the French title at bantamweight and had a very close match against the aforementioned Tommy Nobel for the European title, which he narrowly lost. Sam could not resist the offer. It was as much for the pride and kudos as for the money.

Criqui was approaching his peak and was moving up to featherweight, at which weight he would go on to win the French, European and world championships. Sam was really up against it, giving away eight pounds and eight years to the Frenchman. Sam was comprehensively out-boxed from the start and probably never saw the big right hook that smashed into his left temple. Finally, the end of the road. Sam returned home to his wife and children, one of whom Dave, would follow in his father's footsteps. But for Dave there would be nowhere near as many, although he still managed to rack up over fifty fights.

Jack Gold was a very close neighbour of Sam Kellar but a little younger. He attended the Judean Club where he was taught to box and had his first professional fight in 1910, which was a hard-fought draw. Jack was then matched against Jack Bunner. Why he was matched against Bunner is difficult to fathom, as Bunner was already an established boxer with almost forty fights behind him and had won most of them. As it happened Jack boxed well and Bunner had to secure the victory on a narrow points decision.

The next three fights were against less experienced boxers and Jack won these before facing another seasoned professional in the shape of Tom Gibbs from Poplar. Jack was knocked out in the first round. Again, Jack got up ready to face his next opponent. He was obviously resilient and he needed to be. On 11 June 1911, Jack turned up at the Judean Club to fight the unknown novice boxer, Kid Kelly from Stepney. He was first up on the bill. Ted Kid Lewis was also boxing that night. Shortly before Jack was due to go on, he was approached by the promoter. He was asked if he would be prepared to fight another match later in the evening because one of the boxers had pulled out. Remember, Jack was about to face Kid Kelly in only his tenth fight. Oh, the exuberance of youth. Jack said yes, he would!

Jack strode out to face Kelly and duly lost the match over six pretty dour rounds. Kelly collected his meagre purse and left. Jack took a back seat in the audience to watch the great Ted Lewis perform. A little later he went back to the changing area to prepare for his extra bout. I don't know if Jack knew who he was about to face. Possibly he did but it mattered not. Jack again made his way ringside for only his eleventh match and the second one in less than two hours. Waiting for him was Barking's George Moore. Moore was a very senior professional and had fought some of the greatest lighter weight boxers around, including Johnny Summers, Young Joseph and Alf Reed, as well as Cockney Cohen. He had narrowly lost to the outstanding Welsh featherweight world champion Jim Driscoll and managed to hold the world bantamweight champion, Pedlar Palmer, to a draw. Well, fortune favours the brave as they say and it is possible that Moore may have, with some reason, underestimated his opponent. Shortly after the start of the first round George dropped his hands slightly and young Jack smashed a big uppercut onto the exposed jaw of

Moore. George hit the canvas and was counted out. Against all odd,s Jack Gold had beaten one of the best boxers around. A shock result at the end of an extraordinary night of boxing for Jack.

That result could have propelled Jack onto bigger and better things. Sadly, that was not the case. Jack only won six of his next fifteen fights. His whole career was one of inconsistency and as a result Jack Gold's name would more often be found on the bottom half of the billboard posters rather than in the top half. Still, Jack was one of the great journeyman Jews and fought all around London as well as in Philadelphia, New York and Paris over a twelve-year career, clocking up 105 fights.

Born in the Euston area of North London, **Tommy Hyams** was one of North London's outstanding journeymen boxers. In a career of just over twelve years he climbed into the ring almost 200 times. That's around one fight every three weeks! A durable boxer who never came anywhere near to fighting for a title, nevertheless, during his time on the road he managed to beat a few excellent fighters. Tommy boxed all over England and most of the top London venues of the day. He had just two fights outside the country, in France. He fought against Maurice Holtzer, the brilliant rising star in French boxing. Tommy fought him to an incredibly close decision over 10 rounds, just losing to what many suspected was the home venue factor.

Holtzer was to go on and win the featherweight European title a couple of years later and defend it twice before drawing a world title fight in 1938. Hyams second French fight was even better, defeating the excellent European lightweight champion, Maurice Arnault in a non-title fight in Paris in 1937. Back on British soil he claimed victories over the likes of British featherweight champ Johnny McGrory, Packey McFarland, Harry Kid Farlo and the legendary veteran journeyman boxer,

Len Wickwar.[1] Tommy Hyams also had a series of great fights against British bantamweight East End boxer Dick Corbett. He was later matched to fight the very colourful and equally exceptional American world bantamweight champion, Panama Al Brown at the Ring Venue in 1933. On paper, it was a complete mis-match and although Tommy was knocked out flat in the ninth round by one of the world's all-time great bantamweights, it was still regarded by many as a great effort, Tommy having been floored eight times before the referee called a halt.

Unless you were one of the champion boxers of the day or one of the great journeyman boxers fighting several bouts in a month for years on end, then the small purses were often insufficient to look after a family. And families could be large. The big wholesale markets provided much casual work for many. Men stood outside the dock gates waiting for a boat to dock in the hope that it may need a few extra hands for unloading. 'Standing on the stones' was the term those part-time dockers used. It was a hit or miss affair.

There was a thriving area around Whitechapel that became the hub of the garment trade. In Whitechapel High Road, men could be seen waiting outside the small factories in the area in the hope of some casual work. This work was known as piece rate work paid by the number of garments that a person worked on. Some were skilled machinists, some were pressers. Pressing was a demanding job and in those days the conditions would have been dreadful. They were true sweatshops. The machinists worked in areas that were only marginally better. Jack Nathan, who was the father of boxer and referee Sid Nathan, was a machinist in a clothing factory. Sid Nathan recalls that his father came home totally exhausted after working a shift.

As part of the Jewish Museum's 'Oral History of Jewish Life', Frank Russell was interviewed about his time working in his father's clothes business:

> If we got a large order in and had to fill it quick like, we often needed a couple of extra workers. He (his father) might tell me to go down onto the street and get an under presser or a cover stitcher machinist. We had one of these casual machinists worked for us. One day he was working a long shift right through to the late evening. That evening he says to my father that he would have to go out and he would be back in half an hour. He disappeared and came back about half an hour or so later. I asked my father if he had to go home for a meal. "No, he's a boxer. He has just had a fight" he said. He had gone to the Whitechapel Pavilion, a few yards down the road, had a fight, then come back and carried on working. His ring name was Kid Silver.

Kid Silver's real name was Johnny Silver. Kid Silver's time in boxing was short-lived. He is only recorded as having around a dozen fights, so he was no journeyman, unlike his namesake Harry 'Kid' Silver.

When young boxers take their first tentative steps as a professional it is very unlikely that they would be pitched in against more senior pro fighters. These young, very green boxers would mainly fight other young debutants or those who had just a few bouts under their belts. Two such boxers appeared at the Devonshire Club in Hackney in August 1936 to contest just a four-round match. These two had a bit in common. Both Jewish, both the same age and both came from Clapton, which was no more than a mile away from the Hackney venue.

Harry Silver also used the nickname of 'Kid'. He was stepping into a professional ring for the second time but his opponent,

Mick Hyams was making his professional debut that evening. The crowd there that night would have had little knowledge of either boxer, although they had both fought on the same amateur circuit. These matches, normally first up on the bill, were three or four round affairs and I suspect nobody there would have any idea who would most likely win. In horse racing parlance, Harry Silver was a previous course and distance winner as he had fought his debut over four rounds at the same venue two months earlier and won, so he may have been a very slight favourite.

After three rounds of fairly mundane boxing, Mick Hyams delivered a low blow and was disqualified. The bout was eminently forgettable and told little of how these two men would progress. History shows that their lives from that point on went different ways. For Mick Hyams, that was to be the last time he ever pulled on a pair of gloves and he went on to carve out a reasonably decent business career. Harry Silver's feet remained firmly on the boxing road. Harry became another very good journeyman and an ever-present figure around the boxing scene for over twenty years. Silver was highly successful around the London venues over the next three years. His record of losing just twice in his first thirty-five fights looked to have a little bit more about it than that of an average journeyman boxer. His career was impressive for someone who never got a sniff at a top championship match. Harry Silver fought eighty-five bouts, winning sixty-one, drawing eight and losing just sixteen. What puts Harry in the journeyman bracket is two things. Firstly, Harry never fought any past or future national champions nor any such contenders, so Harry always went into the ring with a decent chance. Secondly, Harry went into rings all over the country and a few overseas as well.

When Harry eventually retired, he could rightly claim that he had turned out at Liverpool's Anfield stadium and Leicester's

Filbert Street ground. He also mixed it with the rugby lads, appearing at Welford Road, Leicester and Pontypridd. Some of the other weird and wonderful venues Harry graced were places like Canterbury's skating rink and the Wandsworth Greyhound track. In between, he boxed at some top venues like Earls Court, Seymour Hall and Alexander Palace. From Southampton to Perth and from Brooklyn to Brisbane, Harry clocked up the miles. He could also boast he appeared on Broadway as he fought twice at the Broadway Arena in New York.

Alf Simmons, enjoyed an outstanding amateur career. His boxing abilities as an amateur were well noted and he climbed into some prestigious rings in his first few professional fights. In early 1919, he easily won his first three fights before slipping up in his fourth bout. Some inconsistences were beginning to creep into his boxing and his next dozen or so results were mixed. Alf started to box at smaller venues for the next few months but his form gradually improved and he strung together a series of impressive wins during 1921.

He was beginning to climb up the rankings. In 1922 he was offered a chance to box regularly at the Premierland. He continued winning, but at the end of the year his inconsistences returned. Alf tried his luck in Australia, South Africa and along the Eastern Seaboard of America but again with mixed results. Alf realised that the top of his particular tree was unreachable, so he knuckled down to preparing as best he could for retirement. Alf was still capable of some decent results and carried on boxing regularly around London until well into the 1930s. In April 1931 he fought fellow journeyman Fred Green from Blackfriars. When the two met at Green's home venue, the Ring, they had jointly fought 340 matches in twelve years. They both realised they were approaching the end of the road. On the night though, they produced fifteen rounds of classic welterweight boxing. Alf lost... just. Alf

Simmons fought only four more times after that and lost all four. He fought his last match at the Mile End Arena in August 1933 to bring to the end this journeyman's travels. Fred Green retired around the same time.

Boxing brothers are fairly commonplace in the sport and we will look at Jewish boxing families a little later. In Bethnal Green, the Corbett Brothers had an astonishing number of fights between them and they both reached the top of the sport in this country. They jointly fought well over 400 matches between the two World Wars. They were not Jewish but they followed in the footsteps of two other very durable Jewish boxing brothers who were initially active in the same area a decade or more earlier.

Harry and Alf Mansfield were born in Aldgate but moved a mile or so northeast to Bethnal Green. Apart from changing addresses they also changed their names. The family changed its name from Ginsberg to Mansfield. To confuse things further, Harry Mansfield more often than not boxed under the name Jack Jones. Harry was the elder of the two and his career turned out to be more eventful. Harry's story will be told a little later.

As for Harry's younger brother Alf, his road was littered with the potholes of failure. Alf attended the Judean Club as a young boy, he was a quick learner and progressed well until turning pro in early 1910. For Mansfield, fights came thick and fast. In his first year in the professional game Alf fought forty-three times, all but seven at the Judean club. After that he fought whenever and wherever he could. In total, he appeared on 130 undercards in both this country and in America over ten years.

Unlike Judean's favourite son, Ted Kid Lewis, Mansfield knew from his several early defeats at the Judean and the many more that accompanied him on his travels, that it was unlikely he would be challenging for higher honours in the game. Instead, he carved out a living. Alf ended his career in 1920 when he stepped out of the ring at the Pitfield Street Baths in Hoxton which, coincidentally, was where his famous fellow Judean club member, Ted Kid Lewis, would also finish his career. Many would follow Alf's journeyman footsteps but very few would follow in Ted's.

Another Judean graduate was **Fred Halsband**. Like the incomparable Ted Lewis, Fred was a firm Judean favourite. He showed tremendous early promise. In fact, his early boxing stats were superior to Ted's fight record. By coincidence, they both had their debut pro fights in 1909 and both lost but after that, there was no stopping the likeable Halsband. Fred was sensational in his first couple of years and nobody who witnessed his early battles would have believed he would end up one of those also rans. After that first loss in June 1909, Halsband's hand was raised thirty times at the end of his next thirty-two fights, with the other two bouts ending in draws. He was racking up fight after fight in quick succession. In the month of October 1910 alone, he boxed an incredible twelve times in thirty days against decent opposition. In hindsight that effort was to prove to be a bit too much and the odd loss crept in. By 1912, Halsband's boxing was becoming a little more inconsistent. By now, Ted Kid Lewis had scythed through the lighter ranks and started fighting at slightly higher weights. Halsband had boxed most of his contests at featherweight or lightweight. In August Ted caught up with his Judean colleague on the scales and they fought a featherweight match against each other at Premierland on 31 August. Against the odds, Fred produced an excellent display of boxing to claim a hard-fought match against Lewis.

It was to prove to be the high point of Halsband's career. He fought a return match at the National Sporting Club a couple of months later, where Lewis gained revenge. At this point in his career Halsband decided on working for the Yankee dollar. Following a couple more defeats, he decamped to America in March 1913. Deep down, Halsband knew it would be a tough ask to make an impact Stateside, and so it turned out. He fought eighteen times in as many months with very mixed results. The time in the States was not a complete waste, however. He fought the Australian lightweight champion, Jack Read, at Rhode Island Athletic Club in March 1914 and produced a win that ringside reporters described as the best fight ever seen at that venue.

Fred returned home a few months later with a fair bit of prize money and entered the fray once more in British rings. He was given a chance fight an eliminator for the British featherweight title in 1915 but was knocked out by Duke Lynch in the tenth round. Like so many, Fred answered the call to arms and joined the army to fight on the Western Front. He survived the war and managed to step into the ring a few times for some matches, but he was approaching the end of his career. Halsband fought on until 1921. In July that year he fought his last contest at Stamford Bridge Football ground against a very poor boxer. Although that particular venue had a reputation for being a graveyard for London Jewish boxers, Joe just about held on to his dignity by drawing the match before stepping into retirement after more than hundred bouts.

After the Second World War, the public flooded back to the venues and boxing in London continued at a pace through to the end of the fifties. The decade saw a change for the better in the financial positions of most of London's working class and more and more leisure time could be enjoyed. As the fifties gave way to the sixties, the demographics of the inner city changed as well. The large Jewish communities were gradually being replaced and less and less boxing could be seen in the old-style venues. Less paying punters were turning out for an evening's boxing entertainment in the dimly lit and smoky boxing halls of the capital. TV had arrived in the British front room and those venues that hosted two or three shows a week were fast disappearing.

The journeyman who fought whenever and wherever he could, racking up over a hundred fights or more, was becoming rarer. The Jewish journeymen had reached the end of their journey. For sixty or more years they had travelled in hope and found some small success in their labours, but the times had eventually caught up with them. Boxing fans could see two fighters go toe to toe in the comfort of their armchairs rather than turning out on cold winter evenings to witness the sport in dingy, cramped surroundings.

9

TOE TO TOE – FACE TO FACE

Considering the many years that some Jewish boxers in London plied their trade, it is no surprise that they met each other more than once. On a few occasions, they fought out a championship match against each other, but it was those who fought further down the bills that so often ended up being matched together, sometimes on several occasions. It took a while for two great champions to get together but in 1934, the two best lightweight boxers in the country at that time, Jack Kid Berg and Harry Mizler, faced each other at the Royal Albert Hall for the British lightweight crown.

Jack Kid Berg (Whitechapel) v Harry Mizler (St George's)

This fight was one of the most eagerly awaited matches between two Jewish boxers; a mouth-watering prospect. What added to the mix was the fact that they were both born within a mile of each other and each had contrasting styles of boxing. The Whitechapel Whirlwind as Jack was called was facing a younger more classically styled boxer in Mizler. Many thought that Berg's best days were behind him. Mizler was the favourite on the night but Jack Berg had a history of raising his game in the big fights. Berg had often been written off before a big fight only to prove the pundits wrong.

Mizler started off well but from about the third round onwards he spent more time defending than attacking. Mizler had an excellent defence but Berg was in tremendous form that night and as the fight wore on Jack was getting through a lot more. By the eighth round it was getting to be a little one-sided. Mizler tried to raise his game in the ninth and managed to push Jack back, but in the tenth Jack again proved the more aggressive fighter and by the end of the round was hitting Harry at will. Harry walked back to his corner and within a few seconds the white towel appeared from Mizler's corner.

After the contest, both boxers spoke to the press. A beaming Jack Kid Berg saying: 'I've fought for my country twice in world championships, once over here and once in America. This is the first time I have had the opportunity to fight in London for a British championship and won at the first attempt. I am prepared to fight any lightweight in the world.'

Harry Mizler was heartbroken: 'I am terribly sorry. Both my hands went by the end of the second round. I did my best to carry on. Berg has certainly not gone back. He is still a great tearaway fighter, and I wish him good luck in his role as champion.'

Mizler's hands healed and he went from strength to strength over the next few years. Jack Kid Berg also carried on fighting at a high level as well. It would be just over six years later that they next faced each other. They met at welterweight in a non-title fight at The Cambridge Theatre in London's West End. Mizler was at the peak of his career but Jack was, by now, fighting on borrowed time. This time Mizler was long odds-on to win well inside the distance. Yet again, the enigma that was Jack Kid Berg dumbfounded the boxing world by defeating Mizler, again on points over ten rounds. It was one of the biggest upsets in British boxing for many years. Those two headline boxers only fought each other twice but the fighters further down the pecking order often came up against each other on regular occasions over the years.

Young Josephs Nipper (Aldgate) v Kid Levene (Aldgate)

For young London Jewish boxers that were entering the professional ranks in the early years of the twentieth century, the Judean Club in East Stepney was the place to be. Its ring was part of the conveyor belt that propelled London Jewish boxing to prominence. As young novice boxers, Jewish lads would compete against each other regularly before moving on to bigger and hopefully better things. It was not unusual for a couple of lads to fight each other two or three times in their early days and then go their separate ways, possibly to never meet again inside the ropes.

On 31 October 1909, a couple of flyweights, Young Josephs Nipper and Kid Levene were matched up. The kid was fighting in just his second match and Nipper was fighting his tenth. The few extra fights that Nipper had under his belt told somewhat, and Kid Levene was overpowered and knocked out in the third round. Nipper was having a fine run of results and continued on his way. It is always interesting to look back at a boxer's earliest matches and especially some of the novice competitions they appeared in. Some experience one or two bad defeats and called it a day. Others bounce back and carry on. The Kid bounced back and the following month was at the Judean to win his third match, before facing the Judean's rising star Ted Kid Lewis where once again he was knocked out in the third round. It would have been no surprise if the Kid started to harbour thoughts about whether or not he should persevere; but persevere he did.

On 2 April 1910, five Jewish lads from London travelled down to the Brighton Dome for a boxing event. Most were still making their way in the sport. One of them however, Jack Daniels, was already a fine, experienced boxer and would be fighting his eightieth match that day. It would be some comfort to have him with them as a couple had probably never been outside of London until then. Two of the other four were Kid Levene and Young Nipper. They were again matched up. Again, Nipper won.

So, it was fought two, lost two for the Kid and perhaps at this point he should have decided to side-step the Nipper in future. Instead, the opposite happened and these two Judean old boys fought another six times against each other.

Three months later they were back at their old hunting ground the Judean Club for a six-round bout and it looked like the patten had been set when Young Nipper won for the third time. Another two fights followed early the following year. Both were close affairs, with the two battling out a draw followed by a narrow points win by the Nipper a week later. Later that summer, yet another tight match ended all-square. In November 1912, the pair moved on to the Wonderland arena to continue the saga. Different venue, same result; a draw over six. By this time Young Nipper was approaching eighty fights. Both boxers were still fighting around the country for some reasonable paydays, especially Nipper, but still Kid Levene was turning up like a bad penny, snapping away at him, trying to get a result. In March 1913, the rather odd venue of the Thames Rowing Club at Putney hosted the final match between the two.

A few weeks before this final encounter, Kid Leven had fought a gruelling ten-round match in Liverpool and lost heavily on points. Coming into the match against Nipper, the last thing the Kid wanted was another hard-fought match. Unfortunately for Levene, that is what developed and although it was scheduled for just six rounds, Levene was thoroughly outboxed and was lucky to see out the full distance. Young Josephs Nipper won at a canter.

Levene, who had earlier twice fought and lost to Ted Kid Lewis at bantamweight, went on to tackle another world-class boxer, Jimmy Wilde, in two matches later in 1913, which he also lost. After that he retired. Meanwhile Young Josephs Nipper fought on steadily, before losing heavily to a fairly mediocre South London fighter in October 1916 and hanging the gloves up.

Tommy Hyams (Kings Cross) v Dave Finn (Stepney)

Tommy Hyams could fall into the previous section of journeymen, but he was a little bit more than that. Tommy and Dave had both fought at various weights during their career so it wasn't until later that they first climbed into the ring together. It was November 1933 and by this time Tommy Hyams had fought ninety times before, his younger opponent Dave Finn, a mere fifty-five times. These two lads certainly knew their way around a ring! In a reasonable eight-round fight, the more experienced Tommy won a points decision.

It would be another two years before their paths crossed again. This time Dave Finn secured the win in another close match. This was before Finn went over to America to fight a series of fourteen matches against some good American boxers. Finn returned to England in 1937 and in November the following year was matched again with Hyams for their third fight. In a rather controversial encounter, Tommy was disqualified in the fourth round. Hyams was livid and demanded another match as soon as possible. The promoters duly obliged and two months later they squared off against each other for the fourth time. In a tremendous match at the Ring in Blackfriars, the two boxers fought themselves to a standstill with Tommy Hyams, against the odds, gaining the narrowest of victories.

The Daily Herold wrote:

Tommy Hyams and Dave Finn, contenders for the lightweight titles, had a great ten round fight at the Ring last night. Nothing to choose in the first half but Hyams did the forcing from the half-way stage and connected well with a left to the face. He also used the short right to the body well. Finn tried to keep the fight at long range, but was not always successful, which resulted in some furious spells of close-up work between the two. The last two rounds they both stood up well to each other's punches but

Hyams just had the best of some left-hand work. A close and very enjoyable match.

Promoters loved these sorts of close pairings and so, on 8 May 1939, they once again sat opposite each other preparing to do battle for the fifth and what would be the final time. For Dave Finn it would be his 135th career fight and for Tommy he would be touching gloves for the 170th time. A packed Ring waited to see these two great resilient Jewish boxers fight it out again. At the time they were both still regarded as strong British and European title contenders.

The fight started at a furious pace and the crowd looked as though they were in for a real treat but unfortunately it was not to be. The referee stopped the fight in the fifth round for an alleged low blow by Dave Finn. Tommy apparently did not complain too much about the punch but to the audience's obvious disgust, the ref thought otherwise and the match was brought to a premature and unsatisfactory end. A great shame that this series of epic encounters concluded in such a way.

Once war was declared a few months later, both boxers began to fight less. Tommy Hyams retired in 1942 but Dave Finn fought on until 1946. Neither of them fought for a British title but between them in almost 370 fights they provided some great entertainment for London audiences. Dave Finn was another boxer who defied the odds and lived until his nineties. They were a tough and durable breed.

Kid da Costa (Mile End) v Ted Kid Lewis (Aldgate)

Sunday 29 August 1909 dawned clear and bright in the East End of London and two young boxers looked forward to their debut bout of official professional boxing later in the day. Both packed their bags and headed off to the Judean Club in Stepney that afternoon. One of them, Kid da Costa as he was called, waited patiently in the cramped changing area of the club, contemplating his opponent for the day. Da Costa had heard some rumours about his opponent from his amateur days but the two debutants had never met. A few yards away his opponent was lacing up his gloves. They were the second match on the bill that day. In a few minutes, Kid da Costa was about to face the legend that was to become Ted 'Kid' Lewis.

Six rounds and forty minutes later Kid da Costa returned to the changing room as the victor. I am not sure if da Costa savoured his win but he should have done. That was to be the pinnacle of his boxing career. Two heavy defeats later and da Costa packed in the fight game and spent the next twenty years watching his defeated opponent on that day go on to conquer the world.

Ted Kid Lewis' exploits have been well documented. The great man lost very few of his matches over an immense career. Did Kid da Costa dine out on the fact that he once beat the great Ted Kid Lewis? He should have done. Once Lewis got that defeat and one other out of the way in his early days, he started to propel himself toward the top with victory after victory. Very few people had an answer to his all-action, hard-hitting style.

Jack Kid Greenstock (Bethnal Green) v Ted Kid Lewis (Aldgate)

A year later another young Jewish debutant arrived at the Judean Club for his first professional fight. He was about to be thrown into the lion's den to fight the rapidly improving Ted Kid Lewis. He was Jack Greenstock. Kid da Costa had known very little about Lewis when those two fought. Jack though, who was only seventeen at the time, already had a good idea of what he was about to face. A baptism of fire. Lewis arrived on the back of seven straight wins inside five months. Whoever trained young Jack however, must have done their homework on Lewis. What Jack found to nullify the Lewis style of boxing was almost certainly his defence and counter punching. It was enough to earn him a draw. It was a bit of an upset and Ted Kid Lewis arranged a hurried return match. Eight days later they fought a return. It was much the same as the first fight. Lewis could not break down the determined defence of Greenstock, who produced another display of sound defensive boxing. Same result... A hard-fought draw.

Lewis went away and scratched his head. A year passed and Lewis was still relentlessly climbing the ladder to the top when they were next matched. In May 1911, they faced each other for the third and final time. It was Lewis's fifty-fifth fight. It was still only young Jack's tenth. Once again Greenstock defied the odds and ground out another draw. Only the tough American world welterweight champion Jack Britton had a better record against Lewis in their epic series of twenty matches that took place between 1915 and 1921. So, it was just the excellent world champion Jack Britton and the rookie crafty Cockney kid who ever managed to blunt the brilliance of Ted Lewis.

Fred Housego (Paddington) v Mike Honeyman (Woolwich)

Boxing ran in the Housego household. His brother and cousin both boxed around the same time as Fred. Fred was a good solid pro and racked up around 125 fights, boxing all round London in a career spanning seventeen years. Travelling around London must have also run in the family as the famous London cabbie, Mastermind Champion and later radio and TV presenter of the 1980s and 1990s, Fred Housego, was a direct descendant.

When Mike Honeyman met Fred Housego for the first of three meetings in the summer of 1916, Fred was already a veteran of over seventy fights. Mike was just beginning to establish himself as a possible contender for the featherweight title. In the first two fights of that summer against Fred, Honeyman lost fairly convincingly. It was a setback for Mike and lessons had to be learnt if he was to progress to fight better men. Honeymen worked on his game and in the third match a few weeks later he boxed much better and gained the verdict after fifteen rounds of very tactical boxing. Mike had learnt his lesson and the following year, when the two met again at the Ring in Blackfriars, Mike again beat Housego in a great fifteen-round match.

From that fourth and final match against the durable Housego, Mike Honeyman then put together a string of outstanding performances. He fought twenty-five times over the next three years, losing just twice, before fighting and winning the British featherweight title in 1920 against Salford's Billy Marchant. Honeyman looked back on those matches against Housego as a turning point in his career.

Joe Conn (Bow) v Mike Honeyman (Woolwich)

Not every all-Jewish fight was edge of your seats stuff. Some promised much but failed to deliver. Mike Honeyman and Joe Conn were a pair of well-travelled boxers and on paper reasonably well matched. By the time they met in early 1923, Mike was an ex-featherweight champion and Jo Conn was the very solid boxer who fought Jimmy Wilde in that close duel in the sun match at Stamford Bridge a few years earlier. The sun wasn't about to shine on this match though. The fight took place at the Ring on a bitterly cold day in January.

That winter was an exceptionally cold one and there had been thick snow falling most of the afternoon. The arena that night was barely half full when the two arrived in the ring. The fight was scheduled for fifteen rounds but after five rounds most of the audience probably wished that it was an eight- or ten-round match. It was a poor offering from two boxers that the reduced crowd had expected more from. Very few meaningful punches were thrown. Honeyman was doing a little bit more than Conn but in the sixth Conn landed a punch which sent down the ex-champ for a count of eight. That was about as exciting as it got. Honeyman, the slightly younger man, perked up slightly and eventually ground out a narrow win on points.

Harry Lazar (Aldgate) v Harry Silver (Clapton)

By the start of the 1930s the amateur boxing set up was churning out great young boxers from all backgrounds. The more specialist boys' and men's amateur boxing clubs were ensuring that the young men who first learnt to box under the watchful eyes of top coaches would be more than ready to make the transition from amateur to professional. Most coaches would have known whether or not their young charges would stand a reasonable chance of reaching the top.

Harry Lazar was a real prospect and turned pro at the age of just fifteen in 1938. Harry Silver was a similar proposition. Silver was eighteen months older than Lazar and he, too, turned professional at fifteen. They met professionally just the one time on 29th February 1940. Both had enjoyed tremendous starts to their professional careers.

When they met, Silver had won all but five of his 56 fights to date. Lazar had slightly the better record, having lost just two of his forty-one fights. The old coaches of both must have looked on proudly as their protégés marched on towards the top. Surely this eight-round fight would just be a precursor to a championship title fight between the two a little further down the line. The battle of the two Harrys was staged at the Empress Hall, Earls Court, and fought at lightweight. The odds were more or less even so most observers were looking to see which of the two may have the edge.

Silver had just that little bit more experience overall and looked confident, but Lazer had excellent footwork and an array of good counter punches. The fight went the full distance and nobody ringside had a clue who was the winner. A draw looked the most likely result, but the decision was given to Lazar. As a pointer to who would be the first to challenge for a title, the fight gave little clues. In the event, neither Lazar nor Silver made it to a championship fight. It was an indication of just how strong the middleweight divisions were in British boxing during those times.

Harry Silver (left) with stablemate Eric Boon and manager Jack Solomons. This photo was taken in December 1938. Boon had won the British lightweight title the week before. Harry Silver was Jack's latest protégé and would be tipped for big things. Unlike Eric Boon, Harry never got close to challenging for major honours and turned into a solid if unspectacular journeyman boxer.

10

THE MAN IN THE MIDDLE

Boxing referees have always presided over boxing matches since the early bare-knuckle days. In fact, in those early days, the referee was ever-present and often accompanied the boxer's seconds. So, when Jack Broughton was slugging it out on a patch of ground in a ring made up of spectators, there could be five men prowling around the ring at any one time. Paradoxically, once the organised gloved version of the sport came along, it was fairly common to see the referee officiating from outside of the ring. This practice lasted up until the 1930s when it was thought that boxer's safety could be compromised if the referee was not in a position to physically step in straight away to end a fight and prevent serious injury.

There were some tremendous characters who refereed over the years and many of them had spent time inside the ropes as boxers. Ex boxers were encouraged, especially by the BBBofC, to apply for a referee's licence. The thinking was that a decent ex old pro would know what to look for in terms of scoring the contest and penalise any illegal punching or moves that took place.

Over the course of their careers, some referees could handle well in excess of 500 boxing matches. The well-known referee Harry Gibbs officiated on close to 1,000 bouts of boxing during his illustrious career. Gibbs was a Londoner but not

Jewish and although he boxed in his youth, he only fought four times professionally. At a couple of London's most popular venues a day's boxing could consist of up to twenty contests. The Wonderland Arena, for instance, sometimes hosted as many as ten novice three-round matches in the afternoon, followed by ten senior contests of between six and twenty rounds each in the evening. On occasion just one referee officiated at every match on these bills.

Many of the Jewish referees that progressed from boxing had a reasonable fight record behind them. British champion boxer Matt Wells handled many contests. His Lynn AC amateur clubmate, the gifted Rube Warnes, refereed a few fights as well.

Jack Hart was very popular both during his time boxing and over his lengthy refereeing career. Jack was born Moses Solomon at the turn of the century. He was an average boxer who fought twenty times before retiring in 1924. He applied for his refereeing licence shortly after this and once he had passed the appropriate tests, he took control of his first bout in 1926. He officiated at over 200 contests, his last match being the Walter McGowan non-title fight against Felix Brami at the Royal Abert Hall in 1965. Jack refereed two matches featuring the Canadian heavyweight, Larry Gains. They were both great matches. The first was against ex World champion Primo Carnera. The Ambling Alp met the Toronto Terror at the White City stadium in 1932. It was a big production and heavily advertised. In the event, just over 70,000 people attended, a record for a British boxing match at the time. The second was Gains' much-anticipated match against Len Harvey. This match was for the British Empire heavyweight title and was staged at the Harringay Arena in 1939. It was a really tough bout of boxing with Gains suffering a bad eye injury in the twelfth round. The following round Jack inspected the injury to Gains, stopped the fight and awarded the win to Harvey.

Angela Buxton and Althea Gibson in action at Wimbledon; two so-called minority athletes winning a major sporting event.

Daniel Mendoza's great-great-grandson Peter Sellers, in action as Inspector Clouseau, showing off his physical combat skills with his illustrious forefather pictured in the background.

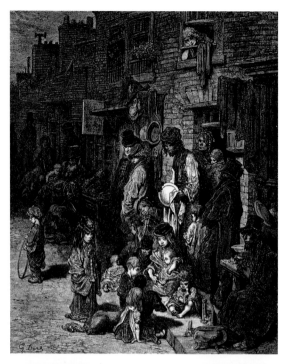

Street life on the cobbles. Wentworth Street *circa* 1870, part of the retail and business area which became known as Petticoat Lane and famous for its street markets. (Engraving by Gustave Doré in *London Life*)

The dark and sinister Old Nichol Rookery *circa* 1890. It was a breeding ground for both boxers and criminals.

Bernhard Baron House, home to the Oxford and St George's boys' club founded by Basil Henriques.

Above: A military camp at Deal in Kent in the summer of 1914, run by the Jewish Lads' Brigade. Sitting in the middle row, third from the left is Arthur Henry, a senior manager at the Stepney Lads club who arranged much of the gymnastics and boxing activities. He fought in the First World War as a lieutenant and was killed on the Western Front in 1917.

Below: Great Days in America. Ted 'Kid' Lewis fooling around with his good friend Charlie Chaplin.

Johnny Brown's Lonsdale Belt. He won this outright, the first Jewish boxer to do so.

One of the famous Star of David pairs of boxing shorts that were worn throughout the great Harry Mizler's career. They are exhibited alongside the gloves of Dave Finn, one of the legion of great journeyman Jews. (By kind permission of the London Jewish Museum, all rights reserved by LJM)

Harry Mizler continued to help out with his family's fish business whilst still boxing at the highest level.

The Battle of Cable Street. Note the women in the upstairs windows, ready to hurl down whatever comes to hand should Mosley's blackshirts or the police charge the barricades.

London Jewish boxers relaxing at a training camp in 1927. Seated second from left is Phil Lolosky and far right is Jack Hyams (Kid Froggy), both of whom were in training for upcoming fights. Standing at the back is their manager and trainer, Dave Phillips.

Gentlemen's boxing night at the sport's HQ, the National Sporting Club.

The Ring venue at Blackfriars, run by Dick and Bella Burge, hosted important fights from 1910 onwards.

Bella Burge, with her background in music hall, worked tirelessly to keep shows going on at the Ring. Seen here in the centre, on her left is the legendary music hall star Marie Lloyd. After the death of her boxing husband Dick, Bella became the close companion and confidante of Marie Lloyd for many years.

Left: Friday night is boxing night: British boxing at the peak of its popularity. This is a clipping from the *Radio Times* in 1938 advertising an upcoming boxing bout at the Devonshire Club. Jewish London boxer Kid Silver fought and beat Portsmouth's Billy Pleace that night.

Below: Sid Nathan, boxer, referee and ringside judge for over sixty years. Dave 'Boy' Green is in action.

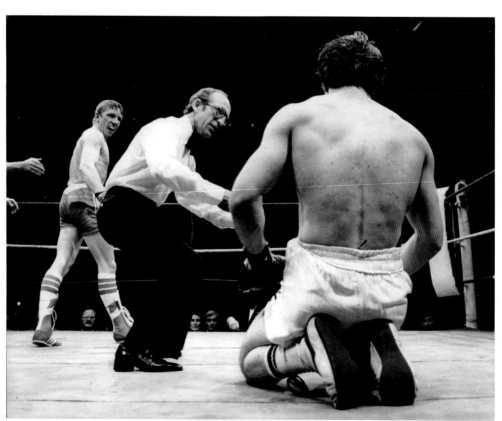

Referees Moss Deyong (left) and Sam Russell (right), top London officials who worked all over the capital.

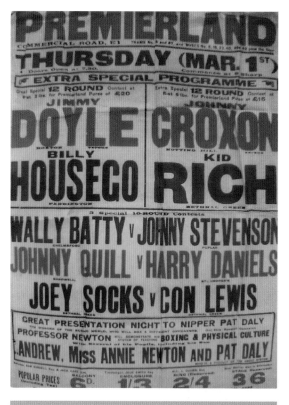

The inter-war years were the peak period for British boxing, with events taking place everywhere across London from east to west. Above is a poster from Stepney's Premierland advertising several Jewish boxers, and below is an advertisement for Boxing Night at the Royal Albert Hall in Kensington, arranged by the Jewish Sportsmen Committee.

The opening of York Hall, Bethnal Green, in 1929. Named after the Duke of York and he can be seen here in the foreground, next to Bethnal Green's mayor, George Bayley. York Hall is still one of the world's premier boxing venues and regularly hosts some of boxing's great championships.

All the boys in the Lazarus (Lazar) sporting family boxed, as did a couple of the girls. Harry and Lew Lazar (left) were excellent boxers but Mark (right) swapped his gloves for football boots, playing for four professional football teams in London.

Heavyweights Cassius Clay (later Muhammad Ali) and Henry Cooper are seen sitting either side of Jack Solomons and his lifelong friend, the great entertainer Bud Flanagan, at a lunch for the two boxers prior to their fight in 1963.

Britain's Mr Boxing, Jack Solomons, walking through Soho with Cassius Clay. It was Solomons who matched the young future boxing legend against South London's Henry Cooper.

Above: The other Jewish boxing supremo from the golden days of London boxing, Harry Levene. Sitting next to Levene is heavyweight Billy Walker and also in attendance are promoter/managers Al Phillips and Mickey Duff.

Right: Micky Duff, seen in his later years with his boxer Robert McCracken. Duff was the leading British promoter during the latter half of the last century and into the first few years of this one.

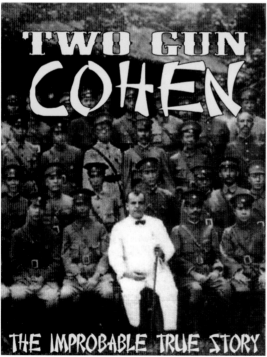

Above: 'What do you guys call this game?' Muhammad Ali at Lords. Boxing promoter and media mogul Jarvis Astaire stands behind Ali trying to explain the finer points of the English game to the great man. Ali came away none the wiser. At this point, Astaire was the managing director of View Sport Ltd.

Left: Morris 'Two Gun' Cohen, aka Cockney Cohen, borstal boy, boy boxer, prize fighter, war hero, bodyguard, gun runner, spy, military leader and influential political activist. The radio play and the couple of books on him probably do not do justice to this East London character. Seen here with Chinese leader Chiang Kai-shek and his staff.

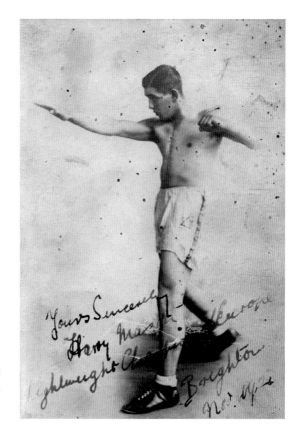

Right: The well-travelled Harry Mason, as skilled with a violin and bow in his hands as he was with gloves on his fists.

Below: The conjoined Hilton Twins from Brighton, who went to America to star in vaudeville, were the love interest of Harry Mason for a short time.

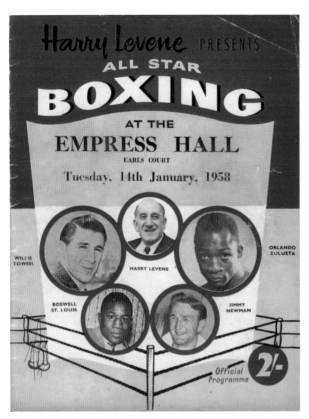

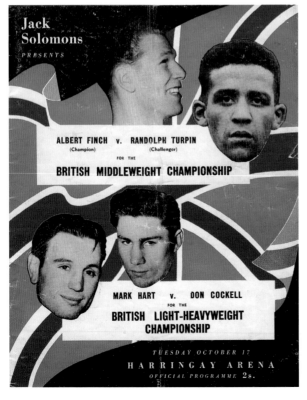

The two great rival Jewish boxing promoters who dominated the British London fight scene either side of the war. Harry Levene often used the Empress Hall in Earl's Court to stage his promotions. Jack Solomons staged a lot of his big fights at the Harringay Arena.

You sometimes see old black and white comedy films featuring boxing. Often a good visual joke is watching two big men supposedly slugging it out when a small hapless referee tries to separate them and gets accidentally knocked out by a punch. All good fun. Actually, there have been several cases of the referee being 'taken out' by an accidental wayward punch. Jack, though, was once on the receiving end of one that was not.

Jack Hart officiated with a cool head for forty years and rarely had any problems in the ring apart from one incident that occurred in October 1927, when Hart was officiating a bout between Kid Brooks and Young Stanley. It should have been standard fare. Both were experienced professionals. Stanley had fought over fifty times at this point. The contest was a very close one from the start and after a few rounds a bit of 'niggle' crept into the fight with complaints from both boxers and their respective corners about foul play. The match went the full distance, but Hart had to keep pulling the two fighters apart and was constantly warning them about their behaviour.

As soon as the bell sounded for the end of the match, Hart called the boxers together and acrimonious fight or not, it was a close call. Hart however, raised Kid Brooks hand immediately, seemingly never having looked at his score card. This incensed Stanley. As Hart turned to leave the ring, he ran straight into a huge straight right hand thrown by Stanley. Jack staggered backwards and nearly fell through the ropes. This was not a slapstick comedy routine and the two corners had to step in to prevent Stanley going after Hart. Sometimes in those days incidents like this could be overlooked as something that happened in the heat of the moment and an apology may have been sufficient. Unfortunately for Young Stanley, there was a representative of the boxing board present. He was not impressed and Stanley was hauled before the board. These days, such an incident would result in a boxer losing his licence. Stanley was only banned for six months.

As for Jack Hart, he moved onwards and upwards becoming a really top official. He mostly worked in this country but he did handle two world championship matches in Africa during the sixties featuring Dick Tiger and Sugar Ramos.

Unlike Jack Hart, **Sam Russell** had a lengthier and more successful career with the gloves. He won thirty-one of his forty-one fights in five years of boxing. He also managed a couple of fighters as well. It was though, his time as a top referee that was impressive. Sam took charge of some truly great bouts of boxing over a thirty-year period. He worked with some great British boxers as well as some American boxers who occasionally came over to fight.

The men that he instructed in the ring, many of whom were fighting for top honours, read like a who's who of British boxing, among them Jack Berg, Harry Reeve, Harry Mason, Teddy Baldock, Al Foreman, Len Harvey, Johnny Hill and Randolph Turpin. The list goes on. Sam will best be remembered for handling the Bruce Woodcock v Freddie Mills title fight at the White City Stadium, when Woodcock battered Mills round the ring for the best part of twelve rounds. Mills went down time and time again only to keep getting up. This blistering bout of boxing was ended by Woodcock in the fourteenth and penultimate round, with a devastating right-hand cross that put poor Freddie out cold.

In 1925, Sam refereed the match between Teddy Sheppard and Billy 'pop' Humphries. At that time Sam was one of those referees who would mostly officiate from outside of the ring. In the sixth round of the fight, Sam noticed that Sheppard was hanging onto Humphries for long periods and making little effort to throw any punches. Sam sensed something was wrong and entered the ring and on inspecting Sheppard, immediately stopped the fight. As

Hart ushered Sheppard back to his corner, Sheppard collapsed onto the canvas. Help arrived but Sheppard died on the ring floor. There had been a few deaths in the ring during the early 1920s and an enquiry was conducted. No legal action was taken against any party that was involved that night but following these deaths, referees started to officiate a lot more in the ring. Within ten years or so, all matches required a referee to be present in the ring at all times during a fight.[1]

Most bills of boxing in later years featured anything from six to ten bouts of boxing. In the longer events, normally several referees could share the officiating duties. The BBBofC was raising the standard of refereeing. Once referees started controlling the fights from inside the ring rather than sitting ringside, the need increased for them to be strong, fit, quick-witted and observant. At a boxing event that took place at the Drill Hall in Dover, Kent, in 1932, eight bouts of boxing were fought and every one was refereed by Jack Hart. It was unusual but that night, Jack was present in the ring for almost sixty rounds of boxing. Over three hours of concentration whilst weaving around the ring: some feat. On other occasions, it may be that just three or four bouts of boxing that were staged. Often a matinee event of novice and debutant boxers were put on. These were normally limited to three or four round matches so the whole event could well last no longer than ninety minutes. One such event took place on Sunday 9 September 1900.

Moss Deyong from West Stepney entered the ring in Spitalfields on that date to fight in his first professional match. Moss was of mixed Dutch/Jewish descent but not much more is known about his background. I do not know if he had his sights set on a professional career or how good a boxer he was. I can find no trace of the weight at which he fought. What is certain is that nothing that happened that afternoon would have entered his head as he climbed into the ring. As is perfectly normal for a debut fight, Moss was given a three-round contest against another debutant. On this day Battersea's Mike Morris was his opposition.

At the start, all seemed fine, with Moss steadily gaining the upper hand. Again, I have no idea of the exact events in the third round but after receiving further punishment from Deyong, his opponent, Morris, was knocked out and lay on the canvas unconscious for some time. The two sets of corner men managed to gradually bring him round and he returned to his dressing room. Any euphoria of winning his first bout soon disappeared when Moss learnt that Morris had slipped into unconsciousness again. Initially, after hospital treatment, Morris improved.

It appears that with the events of the match turning so sour, Deyong did not rush back into the ring to fight again. His worse fears were then realised when, a few weeks later, Mike Morris died. Young Moss Deyong did not box again. It is possible that Moss blamed himself for the death or maybe he thought that the officials could have done more. I know not, but he turned his back on the sport that he loved. In boxing circles nothing much was heard about him for almost another eleven years, until his name appeared on a list of available boxing referees.

His time in the ring as a professional boxer lasted no more than nine minutes but his time in the ring as a referee lasted forty years! Deyong handled fights all over Britain at all the top venues. He officiated on championship matches and also refereed the odd contest in Europe. In 1911, he was retained by the Judean Club to referee. Deyong was quite big, tough, and looked it as well. The owners there were experiencing a few problems with some of the younger boxers arranging the outcome of a fight to suit themselves by feigning injury during the match. Moss could spot this type of thing early and within a few short months had cleaned up the problem. He was, though, most associated with the Ring venue at Blackfriars and Premierland in East London for many years before he started looking after some prestigious matches at places further afield like the Royal Albert Hall, Manchester's Belle Vue Arena and the St James' Hall in Newcastle.

He handled well over 300 bouts of boxing, including many British, European and world title fights and several exceptional non-title contests, including the great bantamweight and former world champion Teddy Baldock's swan song against rising star Dick Corbett at Clapton Greyhound Track in September 1931. The two Cockney lads fought out a twelve-round classic in front of 20,000 vociferous East Enders. Moss oversaw his last match in 1950. He was considered a very competent official and a safe pair of hands. Occasionally an eyebrow was raised when it was thought that he stopped a fight slightly prematurely. Given his boxing baptism, it was no surprise that he refused to let a boxer take any more punishment than was the minimum norm. It was a surprise therefore, when Moss came in for some criticism over the handling of one of the greatest fights ever to take place in a London ring.

Moss Deyong was appointed to take charge of the Harry Mizler v Gustave Humery fight that I covered earlier. In that fight Mizler suffered round after round of knockdowns and standing counts. Seven rounds of them, in fact. Many there that night, including Mizler's own corner, by all accounts, were surprised that the fight was not stopped. During the blackest times during that fight, Mizler convinced both his corner and the referee that he was capable of continuing. As you know, this was proven to be the case. From being a second or so away from defeat on many occasions throughout the first half of that fight, Mizler produced the most remarkable of turnrounds to stop the impressive Frenchman. So, Moss Deyong got it right, although despite the result, some continued to believe that the fight should have been stopped. I think that fight may possibly have been the exception in terms of his general approach to refereeing and it paid off for Harry Mizler.

For well over thirty years, **Sid Nathan** took control of some of this country's greatest fights. He and Harry Gibbs were considered two of Europe's greatest post-war boxing referees. Sid had boxing blood running through his veins and as a boxer himself, he probably spilt a bit of it along the way. Sid, if you remember, was one of the boxers that came through the Jewish Lads' Brigade. Sid had tasted the atmosphere of the professional boxing game early in his life. His father, the clothes machinist, was also a boxer. Sid said that as a young boy, he was once carried around the ring by Ted Kid Lewis whom Sid's dad knew well.

According to Sid's granddaughter, Georgina Morelle, her great grandfather boxed under the name of Jack Arbour and took his ring name from Arbour Square near to where he lived. Records are vague. Some show his name as Arbour and some as Harbour. Being a Cockney, it must 'ave been Arbour, surely. It looks like he had a dozen or so fights around 1910 and he also had a few fights under the name Jack Nathan. To confuse things even more, Nathan was not the original name, that was Natalsky. One thing is sure though, Sid was surrounded by boxing all his life. Sid was an avid watcher of the game before he pulled on a pair of gloves professionally. After his boxing career was cut short somewhat by the Second World War, he took up refereeing and his years spent as an A-list referee were truly exemplary. With about 1,200 bouts of boxing under his belt, Sid's time as a boxing referee was more or less controversy-free. That in itself is remarkable. Even his illustrious colleague Harry Gibbs had a couple of controversial fights, not least of which was Gibbs's verdict in favour of Joe Bugner over Henry Cooper, which even today is viewed as a very poor call indeed.

Most experts agree that by and large, Sid got it more or less right 1,200 times. His style of refereeing facilitated this. If and when he noticed that a boxer's punching or movement may have resulted in him having to stop the fight and warn the boxer of his actions, Sid was always ahead of the game and would issue his instruction whilst letting the fight flow on. There is an old maxim in sport that says that the best referees are the ones you don't notice during a match. Nathan was one of those men. After having to retire from his time in the middle, Sid became a senior boxing judge and scored eighteen world championship contests. He continued in the game well into his eighties. His longevity in the sport means that in his time, he can claim to have been in the ring with two British world champions, Ted Kid Lewis and Frank Bruno, a span of about sixty years!

Sid Nathan, as a boxer, fought over half his bouts at the Devonshire Club in Hackney, the first being in 1939. On March 1995, Sid sat down ringside to judge what was to be his last boxing match, the world middleweight title fight between Robert Allen and Ricardo Raul Nunez. Fittingly for this great Londoner, the match took place at one of boxing's great venues, York Hall in Bethnal Green, just a few hundred yards from the old Devonshire Club site. He remained as fit as a flea until the last months of his life. Sid died peacefully on 2 April 2016 in Barnet, North London.

Back in 1988, even before he stepped down for good, Sid reflected on his time in boxing: 'Boxing has been my life. I was just a Jewish kid from the East End, but boxing has enabled me to travel the world, and meet some wonderful people. Experience that money can't buy. I've been fortunate and I appreciate it very much.'

Such was the sheer number of boxing contests that took place at the Wonderland Arena in Whitechapel during its relatively short life of eleven years, the list of referees that officiated there is extremely lengthy. At its height it could be running two shows a day. You would need a fair roster of referees to call on in order to cover that number of matches. There appeared to be no shortage of such men. Very few would be termed 'A' star referees that officiated at the more prestigious matches in later years. These were often men that had boxed a little bit in their earlier days and had enough authority about them to control a match.

As befits a venue that had a reputation of showcasing Jewish boxers, the men in the middle were also predominantly Jewish. Look down any bill of boxing at the venue and names like Dave Fineberg, Richard Josephs, Ben Cohen, Victor Mansell and Gershon Harris would often indicate the men in charge. Some of these men could well have handled over three hundred contests at the Wonderland alone. **'Jolly' Joe Hyams,** of whom I could find no record of ever having fought an official professional boxing match, handled almost 400 fights in his relative short career of just over two years and every single one of them was at the Wonderland. **Dave Jacobs** must have spent more time in the ring at Wonderland than he did at home. In less than six years at the venue, he took charge of almost 1,200 fights. There are instances of some referees handling an entire bill of boxing of a dozen fights by themselves. Although much of the officiating was done ringside, it would still require up to four hours or more of non-stop concentration.

11

ENTERTAINMENT VALUE

London's boxing history can be traced back to Jack Broughton, the so-called 'Father of British Boxing' and James Figg, England's first heavyweight champion. They were instrumental in establishing the first boxing booths that appeared in the West End of the capital from around 1725. The unregulated bare-knuckle sport was popular at these booths but in these formative years the sport often found its home wherever it could. From the cobbled backstreets of the inner boroughs to the more open spaces on the outskirts of the city. Variety halls and public houses were also used in those days.

As the popularity of pugilism grew throughout the eighteenth century, by the end of the century the sport had become established nationwide and a great deal more regulated. More purpose-built boxing arenas were needed to help develop this next stage for the sport. Town halls, swimming baths and community halls were used and continued to be used for many more years, but at the turn of the twentieth century larger purpose-built arenas appeared around the capital. These were to become focal points for London boxing.

One of the first to appear was the **Wonderland** in Whitechapel High Road, which around 1900 began to showcase the many Jewish boxers who lived locally. It became a very important venue in the development of London boxing. They would often hold novice tournaments, over three and six rounds, at the various weights to ease young boxers into the fight game. The money for these tournaments was poor but for many young Jewish boxers, this was the ring they climbed into for their first professional fight. These tended to be staged as matinee performances and the evening shows were for the more senior fighters. It was very popular.

In an article in *The Era* publication wrote in May 1896: 'Enterprise in the world of amusement has never been wanting in the East, as its large and well-equipped variety temples and its elegant and up-to-date theatres amply testify.' It was referring to the many music halls and entertainment arcades in the area and the involvement of the Jewish entertainment entrepreneur Jonas Woolf in setting some of these up. By today's standards, some of the sights that could be seen in the arcades and the acts that performed in the halls would be considered quite unedifying, not least in the way which some of these acts were kept and the manner in which they were treated.

Woolf took over the old Effingham theatre and handled a couple of smaller entertainment arcades. He changed the name of the theatre to the Wonderland in 1896. Across the road was a so-called 'amusement parlour' that was run by Tom Norman who exhibited John Merrick, The 'Elephant Man' in a back room. One of Woolf's 'acts' was a young lady called Miss Virginie Brisou from Paris. His posters advertised: 'Next to Anak the Giant (he was an Irishman of around seven foot-plus) you will see seated, the "lady with the lobster claws", an extraordinary freak of nature. The claws, in the place of hands are over ten inches long. She can sow, embroider and play the piano.'

Initially, the Effingham theatre was used as an exhibition hall and 'theatregraph', which was an early form of cinema. It was not too successful. Woolf though, had witnessed the rise of boxing in the capital so he introduced boxing into his venue and the sport found its first home in East London. Back in the early days of bare-knuckle boxing, there had always been an element of showbiz in the proceedings. Woolfe developed this, and the transition from entertainment venue to sports venue was a seamless one.

As the Wonderland developed, Woolfe was joined by Harry Jacobs as a co-promotor. Jacobs came from a boxing background and had run the Mile End Paragon Music Hall that had also featured boxing events. Harry was committed to the sport. He was instrumental in securing some of London's best boxers to appear on the bills at the Wonderland. It drew big crowds, due in no small part to featuring Britain's big star boxers and great champions of the day, like Bombardier Billy Wells, Pedlar Palmer, Johnny Summers, Pat O'Keefe and Bill Ladbury. But it was the Jewish boxers coming through that featured heavily on its bills. They were to form the cornerstones of boxing events at London venues for many years.

Apart from promoting Jewish boxing, The Wonderland also featured a few black boxers in official regulated boxing matches. According to all official records, Britain's first black national Champion was Dick Turpin, the elder brother of Randolph Turpin who was Britain's first black world champion. However, forty years before Dick's title, Andrew Jephtha, a black (Cape Coloured) South African, fought and won a British and British Empire title at the Wonderland in 1907. There were, though, a couple of anomalies with this promotion, so it is absent from official record books.[1]

There was one boxer whose name is associated with the Wonderland more than many other. He was a little-known boxer who had an extraordinary career in some respects. **Bert Adams** was half Jewish and lived all his life in Spitalfields. He fought his debut match in Croydon but after that he plied his trade mostly around inner London. After competing in a couple of fights in a novice minimum weight competition at the Sporting Club in

Covent Garden, he went on to define boxing at the Wonderland. He fought his first match there two weeks after it opened its doors in 1900 and he fought his last fight there, two weeks before it closed in April 1911.

Over the eleven years Wonderland was open, Adams competed almost 150 times at the place, 140 of those between 1900 and 1908. He finished off fighting at the Premierland, which took over the mantle of Wonderland. He fought fellow Jewish lightweight Jack Gold three times in six weeks in 1912, before retiring later the following year in 1913. His boxing record was average. Although his career may have been so-so, it was prolific. Bert is recorded as having 206 matches, although it is possible that he may have had more unrecorded fights. After his debut, he only fought in two rings outside of London, once at Merthyr Tydfil and once in Sheffield. He was a proud Londoner and a great Wonderland stalwart.

So, in the shape of the Wonderland arena, East London had its boxing home, but within a few years of its opening, Central and South London were looking to build arenas to showcase the sport in their part of the capital. By the end of 1910 some splits were starting to develop between Woolfe and Jacobs. With better and bigger venues beginning to open, Wonderland would have to respond. It failed to do so. On 12 August 1911, Young Johnny Cohen knocked out Harry Williams in the last fight on the Wonderland bill that night. Once the two boxers left that night, Jonas Woolfe turned out the lights and locked up the arena. The following day, the Wonderland had gone, completely gutted by a mysterious and devastating fire. It all looked a bit suspicious, but nothing was ever proven. Some of the earliest history of the gloved version of the noble art performed at the Wonderland was now buried amongst its ashes.

In June 1901, ex boxing champion Dick Burge met East End girl Leah Belle Orchard. Little is known about the early life of Dick Burge, who was boxing around the time that the gloved version of the sport began to take over from the bare-knuckle version. Records show him as holding both the lightweight and middleweight English and British titles between 1890 and 1897. He was born and grew up in rural Gloucestershire but moved to Newcastle, where he first fought. We do know that by the end of the nineteenth century he was living and boxing in London and that is where he met Leah Orchard, who by then was known as Bella Lloyd.

Bella Lloyd was Jewish through her mother's line. Both her parents came from Britain, but her father was a florist and for many years lived and worked in New York. Bella was born in America but following the death of her father when she still a very small child, the family moved back to Whitechapel where her mother originally came from. Both her parents were artistic and Bella developed a flare for the arts. She became an accomplished LLondon music hall performer singing and acting under the name of Bella Lloyd. She also occasionally worked in the makeup and wardrobe departments of the theatres. It was whilst performing as a thirteen-year-old in a Christmas pantomime with two other actresses, Grace and Alice Lloyd, that she met their sister, the renowned music hall entertainer, Marie Lloyd. To clarify, Lloyd was their stage name (Wood was their family name). Marie Lloyd and Bella became friends over the years and remained so until Marie's early death in 1922. Bella often worked as Marie's dresser and makeup assistant and became her very close confidante, as well as performing herself.

Dick and Bella's marriage in October 1901, just four months after they met, certainly had a showbiz feel about it. 'Music hall star marries champion boxer' would have been the headlines. They made a colourful couple. How much Bella knew about her new husband's boxing background I do not know. It may not have mattered much to her that during the course of Dick's boxing career many of his match results, including some top-billed fights, were the subject of serious speculation about their legitimacy. Burges's fights against Ted Pritchard in 1894 and his title fight against Jem Smith the following year were investigated as possible betting scams. Nothing was proven and a later fight against Arthur Ackers was also highly suspicious. In January 1901 he fought Jerry Driscoll back on his old hunting ground of Gateshead in the North East.

By this time Burge's reputation was preceding him and when it became apparent that this fight was not progressing as it should, with neither boxer throwing any meaningful blows, rather than warning the boxers, the referee stopped the fight halfway through the second round and called the match a 'no contest'. He informed the boxers that he would be reporting the matter to the governing body. Dick Burge announced his retirement the next day!

Five months later he met then married Bella and a new, easier chapter of his life was supposed to begin for Dick. Sadly, that was not the case. Unknown to Bella, the previous year, Dick along with a couple of very sophisticated conmen that he fell in with, pulled off a massive fraud involving Liverpool banks. The amounts of money where huge, almost £180,000 was obtained illegally and mixed with counterfeit notes, which were then laundered through racecourse betting. A few months after their marriage the scam was detected and Burge was caught and convicted. Poor Bella, a new bride of six months, was left to fend for herself while Dick was sent away for 10 years hard labour.

He served less than eight and when he got out, he went back to Bella and, determined to go straight, he teamed up with Bella to open a boxing arena in Blackfriars. It was rumoured that Dick had stashed away some of his ill-gotten gains, which helped pay for the conversion of an old chapel in Blackfriars, South London, and turn it into a leading London boxing venue, The Ring.

The Ring opened its doors to the public in 1910. It was a unique venue as it was completely round in shape. South London had its major boxing venue. It advertised the place as providing, 'upper class boxing at working class prices' and it delivered on that promise. It was tremendously popular over the next thirty years or more and attracted all the top boxers of the day. It hosted many championship fights. Bella very often attended the boxing sessions and helped to bring a bit of pazazz to them. It is not known if her friend, Marie Lloyd, ever climbed through the ropes to give the crowd a rendition of her Cockney masterpiece, *Don't Dilly Dally on the Way*, or *My Old Man (Said Follow the Van)*.

At the outbreak of war, the patriotic Burge enlisted in the Surrey Rifles. Bella was left to look after the venue and keep it running by herself. She had great empathy for the young men that were going off to war and would often address the audience from within the ring, prior to the start of events. Many of the young men she spoke to in the audience went off to the front line, never to return. Neither too, did some of the boxers she promoted. These were dark days, but Bella kept up everyone's spirits. She became a firm favourite within the boxing fraternity. During the Boer War, fifteen years earlier, and at the height of Bella's music hall career, one of Bella's most popular musical songs was the prophetically titled *The Girl You Leave Behind You*:

> The troopship was just upon starting
> The soldiers were ordered to war
> And I saw my true love departing

Perhaps to return never more
The tears dimmed his eyes as we stood on the strand
And I could not speak – only press his dear hand
He said, 'Tis to fight for old England I go'
I answered 'I know dear' then soft and low,
'Now your country calls you far across the sea
To do a soldier's duty, for England, home and beauty
Think of those who love you, and all the ties that bind you
And soon come back, my own dear Jack
To the girl you leave behind you.'

Dick Burge did not come back to the girl he left behind. After making it through to within a few months of the war's end, he developed pneumonia and died. Bella, who stood beside him throughout his life, carried on with the business through the 20s and early 30s and she continued to promote some excellent fights there. She was much loved by the boxers that fought at the Ring, but the place started to decline somewhat as more comfortable venues opened. By the outbreak of war in 1939 it was struggling financially but Bella soldiered on until two German 500lb bombs that fell onto the building in 1942 delivered the final knock-out blow to this iconic venue.

The couple were big names in the boxing world and Bella in particular gained a tremendous reputation. In those days, boxing was a totally male-dominated sport and for a woman to make the sort of impact that Bella did was truly exceptional.

Around the time that the Ring first opened for boxing, an old but large warehouse in Back Church Lane, about half a mile away from the defunct Wonderland, was being re-developed for entertainment use. It was a very large building and had the potential to hold many thousands of customers. With no nearby large boxing hall around, Harry Jacobs was taken on to run the project and it was to become the next great East London boxing venue for the following twenty years.

Premierland, pronounced 'Pree-mier-land' by its patrons, was to become even more popular then the Wonderland. It, too, became the ring that showcased a lot of up-and-coming Jewish boxers. It went on to stage a huge number of events, although it only ever featured one championship fight. Unlike some other boxing venues, its façade was less than inspiring, but it was well lit up to stage its opening event in December of 1911. Hundreds of posters had gone up previously all around the area advertising the event, and a couple of thousand turned up to get in to watch an impressive nine-fight bill of good solid boxing.

Sunday, especially in those days, was still very much a day of leisure for the various Jewish communities. In London, Sunday morning was often spent visiting one of the thriving street markets that could be found around the capital. In East London, Petticoat Lane, Hoxton Market, Ridley Road and Club Row markets attracted large crowds. For many, this was followed by a trip to the pub for a lunchtime drink or to the famous Bloom's Kosher Restaurant for a salt beef sandwich. Later in the day, many boxing fans would wander down the Commercial Road to take in either an afternoon or evening bill of boxing at the Premierland or the Judean Club.

Harry Jacobs ensured the earlier Premierland events featured some of the top Jewish boxers around, as it was estimated that half the audience was Jewish. Salt beef sandwiches, jellied eels and fruit were sold on site. Boxers like Harry Reeve, Ted Lewis, and Harry Mansfield were regular attractions in the formative years. By the end of the following year, the place was electric on fight nights. Betting was rife and the crowd noisy. Harry Jacobs was the go-to promoter in London.

Despite its popularity throughout the period it was open, the venue as a business struggled from time to time. In its earlier years, Jacobs' promotional skills drew huge numbers of cash customers and seemed successful. There is an old Jewish saying in business: 'Loads of dough in the till but none in the bank'. It is as true today as it was then. There was some bad mismanagement and by the summer of 1913 Jacobs was going bankrupt and so he sold out to Harry Morris and Jack Callaghan, two experienced managers and promoters who put the venue back onto a sound footing by featuring more shows but less bouts on each card.

In December 1914, after the outbreak of war, the Premierland stopped its boxing events and the premises were used as a cinema until 1921, when boxing was again staged at the venue. Initially, two new men were at the helm. Joe Morris, an extremely capable boxing manager and matchmaker, joined up with boxing superstar Ted 'Kid' Lewis, but in 1922 the lease was taken over by Ted's brother-in-law, Manny Lyttlestone, and he was joined by local sportsman and up-and-coming promoter, Victor Berliner.

A big re-launch was undertaken in 1922 and with the matchmaking and promotional skills of Morris and Berliner coupled with the management skills of Manny Lyttlestone, Premierland once again became one of London's top boxing venues. By 1925 the place was buzzing, with big fight nights and huge crowds present. Jewish boxing was reaching its peak in these inter-war years. Great champions like Jack Kid Berg, Young Johnny Brown, Harry Mason and Al Foreman all boxed there, and also several other London-based non-Jewish boxing champions fought there regularly. The great world bantamweight Teddy Baldock, and British champions Johnny Summers, the Corbett brothers, Johnny Curley and Kid Pattenden travelled the short distance from their homes to climb through the ropes at Premierland.

Jewish boxers who made their mark at
Premierland. Al Foreman (right), who won
the only British championship fight at the
Venue. Below are the two great Brown
brothers, British champion Johnny and
little brother Young Johnny. The Browns
fought a total of almost sixty matches
there.

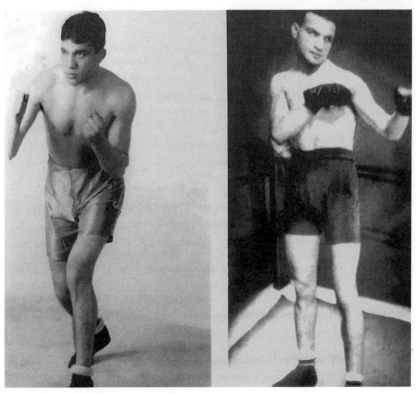

Of all the London Boxing arenas that came to prominence during the first half of the twentieth century, Premierland after the First World War was, more than most, probably the most atmospheric and interesting of all. It was not an attractive place. It was not a comfortable place either, and as mentioned, it only hosted one championship title fight. What makes the place so memorable was that it encapsulated so many aspects of London life and the sport of boxing. It staged a huge number of fights over the years. In its early years, before the First World War it would often hold bills of up to fifteen matches. Some of these bills featured a series of novice fights, normally up to eight, 3- to 6-round bouts aimed at giving young London boxers a 'gentle' introduction to the professional game.

At any given boxing match there, if you were in the know, you would find East End music hall and West End theatre stars sitting next to London underworld figures. Betting was not allowed on the premises but at every bill of boxing you would see 'Street Bookmakers' leaning inconspicuously up against one of the iron stanchions holding up the glass roof, their bookie's runners buzzing around the stalls collecting bets. East End gangster Jack Spot cut his early criminal teeth running for a bookmaker at the Premierland. Kosher and non-kosher food would be consumed and patrons could be seen swigging from hip flasks before leaving to finish the night's entertainment off in one of the many pubs that surrounded the venue.

It was a couple of matches that took place here that prompted the authorities to look seriously into introducing greater safety measures for boxers. At the Premierland, there were no official weigh-ins and there was very rarely a trained medical person on call at ringside. The boxers relied on their cornerman to administer any minor first aid and pull them out if they were taking too much punishment. Ring deaths happened, and still do, but it is extremely rare now.

The death of Teddy Sheppard at the venue in 1925, referred to in the previous chapter, prompted the authorities to carry out a number of investigations and eventually they introduced a venue licensing agreement for all London boxing venues. Specific requirements had to be met in terms of running a safe event, with the boxer's needs paramount. In 1929, the British Board of Boxing Control was formed and they gradually took a more responsible approach to boxer's welfare. Within a few years the BBBofC would arrange for doctors to assess their conditions in the dressing rooms before the fight and be in attendance ringside during the match.

Set within the dense East London population, the Premierland was not universally accepted during its tenure. It had its detractors. Contemporary reports suggest that crowd violence and gambling were commonplace there and overcrowding was dangerous. One regular Jewish visitor to the hall throughout the 1920s later noted: 'The place was packed to the rafters. For sixpence you just stood on a football style terrace, on steps. Some spectators were most ingenious, they climbed onto the top rafters and hung there.'

Unsurprisingly, complaints from 'respectable' society continued to be sent to the local authorities. In 1928, a Mr Cohen from Bow, East London (a self-labelled 'well known person' in the East End) complained that 'Premierland was a hot bed of gambling and excess drinking. Overcrowding was commonplace and this could lead to loss of life.'

A victory for those wanting to stamp out Jewish misconduct and protect younger, impressionable men from the temptation of Premierland was recorded when the LCC (London County Council) and the Metropolitan Police launched an investigation into gambling and crowd safety in smaller boxing halls in the capital. In late 1929, the management of Premierland was singled out for negligence in turning a blind eye to illegal gambling and allowing dangerous levels of overcrowding to occur.

By 1930, the Great Depression was gathering pace and although crowds were still good, the place was in urgent need of some major repairs. It also had to respond to the question of seating arrangements in the light of the overcrowding issues that were brought to its attention. Improvements had to be made. A lot more seating had to be introduced. Additionally, the glass ceiling needed urgent work done on it and the heating system needed to be replaced. The expenditure was too great and Premierland closed in October 1930 after entertaining London's boxing fans for almost twenty years.

Eight miles north of Premierland and the Wonderland arena in Whitechapel, the **Alcazar** was constructed in Edmonton, North London, to cater for that area's local boxers. It opened on 28 June 1913. The Alcazar boasted one of the earliest cinemas on site, which was very popular. The building stood on Fore Street and featured a facia of whitewashed alcoves which made it look like a Moorish palace. It was strikingly different to the properties that surrounded it. Behind the cinema was a large ballroom. It also featured roller skating and wrestling events and it was here that the boxing was mainly held. A couple of odd boxing promotions were held in the early days, but no boxing was featured during the First World War. After the war, the cinema and ballroom were still attracting large crowds and it was not until 1925 that boxing reappeared at the Alcazar.

What made the venue unique were the picturesque gardens behind the building. In warm weather, fights were held outside in a ring that stood amid sloping grass banks, fruit trees, flower beds and a stream. The ground was a sort of amphitheatre, bound by the gardens of the adjacent fairly well-to-do houses. On balmy autumn and spring evenings thousands sat in deckchairs or on grass around the ring; their sporadic yells rivalling the roar heard up the road at White Hart Lane whenever Spurs scored a goal. As daylight faded, the gardens were lit up by countless coloured fairy lamps, which gave the shows a special ambience. Outdoor fights were usually advertised with the proviso, 'In Hall if Wet', but in the colder months all fights were held indoors.

It was a unique and pleasant place for an afternoon or evening's entertainment and plenty of Jewish boxers were featured at the venue. North London's Bloomfield brothers and Nat Franks from Dalston boxed there in the early days of their careers. Franks, a light heavyweight, fought a remarkable six, twelve-round bouts of boxing in little more than a week in

The Alcazar, North London's answer to East London's Wonderland and Premierland venues. Set in a pleasant leafy location with a very attractive façade, its image was somewhat at odds with the fierce fights that could take place inside.

1932. Bethnal Green's popular Kid Rich boxed several times at the venue. Probably the most well-known boxers that fought there were Professor Andrew Newton, the mercurial Nipper Pat Daly and one of the country's greatest journeyman boxers, Billy Bird. The Alcazar closed in 1935 and the building gradually fell into disrepair. It was later badly damaged by German bombing in 1940 before a V1 strike in 1944 wiped the place off the London map for good.

Nearer the centre of the capital, the go-to venue from the early twentieth century would have been the **Holborn Stadium** in High Holborn, just a short walk from the West End. It was one of the three arenas that featured in Alfred Hitchcock's 1927 silent film *The Ring*. Bombardier Billy Wells was in the film, uncredited. The Holborn held its first fights there around 1910.

Sid Nathan performed there a couple of times. He spoke fondly of the place in an interview he gave just prior to his death. Sid, who you may recall, was an ex Jewish Lads' Brigade junior boxing champion had fought around a few of London's less than salubrious venues. Over the course of his boxing and refereeing career, he ranked this venue as one of the better ones around in the thirties and forties, both for its atmosphere and for the comfortable conditions for both the boxers and the audience.

Just a few miles north of here was Alexander Palace. It was also used for the occasional match and in the eighties and nineties staged a few quite big fights. The Ally Pally was a multi sports/ entertainment venue and some older readers may even remember the horse racing course that was there until 1970. Pre-war, a few more boxing venues came on stream. The iconic **York Hall** in Bethnal Green built in 1929 was to become the leading venue for boxing after the war. Jack Solomons' Hackney club, the **Devonshire Hall,** that operated through the 1930s, featured plenty of Jewish boxers until it, too, became a victim of the Luftwaffe.

Jack though, moved his promotions to the **Harringay Arena**, near Wood Green in North London. This Arena was to feature some outstanding fights over many years including some great championship matches. On 17 September 1957, one of the great nights of British boxing took place at the venue. An outstanding card of boxing.

Top of the bill that night was a Wales v England contest, the British and Commonwealth heavyweight title fight between Cardiff's title holder Joe Erskine and South London's Henry Cooper. Erskine won a points decision over fifteen very close rounds. Also featured that night was the great Randolph Turpin fighting a light heavyweight match against French Algerian, Ahmed Boulgroune, which Turpin won, TKO in the 9th. Two fighters, Mick Leahy and West Ham's Terry Gill, both of whom were unbeaten after eleven matches each, fought out an eight-round bout with Leahy getting the verdict. However, for many that evening, the best fight was the classic encounter of fighter v boxer.

The 'Paddington Express' rolled into Harringay that night. The Express was the nickname of Terry Downes, the brilliant and precocious former American Golden Gloves champion, who had recently turned professional. He was on his way to the top and was ready to power his way to victory that night. Terry Downes was to face the crafty and skilful Lew Lazar. Lew Lazar was one of the famous Jewish Lazarus or Lazar sporting family. Downes had dispatched his previous three opponents by knock outs before encountering Lazar. Lew was a different proposition. An experienced boxer, with over fifty fights under his belt, Lew knew his way round a boxing ring when it came to facing a fierce and aggressive opponent like Downes. Over the scheduled eight rounds, Downes came forward continuously and got through with the odd big punch but Lazar was tough and possessed some excellent defensive skills and effective counter punching. It was a tough call to make as to who won. Most observers thought it should be a draw but the Paddington Express got the nod. A great fight on a tremendous night of boxing.

As far as entertainment is concerned, I think at this point it may be prudent to introduce a slight note of caution. It would be easy for the reader to think that the sport, unquestionably hard and dangerous, is always hugely entertaining. Many of the matches described are such. The fact is, that the fifteen-round blood and thunder, all-out action by two great skilful exponents of the game is not served up regularly. The fight bill of an average evening of boxing would, in those pre-war years, be made up of around five or six fights on a weekday, going up to about eight to ten for bigger Saturday night promotions. The audience may have seen a few humdingers if they were lucky, but quite often, they may have had to endure a couple of tepid or even boring bouts.

Mark Lesnick made his professional debut In March 1924. His opponent, Kid Martin travelled over from Queens Park in West London for the fight at Premierland. The Kid was also appearing professionally for the first time. So, two young lads lost their professional virginity that night; but for young Kid Martin, this experience lasted only about a minute. The kid walked right onto one, hit the canvas and was carried away ten seconds later. It was a sensational start for the seventeen-year-old Mark, the young Jewish lad who lived just a few minutes away from the arena.

The Premierland venue proved a happy hunting ground for Lesnick. He fought his first eighteen matches at the venue and won every one. It appeared young Mark was going places. His next match though, was against Doddy Oldfield. Oldfield proved to be a different proposition. Mark could not work him out and of the four bouts they fought over the next couple of months against each other, Mark only won one. It appeared to really knock the confidence out of him. He started going into the ring with an attitude of not getting beat, rather than trying to win, and employed all sorts of tactics to do so. Perhaps he thought he needed to strengthen his defence, but these tactics resulted in Lesnick being involved in some dire matches. His fight against the boy prodigy that was Nipper Pat Daly was a case in point. Mark knew he had his work cut out even to give Daly a run for his money. At that time Daly was high up in world rankings. As it happened, Mark caught Pat on one of his less than brilliant days. *Boxing news* summarised the fight:

> Referee Jack Hart's decision of 'no contest' in the 11th round was a just and correct one. Lesnick was more at fault than the frail-looking Daly, who certainly tried to make a clean fight of it. Lesnick's plan in keeping to close quarters was no doubt a wise one, but he would have been more successful if he had cut out the rough stuff. Young Pat knows a trick or two himself, and he followed suit when Lesnick started, with the result that one of the poorest bouts imaginable was seen.

There was worse. In another match his opponent had a similar mindset to Lesnick's when it came to defence. That bout was halted in the eighth after persistent warnings from the referee about the effort being put in. In those days a no decision could be called if the referee decided that both boxers were merely going through the motions with neither vigorously pursuing the win. A wag made this tongue in cheek comment: 'It was one of the finest eight rounds of ballroom dancing witnessed in many years. I was particularly impressed with their version of the Viennese waltz. As far as the boxing was concerned, the only brief flashes of it were only seen when they unveiled their rendition of the paso doble!'

Lesnick fought all but seven of his contests at Premierland and only ever fought outside London once. His boxing records reads bouts 56, won 31, drew 8, no contests 4, and lost 13, of which 5 were through disqualifications for his use of illegal tactics. The series of four fights he had against the classy Doddy Oldfield in 1925, all of which were over the full fifteen rounds, that ended in a draw, a win and a loss each for each man, were eminently watchable. Sadly, many of his later bouts were not. They could be somewhat sterile affairs and often the butt of observer's jokes.

Over in the central and west side of London, things were slightly different from the rest of the capital. London's West End had been featuring boxing since those very early times when the booths that featured bare-knuckle boxing were operating. The gentlemen's clubs that sprang up during the Victorian era featured boxing matches on a more intimate scale. Larger variety theatres in the area also staged some events. Sadler's Wells Theatre near Holborn featured the sport on several occasions. One night ballet, one night boxing. C'est la vie! The impressive Seymour Hall in Marylebone was often used to stage events.

In 1891, the boxing authorities established what many would regard as the Mecca of British boxing. A venue opened that would be regarded by the aficionados of the sport and by most of the boxers themselves as the place to appear if you wanted to establish your name at the top of the national boxing scene. Unlike all the large boxing venues we have described, this venue was a private club situated in London's Covent Garden and was called the **National Sporting Club.**

By 1891 the Marquess of Queensbury rules had been universally introduced into mainstream boxing and moves were made to establish a high-class establishment to house prestigious boxing matches and a body to oversee both the club itself and professional boxing in general. The gentlemen's sporting clubs that were popular in the capital and featured boxing nights as a form of entertainment for their members were, in truth, little more than drinking clubs. One of the most well-known of these, which featured some reasonable professional fights, was the Pelican Club in Soho. It was run by William 'The Shifter' Goldberg, who was approached by several wealthy men who were backers of the proposed National Sporting Club to help set up and run this new, members only, boxing only, venue in Covent Garden. Goldberg agreed and the National Sporting Club, which became known as the NSC, was opened on 5 March 1891.

Initially, it retained an air of the gentlemen's club about it with dinner being served before the members retired to view the evening's boxing. The ring was set up in the building's large basement area and could accommodate as many as 1,200 patrons who watched the bouts of boxing in quiet reverence. Goldberg and Arthur Bettinson were the main matchmakers and the two of them quickly established the club's prestige. Another of the founding members was Jewish entrepreneur and showman Barney Barnato, who handled much of the publicity for the club. Also working behind the scenes was John E. Harding, a cousin of Jewish champion Matt Wells. Harding later went on to set up the New National Sporting club when it left its Covent Garden base.

The NSC was one of, if not the, earliest boxing authorities in the world. It was determined to improve the status of the sport following on from the bare-knuckle era. It amended many of the original Queensberry rules and added a lot more specific criteria, such as defining the specific roles of officials. It devised a system of scoring bouts and enabled the referee to determine who won a boxing match. In 1909 a ratification vote by the NSC recognised the eight varying boxing weights that had been loosely used since the turn of the century. These weight divisions were universally adopted by world boxing and continue to be used to this day. Their power grew and virtually all world championship fights that were fought in Britain as well as national title matches were staged at the Covent Garden venue. When the BBBofC superseded the NSC, fight venues restrictions on holding top championships fights were greatly relaxed and large and more comfortable London venues like the Royal Albert Hall and Earls Court/Olympia began to feature more top line boxing.[2]

12

SHADOW BOXING

Once the National Sporting Club had been established and the original Marquess of Queensberry rules, together with the NSC's conditions, were universally accepted, boxing became well organised and comprehensive structures were put in place to guide boxers through their careers, from their first tentative steps on the amateur road through to the top of the professional game. Boxing was well regulated and controlled. From the turn of the twentieth century things like venue facilities, equipment and the boxer's health were more closely monitored. Boxer's fighting weights and weigh-ins were closely scrutinised.

In the earlier non-gloved version of the sport there were a few high-profile incidences of match fixing, when a boxer would take a dive. One such example was the title fight between Peter Corcoran and William Darts in 1771, where evidence exists that a sum of £100 changed hands between the two pugilists. After the formation of the NSC, match fixing was thought to have been quite rare, particularly in Britain. In America, with the influence and power of the Mafia, there were cases of match rigging and it tainted the reputation of one or two of their better-known boxers.

Wherever there is competitive sport there is betting. Cricket, until recently that whiter than white sport, has had problems with gambling. Football too, particularly in Italy, has experienced match fixing. Even in this country football has had incidents of irregular betting pattens on games. It would be naïve to believe that, even in later years, the sport of boxing was free from corruption. At its peak, when hundreds of fights were taking place up and down the country weekly, some irregularities surely did occur at some of the bottom of the bill fights in small venues. The more prestigious match higher up the bill were a different case. Barrington Dalby, the well-known boxing journalist and BBC commentator, was also a top boxing referee for many years. He officiated on lots of top fights. He is on the record as saying that only once did he have doubts about a boxing match. If that is the case then boxing, in this country, can afford to hold its head up high when it comes to match rigging.

Betting on boxing matches was big business though, and had been since the earliest bare-knuckle days. When betting offices started to appear on British high streets, several Jewish businessmen took the opportunity to get into the betting business, which for many years had been carried out in relative secrecy. Moishe Cohen was one of the first to open a string of bookmakers, trading under the name of Major Collins. His brother Jackie also owned shops. Even boxing promoters Jack Solomons and Harry Levene opened bookmakers.

I think it is fairly safe to assume that mainstream boxing was virtually free from any form of serious match rigging, but evidence does exist that with the growth of betting the shadow of London's underworld fell on some boxing events in the more minor venues in the capital. Prior to the First World War, a couple of Jewish gangsters were active within the sport. Around 1903 Edward Emmanuel appeared on the scene. He had a serious brush with the law in 1904, when he was found going equipped with a loaded revolver to perpetrate a crime. After that he kept more in the shadows. However, those in the know were aware of his growing powers. He practised extortion but was also in the betting business. He was soon to become known as the Jewish Al Capone. In a recorded statement, the East End villain, Arthur Harding, who knew Emmanuel quite well, spoke about him:

> I remember there was a fight between Cockney Cohen and Young Joseph. Well, there were thousands on the match: two Jewish chaps fighting each other and thousands of Jewish people betting. Cockney Cohen was the favourite; he was regarded the top man of the two. Edward Emmanuel wanted Cohen to lay down. They tried to pay him to take the drop, but Cohen refused. Somebody then stuck a knife in him. I can't remember if the fight went ahead.

I suspect it did not take place, as Emmanuel had probably already set up the bet and if Cockney was going to be non-compliant, Emmanuel would have been better off with the fight not taking place. Boxers on the way to fights would occasionally get threatened by punters who demanded they 'take a dive'. A couple of desperate and insecure ones may have done so, but the vast majority had their boxing licences to consider and laughed off the approaches.

Emmanuel worked the racetracks and surrounded himself with a group called the 'Jewish Terrors' and he later fell in with the Sabini Gang, the Italian Mob, as Harding called them. The Sabini Gang and Edward Emmanuel are both referenced in the *Peaky Blinders* TV series. With Emmanuel away doing the business at the racecourses, the way was open for a new young gun on the block. and that's exactly what they got. No, it was not Morris 'Two Gun' Cohen, who features later. The new man went by the now shocking moniker of 'Darky the Coon', who was actually born Isaac Bogard. He came out of the notorious Old Nichol rookery, possibly the most lawless of all the London rookeries. He set up operations on Commercial Road.

It's thought that he got the name from his very dark complexion. He often dressed in cowboy type garb and carried a gun in a side holster (it was at that time, legal to carry). Even more strange was the fact that he spoke with an American accent! He, too, was into extortion and betting, but he added prostitution to his portfolio and oversaw the various territory divisions of the oldest trade. He kept the warring factions apart. He was said to have fixed the odd minor boxing match on both the licensed and unlicensed circuit. He had a few boxers on his payroll. They were there as protection for the girls. One boxer, Phil Shonck, who allegedly once 'threw' a match, was working as a part-time pimp for 'Darky' when he was later shot in a major turf war. He survived to give evidence in a well-documented trial.[1]

Research on London Jewish boxers and their part in criminal activities in London indicates that comparatively few professional boxers were found to have been involved in serious crime and petty crime tended to be carried out by young amateur boxers who were often part of a street gang. In the bare-knuckle

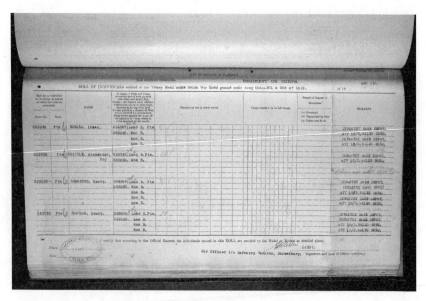

Isaac Bogard wasn't all bad. He 'did his bit'...

unregulated days of the sport, a few fighters did fall foul of the law on more serious offences, but once the gloved version of boxing was established, serious offences committed by boxers were extremely rare.

If any boxer was found guilty of using his fists in a violent way against a member of the public or in the commission of a criminal offence, then both the law and the boxing authorities would come down extremely hard on him. There have been a few such incidents over the years. Possibly one of the most famous was an incident involving former World Bantamweight Champion Pedlar Palmer from West Ham, who, in the course of protecting a lady from being verbally abused, had punched her antagonist and by sheer bad luck ended up killing the loud-mouth. He was jailed for manslaughter in 1907, sent down for five years.

Settling arguments between two boxers outside the ring was a no-no. However, there were ways around this. Simply use the inside of the ring instead. Although it would never happen today, there were a couple of occasions when it did. Two East End Jewish boxers, Kid Herman and Cockeye Davis, had previous history. Both had flirted with the criminal gangs around at the time. They were a couple of novice boxers, with one professional fight each when their paths met again at a greyhound meeting at Harringay Dog Stadium in 1929. According to friends of the pair, they had a wager between them on one of the races. A big argument broke out about the bet and their friends had to pull them apart. They agreed to settle their dispute in the ring, so a match was made between them to fight at the Premierland. Neither the promoters nor the venue knew the background to the fight. Word got round. On the day of the fight most of the people attending came to watch this supposedly insignificant bout at the bottom of the card. Both entered the ring with a large entourage. The place erupted. The management must have wondered what on earth was going on.

The boxers intense dislike of each other was plain to see from the start as they waded into each other. After two rounds neither had managed to land a meaningful blow. Egged on by their respective support, the two came out for the third round and started to use their feet as well as their fists. It developed into a street fight as both men lost their heads. The referee had seen enough and realised that there was another agenda being worked out here. He stopped the fight and called it a 'no contest'. After the match, the referee said he refused to rule on a boxing match when there were as many kicks as there were punches.

I only came across one other case of a London professional Jewish boxer being convicted of a potentially capital offence and that was a case in 1902, in which a boxer who was connected with the notorious Bessarabian Tigers Gang was involved in a serious incident. Max Moses was a well-known boxer in the area and worked as a porter in Smithfield's Meat Market. Max boxed under the name of Kid McCoy and he boxed mainly out of the Wonderland Arena, although he did have one bout at the National Sporting Club at Covent Garden. He was a reasonable bantamweight.

In October 1902, he was involved in a reprisal attack on some men coming out of a music hall. He and three others chased some men across Whitechapel High Road to the White Hart public house in Back Lane, where a vicious fight broke out and one was stabbed to death, two more seriously injured. Moses and two others were found guilty. The fact that the victim was carrying a couple of offensive weapons and had a previous record for violence meant that Moses was only sentenced to ten years imprisonment for manslaughter, rather than murder.

It was after this case and something similar that occurred in North London, that the police were forced to act to clear these gangs and gangsters off the streets of London. The turf wars by the multitude of street gangs gradually became a thing of the past. By the outbreak of the Second World War, the pickpockets, the smash and grabbers and the street con artists that frequented the Victorian and Edwardian London streets gave way to more organised crime. The Maltese Massina Brothers gang took control of the Soho area and later, 'firms' like the Krays in East London and the Richardson gang in South London ruled underworld activities in those parts of the capital.

We again come to the great Jewish champion, Jack Kid Berg and his relationship with one of this country's most notorious gangster, Jack Spot. We know about the great Jack Berg and his impressive fight record, but a little background to Spot, this most famous of London underworld criminals, is required. Jack Spot was born in Myrdle Street, Whitechapel in 1912. His parents were Polish immigrants that came to the area in 1902. They adopted the anglicised surname of Comer, but from an early age he was known as Jack Spot due to the large round birthmark on his cheek. As a young teenager he joined the Whitechapel Gang. It was the same gang that Jack Kid Berg was part of for a few years. Although Spot was three years younger than Berg, they knew each other from an early age. It is likely that Berg was moving on to his boxing career when Spot first hit the streets. His grounding in street crime with the Whitechapel boys was the basis for his future life of crime.

Spot boxed a fair bit. Mainly low-level unlicensed backstreet stuff. As a youth he was big, fit and aggressive. He may possibly have made a half-decent heavyweight. Spot though, pursued crime whilst Berg climbed the world's boxing rankings. By the late 1920s Spot was working as a bookies runner at the horseracing and dog tracks, but he also worked the boxing venues where betting was rife. He steadily climbed the criminal ladder and during the 1930s he helped to bring a significant organised element to London crime by working with many of the leading London criminals. Everyone benefitted, and by the late 1930s he became the effective 'Kingpin' of the London underworld. He already controlled most of East London and when the head of the Sabini family was imprisoned during the war, he started taking over parts of Holborn and London's West End. It was outside a Soho club in the West End that Jack Spot picked up his large facial scar, after being slashed by fellow gangster Albert Dimes. His criminal legacy was now well cemented and he effectively laid the foundations for organised crime that was the basis for the power that was wielded by the Kray and Richardson gangs during the late 50s and 60s.

Jack Spot claimed in his memoirs that he and some of his henchmen were present at the Battle of Cable Street and that he led a charge into Moseley's fascists ranks, but this is unproven and dismissed by some of the left-wing activists present on the day. He did however, after the war, help fund the 43 Group. By 1956, Jack was beginning to take more of a back seat in the London criminal scene and was living in elegant St John's Wood, a far cry from his Whitechapel beginnings in Myrdle Street. In his earlier days, threats to his life would have been common but in May that year, Spot and his wife were attacked in the street outside their residence by 'Mad' Frankie Fraser and about six others. His wife received only minor injuries but Jack was hospitalised, receiving further facial injuries.

Jack Kid Berg was born one street away from Spot in Whitechapel and as mentioned, they were both members of the same gang. It was inevitable that rumours about Berg's possible connections with Jack Spot and his activities often circulated. In fact, whispers about Jack Berg's flirtation with crime on both sides of the Atlantic persisted for much of Berg's life, but it is evident that Berg was never drawn into Spot's inner circle. Jack

Berg was never officially investigated by the police. Spot watched many of Berg's greatest fights and the two remained firm friends until Jack Berg's death in 1991. Spot died five years later.

Although the Kray twins boxed both at amateur and profession levels, they do not feature in this book as they were not Jewish. In actual fact, it has recently been discovered that although the family have primarily Romany and Irish roots, the twins' maternal grandmother could well have been half Jewish. This may account for the absence of any religious bigotry during their reign of criminality. They made no secret of their admiration for Jack

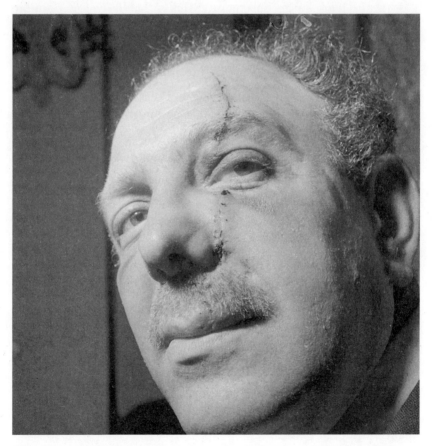

The infamous gangster Jack Comer, aka Jack Spot, the leading figure in London's underworld between the late 1920s and the mid-1950s, had a strong connection to boxing in his early days.

Spot, but they would, wouldn't they? There was though, another Jewish character that they also admired greatly, and he was the complete opposite to Jack Spot in every respect.

Mickey Davis devoted much of his life to the western areas of the East End. Around the outbreak of World War Two, local councils were desperately seeking buildings that could be used as large air raid shelters. In Brushfield Street, Spitalfields, just opposite Liverpool Street Station, stood the City Corporation's Fruit and Wool Exchange. It was a robust steel and concrete warehouse type building, built twelve years earlier. It had quite a deep and very large basement. Mickey Davis was a popular local businessman and was unmistakable. From Russian Jewish stock and well-known as the local optician, he was just four and a half feet tall. He was instrumental in persuading the corporation to give over the basement of their building for use as a bomb shelter, and then organised a shelter committee as chief shelter marshal. He mustered local volunteers to clear the site and set up bunks, tables and chairs and medical facilities. Just in time, as it happened. During the blitz it catered for thousands of people a night. Davis even persuaded Marks and Spencers to install a canteen.

After the war Mickey threw himself into public service and became a prominent councillor between 1946 and 1949. Davies founded the Vallance Road Boys' Club, which is where the Kray Twins learnt to box as twelve-year old lads before going over to the Repton Club. Reggie Kray records in his memoirs: 'Mickey Davis was a really nice Jewish fella that happened to be a midget. He did a lot in the area and although he was very small you never saw him in anything other than a sharp tailored suit. He had a reputation as a bit of a judo expert which must have been an asset against potential piss-takers.'

13

BLOOD BROTHERS: THE FAMILY CONNECTION

So popular was the sport of boxing and participation in it for thousands of Londoners during the first half of the twentieth century that you would have been forgiven for thinking that there was a decent amateur or professional boxer living in every other street in the capital. There is little doubt that back in those days, of all the major sports world-wide, boxing could produce the greatest number of exponents of the sport from just one family. There are examples of four generations of boxers. In London, both the Irish and Jewish communities produced hundreds of families that boasted at least two boxers in one household. Many could have as many as four or five boxers living under one roof.

Starting way back with Dutch Sam, who encouraged his son Young Dutch Sam to take up the noble art with some success, boxing seemed to run in some families. We have mentioned a few of these boxers previously, such as the Housego family and the Browns (Hickman, big Jewish boxing families in the capital. Without doubt though, it was the number of brothers that followed each other into the ring that was impressive. Sibling rivalry is what it's called and there was quite a bit of it in the Lazarus household. Their name may not be familiar with many because, as boxers, they used the name Lazar. Their maternal grandfather, Harry Solomon, was a bare-knuckle lightweight English champion and his daughter, Martha, took a keen interest in the sport. Martha married Isaac Lazarus. Isaac never boxed but he did follow the sport. By 1920 they had settled just off Leman Street near Aldgate East and started to expand the family. They were pretty good at it. Although a few of their children never made it past infanthood, they produced thirteen children over the next twenty years, before moving out to Chadwell Heath near Romford around 1945.

Eight boys and five girls survived, all of whom were taught to box. The eldest boy was **Harry Lazar** who was born in 1922 and was probably the best of the lads. Harry joined the Jewish Lads' Brigade in Whitechapel, where he honed his amateur skills before he turned professional in 1938 and went twenty-five matches undefeated to kick off a great career. He was the first to fight under the Lazar name. He fought all over London racking up 115 bouts of high-quality boxing. Undoubtedly one of Britain's finest welterweights during the 1940s, Harry failed to challenge for any major titles which, given his undoubted skills, is puzzling.

Referee Sid Nathan, who followed the sport avidly outside of the ring, spoke about Harry in later years. Sid thought Harry possessed all the technical attributes a boxer needed to get to the top. His wins against Harry Mizler, Dave Finn and Dave Crowley were testament to that fact. Sid though, claimed that Harry hated training for matches and looking back on Harry's career some observers thought that many of the fights he lost on points were due to him fading in the latter stages. Nevertheless, Harry was one of Britain's finer welterweights. Harry helped teach his younger brothers and sisters to box and by the time he reached his peak, all seven of his younger brothers were boxing at amateur level.

Lew Lazar, who was eight years younger than Harry, was the next to break into the professional ranks. Lew had learned plenty from Harry before he was called up for National Service in 1949. He was posted to Germany as part of the British Rhine Army and boxed for his regiment. He took two Army Boxing Championships during his time there and all his mates in the regiment encouraged Lew to box professionally. Lew took their advice and fought his first professional match in 1951. He went one better than his elder brother by going undefeated in his first twenty-six fights.

Lew failed to take a British championship. He lost his crack at the British and European welterweight crown in 1954 to the very good Liverpudlian, Willy Thom, and two years later, was stopped in his fight for the middleweight title against another talented Liverpudlian, Pat McAteer. He was an excellent boxer just the same. Lew was a real character with a notable presence on both sides of the ropes. Lew helped maintain the Lazarus's sporting

Training session at the famous Thomas A' Becket Gym in the Old Kent Road. Closeness and diversity – the boxing brotherhood – in 1957.

dynasty. His son Paul was a reasonable professional footballer and he had two nephews. One of them, Nicky, played snooker professionally.

London was becoming truly cosmopolitan, embracing all cultures and religions. The boxers featured in the photo are all London-based. From right to left: Jewish boxer, Lew Lazar from the famous Lazar (Lazarus) sporting family stands next to Roman Catholic and British featherweight champion, Sammy McCarthy. Next to Sammy is Afro-Caribbean and World light heavyweight champion, Yolande Pompey. Sadly, this inclusivity did not always exist in society.

By 1954, Harry and Lew's younger brother, Mark, was winning some excellent amateur fights and seriously thought about turning professional. Mark though, had discovered football. In an interview he gave in 2010 he shed some insight into his family life outside the confines of East London when he was growing up near Romford:

It was far different for us from the East End, you hardly ever saw a car, just a few horses trotting up the Southend Arterial Road. We were about the only Jewish family that far out. We knew one or two families that had moved to Ilford, but we were just that little further out into Essex. We used to get called a few names going to and from school, something I never heard as a kid in Stepney. My mum would say if anyone called us anything we should go and sort them out. We did, and me and a couple of my brothers and sisters got a bit of a reputation that made some people wary of us. My sister Carol was a bit of a tearaway. She was probably the best fighter out of both her girls' school and our boys' school! We never spoke about football in our house, it was all boxing. I got into football when I went to senior school more, and was playing football as well as boxing.

At the age of fifteen, Mark started to play for the Wingate Football Club that was an all-Jewish set up and a decent amateur side. He was spotted by Alec Stock, the Leyton Orient manager, and he signed him up in 1957. Shortly after, Mark went off to do his national service, Stock moved over to manage QPR and Mark later joined him there. Rather than becoming a journeyman fighter, Mark became one of the great journeymen footballers of thet era, playing for eight league clubs, making well over 600 appearances in a career spanning twenty years. Mark used his original family name of Lazarus.

The family's youngest boy was Joe. He boxed at amateur level but did not box as a licensed professional. Instead, he boxed several matches on the unlicensed circuit. From all accounts he was very useful and a couple of experienced observers of that 'code' have gone on record as saying that he could have challenged for top professional titles. As it turned out he did not, and occasionally strayed to the wrong side of the law, which did not help. The Lazarus family were a big and successful sporting dynasty and their name is still around today.

As a result of the harsh realities of their lives, the Goodwin family of Spitalfields were another extended London boxing family. They used their fists to improve their lot in life, both inside and outside the ring. The Goodwin family were well-known in the area in the later Victorian era. Never far from London's criminal element, the family scratched out a living in a desperately poor part of London. The Goodwin children knew all about the workhouses that were dotted around London. They had experienced life on the inside.

Once the elder boy, **Jack Goodwin**, escaped these confines, he found a few odd jobs to earn some pocket money. Any real money would have been hard to come by in those dark times. The street gangs came calling and he slipped into petty crime. Jack ran with the Brick Lane Gang but not for long. He was arrested for affray.

Jack had boxed a bit as an amateur and also had eight recorded professional matches. He was a fit young man and a reasonable athlete.

He served a short stint in prison but kept himself fit. Once out, he decided to improve his life. He rented an old building in Hanbury Street near Brick Lane and set up a small basic gym with a boxing ring. Jack started to gain a reputation as a decent trainer and several of the older teenage lads, who had learned their basic skills at one of the Jewish Boys clubs in the area, went on to train with Jack. By 1890 Jack had moved to a larger building and apart from training boxers, his gymnasium was large enough to stage some modest fight nights. It staged around sixty bills of boxing up until 1906. Jack certainly improved his lot in life and in 1921 he wrote one of the first modern-day keep-fit manuals, as well as a comprehensive instruction manual on boxing. Jack had made a break from the temptations of crime and he ensured his younger brothers did too.

Jack trained, advised and guided two of his brothers during their days in the ring. The two brothers, **Joe and Alf Goodwin,** boxed over 200 matches between them. They could be considered journeymen in their own right. Alf fought around Australia for six years and he also boxed in Belgium and France regularly. None of the Goodwin lads was good enough to fight for any major titles. Joe in particular fought and beat a couple of British champions in the shape of Johnny Summers and Joe Fletcher in non-title fights. At the very least, the sport gave them the opportunity to extradite themselves from the crippling poverty that they were born into.

An even more impressive set of siblings were to emerge a few years later. The Brooks brothers, along with the earlier mentioned Mansfield brothers, were the dominant Jewish boxing family in the area. Their father Joseph boxed a bit but it was three of his four sons who were to go on and carve out lengthy careers in the game.

Young Joe, Nat and Harry Brooks boxed a huge number of fights between 1908 and 1929. They could all be considered journeymen, as they all fought around the country and a couple of them fought several matches abroad. For three brothers to amass the number of fights that they did was testament to their grit and determination. Just taking their professional recorded matches alone, the three lads completed a hugely impressive 445 bouts of boxing. Nat and Harry boxed anywhere between flyweight and welterweight over the years, but the eldest boy, Young Joe, boxed all his professional career at featherweight. As far as ability is concerned, looking at their respective records, they probably all boxed at the same reasonable standard. Harry fought Jimmy Wilde for a flyweight title in December 1913 at Manchester, but like so many London boxers, lost to the incomparable little Welshman. Either side of the Wilde fight, he fought a series of seven very close matches against Young Josephs Nipper, all seven going the maximum distance.

Nat fought a number of excellent boxers over many years. He and Ted Kid Lewis split a couple of contests at the Judean Club in their early days, but Nat produced some outstanding boxing against Joe Fox later in his career. Joe Fox was one of a few Leeds-based Jewish fighters with a really impressive record at the lighter weights. He held the British title at both bantamweight and featherweight for three years each, between 1915 and 1924. Nat fought Joe Fox on four occasions in non-title matches and only lost once.

When brothers boxed professionally, it tended to be the younger brothers who progressed more. Perhaps not so with the Lazar and Brown brothers but generally the younger siblings would often be unofficially coached by their elders, and when their time came to enter the ring professionally, they would be guided by them through their early careers. Those three

Jewish giants of the ring, Ted Lewis, Jack Berg and Harry Mizler, were examples.

The Bloomfield Brothers from Islington in North London were an exception. There were only a couple of years between the boys. Both lads anglicised their name from Blumenfield and both boxed at middleweight and later at light heavyweight. **Jack Bloomfield** started his career just prior to the end of the First World War, climbing into the ring on 4 September 1918 for his first fight. In fact he climbed back into the same ring twice more that day.

The National Sporting Club was holding an inter-allied tournament that featured young servicemen who held a professional licence. They were short three-round affairs. First up were the debutants, of which young Jack was one. He overcame a Sgt Raynor, knocking him out in the first round and an hour later beat Cpl Knight via a second round KO. That set up the final against one of the more experienced boxers that the Sporting Club had drafted in. If a young novice came through the earlier matches, the promotors would see just how good he was by pitting him against a more experienced man.

Jack climbed back into the ring a third time inside three hours to face Private Charlie Braddock. So, although Jack was fighting increasingly lower ranks, he was facing increasingly superior competition. Jack squared up against Braddock who was a veteran of thirty-seven professional fights at that stage and had won a good deal of them. It was a daunting prospect for Bloomfield, but he showed what a great prospect the Sporting Club had on their hands by convincingly beating his vastly more experienced opposition on points.

Jack was on his way. Losing just once in his next ten fights, set up a trip to North America to fight a series of six matches against some tough Canadian and American boxers. Although he lost two contests over there, it was a very good return for the still young

Jewish lad from North London. Back home his success continued. Then, as befell so many British middleweights around that time, he was matched to fight the legend that was Ted Kid Lewis, in June 1921. It was a contest for the vacant British middleweight title. By this time Lewis had reached his peak and just maybe was beginning to show some decline on the world stage, but in this country, he was still a force to be reckoned with. The bout was handled by the NSC premier referee John Herbert Douglas and later Douglas would rank this as one of the best fights he had taken charge of.[1]

Jack possessed a big punch but so did Lewis. Both fighters came into the ring at the top of the weight and most observers thought that it would never go the full twenty rounds. They were wrong. A gruelling, attritional contest with frequent flashes of brilliance from both boxers unfolded. Ted Kid Lewis won on points by the skin of his gumshield. Jack then moved up a weight and fought at light heavyweight, eventually winning the British light heavyweight crown in May 1922, stopping Harry Drake in the seventh round. Jack also beat previous British champion Bombardier Billy Wells as well as American-based world light heavyweight contender Mike McTigue. Bloomfield was looking strong enough in the light heavy weight ranks to step up and challenge for the very top honours at heavyweight. The prized purse.

British boxing was desperate to bring through a decent heavyweight to challenge the Americans. In 1923 Wembley Stadium opened its doors for the first time. Primarily a football stadium, Wembley was also used for the 1924 British Empire Exhibition and it was during the summer of 1924 that boxing promoter Arnold Wilson leased the premises to stage an international heavyweight contest that he hoped would fill the stadium to capacity and make him a fortune. The stadium was designed to hold around 100,000 people and Wilson thought that a heavyweight contest between a top-flight American and local lad Jack Bloomfield would arouse sufficient interest to fulfil his plan. The Exhibition was drawing in crowds from all over the country.

Wilson brought over Tommy Gibbons from the States to fight Bloomfield. The press of the day was not overly impressed with this piece of matchmaking, pointing out that the American had never boxed outside North America and in almost ninety fights he had only managed to get one shot at a world title fight and lost. Nevertheless, Wilson was confident that the match would be a big success all round and if Bloomfield won, it could well get him a shot at Jack Dempsey's world crown.

It was an absolute disaster! The public never really bought into the match and only around 24,000 attended. With the promised purses to the two boxers estimated to be about £17,000, and several thousands more spent on setting up and promoting the event, the venture lost a huge amount of money, which bankrupted Wilson. Apart from the financial catastrophe, things inside the ring also backfired with Bloomfield being completely outclassed and knocked out in the third round. Wilson never promoted again and Bloomfield never boxed again. His younger brother did though, and for a longer period.

As I hinted at earlier, Jack's younger brother failed to emulate his big brother in terms of top honours. **Joe Bloomfield** did initially follow in his brother's footsteps and was assisted in this by Jack. For a while it looked like Joe might go on to achieve big things in the game, but history shows that Joe turned into more of a journeyman. He fought at middleweight and was a very durable boxer. He lacked a big knockout punch and most of his fights tended to go the full distance, so virtually all his victories were on points decisions. Bloomfield travelled the country extensively, fighting all over London and the South East as well as further north. He also fought abroad several times but failed to make much impression on foreign soil.

Joe fought regularly and was a veteran of well over a hundred fights. His durability was a crowd-pleaser but he never quite made it into the top echelon of the middleweights. He gave Roland Todd and Len Harvey, both of whom held the British title at some time, very good fights in defeat. More impressive was his series of three fights against the Frenchman Marcel Thil. Joe met Thil for two fights in 1927. Thil had been fighting steadily for seven years and through most of this time was regarded by many as an accomplished boxer. By the time he met Joe in August that year he was starting to show signs of becoming a title contender. Joe fought very well, but Thil showed why he was being tipped in some quarters for bigger and better things, with a win on points over fifteen rounds.

It looked like Marcel was heading for the French and European titles, but Joe had secured a rematch with Thil in October and Joe produced one of his best performances ever and comprehensively beat Thil over twelve rounds at the People's Palace in Mile End. It was a setback for Thil's climb up the rankings and two further defeats at the end of that year by top British fighters Len Harvey and Jack Hood severely dented Thil's hopes. The new year brought fresh hope and determination to Marcel and 1928 saw him reel off eight straight wins before facing Bloomfield once more in November. This time it was on home soil in Paris and Thil made no mistake against Joe and knocked him out in the second round. Thil was firmly back on track and went on to take the French, European and world middleweight titles over the next three years, marking Thil out as one of the best middleweights around.

Joe watched Thil's climb to the top. For Joe that never happened. He announced his retirement in late 1930. A good honest pro who did not quite make it to the top of British

North London's Jack and Joe Bloomfield – brothers in gloves.

boxing, unlike his brother Jack. I don't know if there was much sibling rivalry going on, but although Jack had the prestigious Lonsdale Belt, younger brother Joe had four times as many fights under *his* belt.

According to some accounts, Jack and Joe's parents worked the circus and fairgrounds and the boys' older sister, Rachel, was a performer there. Rachel met and married Samuel Weinstein around 1920. He was a bookmaker and gambler and did quite well. According to Sam's son Mike, his father was born in Holborn and in his younger days was a boxer. I can find no record of him but it is quite possible he fought in the boxing booths that could be found attached to some of the travelling circus and fairgrounds in the South East, so it is quite feasible that Sam met Rachel whilst boxing in one of these booths. Samuel and Rachel settled in Islington and had two boys, Bernard and Michael, before moving to Tottenham. The two boys inherited their family's entertainment genes, changed their surname to Winters and became the very popular Mike and Bernie Winters act. They were constantly on television during the 1960s and 1970s. So, Mike and Bernie Winters were the nephews of the two boxing Bloomfields.

The two famous Brown brothers mentioned earlier were very evenly matched in terms of ability but the elder Brown boy is an outright Lonsdale Belt winner, so maybe he will live a little longer in the memory. What is clear is that they, and some of the other family members, were excellent athletes. The Browns' father occasionally boxed. Apart from being hugely talented boxers, both Brown boys were decent gymnasts and they also played football. Their sporting genes definitely fed through to Ronnie Brown, Young Johnny's son, although boxing was about the one thing he did not excel at.

Ronnie was born in Clapton in 1933 and was a supreme all-round amateur sportsman. He won a great number of various sports trophies over many years. He was an excellent footballer and played for the impressive Leyton Wingate football team of the 40s and 50s. He may well have known Mark Lazarus from his time at the club. Later he moved to Leyton and became a successful Ophthalmic practitioner with a large chain of opticians. Ronnie talks about his father in glowing terms and confirms that the original surname was indeed Eckman. Ronnie explains that both brothers adopted the Brown name when starting off in boxing but only his father, Young Johnny, formally changed his name by deed poll to Brown, when he joined the RAF in 1943.

Apart from boxing brothers, the sport also boasts a fair few father and son boxers. The 'Dutch Sams' and the Aarons, champions from the non-gloved era, are fine examples of 'like father, like son'. In the modern gloved era, I can't trace any Jewish father/son boxing champion boxers but there are a few examples of father and son boxers that both competed professionally. There is mention of the Kellar family earlier in the book. Sam Kellar encouraged his son Dave to box and they both made a bit of money from the game.

Charlie Wise was another boxer who learned his skills from his father. He would spar with him in the back yard of his home in Millwall on the Isle of Dogs. Charlie's birthname was Wiseman and his father Henry was a decent enough amateur in his day who went on to coach a little. Charlie benefitted greatly from his father and turned professional in 1936. Coached and managed by his dad, Wise moved steadily along the professional route. Solid, if somewhat unspectacular in his earlier fights, he went about his business without too much fuss until 1938.

Charlie's win ratio was reasonable up until the middle of 1937, but in one or two fights that year his performances were seen by some as erratic. He was still winning the odd match before he was thrown in against Eric Boon in September. Boon was the big rising star in the lightweight division and would take the British title within the year. Boon dispatched Charlie inside three rounds. A few more inept performances followed. A couple of boxing correspondents who had witnessed the Boon fight and some of Charlie's subsequent fights were coming to the same conclusion.

The boxing fraternity had always been aware of the risks involved in the sport and several deaths in the ring had been reported over the preceding years. What had never really been addressed was accumulative brain damage. Later that year a report appeared in a national newspaper which was focused on the Wise fights but more particularly on his father.

The description 'punch-drunk', one of many terms derived from boxing, had come into everyday vocabulary, but had never been used by the media to describe how a boxer was behaving during a fight.

The *Daily Mirror* had written a piece stating that it was clear to see that a young boxer had entered a ring punch-drunk and firmly laid the blame for this at the feet of his manager or trainer. No names were actually used in the article but from the facts given it was quite clear that this was a Charlie Wise fight at the Devonshire Club. Charlie's father brought a case against the newspaper for libel. The case was heard in 1939 and the mainstay of the *Mirror's* defence was that the article was a general example that they had used and that no specifics were printed. They also suggested that these types of situations in the ring should be made public.

The defence case more or less collapsed when the prosecution proved beyond reasonable doubt that the article was based on Wise's performances. Furthermore, Council for Wiseman, the plaintiff, called several witnesses to testify including Manny Lyttlestone, who was the Devonshire's manager and promoter, as well as Eric Boon. Eric, whom Wise had fought in the match which had first given rise to the newspaper's interest, told the court that before he knocked out Wise, he detected nothing wrong with his opponent. He added that he would have noticed if Wise's mind was elsewhere and if he was physically incapable of boxing. Lyttlestone spoke at length about the checks made before, during and after the match.

The *Mirror's* defence team reluctantly gave up their position that the story was a cautionary tale about boxing safety in general and admitted that in fact the article was more specifically about the Wise matches. Once that was established, they would have to prove beyond doubt that Wise entered the ring unfit to box and encouraged to do so by his father. That they could not do. End of case. The court found in favour of Wiseman and awarded £3,000 in damages for libel, around £100,000 today.

So, the first case highlighting a boxer's mental health in the ring was settled before any meaningful discussion about boxing brain injuries had begun. A few months later the war broke out and any thought about the authorities looking at this aspect of boxing evaporated. As for Wise, before he could box again war was declared. He joined up and served in the forces for most of its duration. Nothing much more was ever said about the Wise situation and surprisingly after the war, in 1946, aged almost thirty, Wise renewed his licence without any problem and had a further six fights before retiring.

14

TAKING CARE OF BUSINESS

When two boxers climb through the ropes to fight each other, the viewing public sit back to enjoy the spectacle. Most would be oblivious to the activities that have gone on behind the scenes to stage the contest. Behind each of the boxers is a team of people that needs to be there to get such an event put on.

All boxing in this country is run by the British Board of Boxing Control and has been since 1929, when it took over from the old National Sporting Club organisation. The Boxing Board administers the sport at all levels and has strict rules and controls in place, starting with the boxers themselves, once they decide to turn professional. The BBBofC issue each one with a licence to enter the professional world of boxing.

Behind the boxers there are a number of different people that are needed to get them to each match, fully prepared and in a fit state to box. Climbing into the ring with them between rounds would generally be their main trainer giving instructions and advice. On hand also would be the 'cut man', the medical backup. Sitting ringside would also normally be the other people that are needed to stage the event; the managers, matchmakers and promoters.

It is easy to underestimate the importance of the boxing promoters and matchmakers. These are the people that negotiate with all parties concerned to get a match arranged. They have to get it right. An evening of boxing could easily become a disaster if they match boxers of different abilities against each other. An audience should sit down to enjoy a couple of hours entertainment. If these guys get it wrong then you could well get several bouts of boxing finishing within a few rounds. It has happened. A bill of six matches could all be over inside an hour or so if mis-matched boxers make up several of the fights being staged that night.

A promoter won't be around too long if he keeps short-changing the viewing public. Those that get it right stay around the game for years. There have been some very efficient, successful and interesting promoters over the years. Some stay in the background, others like the larger-than-life American promoter Don King, often made the headlines more often than some of the boxers. We shall start with the daddy of them all, the legendary Jack Solomons.

Jack Solomons was born in 1900, in Frying Pan Alley in the Petticoat Lane area. Growing up, Jack was in the middle of the two biggest influences of his life. Business was one. Petticoat Lane was a big retail and commercial business area with large wholesale markets close by. It is situated right next door to the City of London. In those days, about a dozen roads made up the Petticoat Lane area and it was full of shops and small offices with street stalls running alongside its pavements most days of the week. The other big influence in young Jack's life was boxing. Dozens of top boxers lived in and around the area. The Wonderland Arena and the Judean Club were just a short walk away. As a young man Jack had his feet in both camps. Jack learnt to box, turned pro and started to fight under the name of Kid Mears. It was a short-lived career. His mother did not like the sport and his girlfriend at the time refused to go out with him if he continued boxing. Having one woman bending your ear was bad enough but having two was just too much for Jack and he reluctantly retired and concentrated on the family business.

His family were fishmongers and had a shop and a couple of stalls in Petticoat Lane and nearby Ridley Road Market. Jack decided to grow the business and went about it single-mindedly. Still quite young, he managed to become a large importer of fish for the wholesale trade. It was during these years that Jack honed his negotiating skills and when he first developed his business – some would argue sharp business – practices.

From a young age Jack used to sneak in to the various music halls and theatres that peppered the East End of London. Jack met Cheim Wientrop in his teens. Cheim Wientrop was better known as Bud Flannigan, the great all-round entertainer. Bud's family were also in the fish business and had a shop in Hanbury Street in Spitalfields. The two would go to boxing events together and stayed life-long friends. Some of Bud's showbiz glitter must have rubbed of a little on Jack, as he often injected a bit of razzamatazz into his later boxing promotions.

Solomons' rise to the top of the world as a boxing promotor started in October 1934 when the doors opened on a new boxing venue in Hackney called the Devonshire Club. It was the brainchild of Joe Morris, an established manager of some great boxers including Mike Honeyman and Teddy Baldock. Morris had enquired about the site of a church hall in Devonshire Road off Mare Street in Hackney and got permission to turn it into an entertainment venue for boxing – and ballroom dancing.

He needed a fair bit of backing so he approached Jack Solomons and a couple of other businessmen to provide some capital. Morris and Solomons knew the fight game well and could get some good fighters to feature at the club. The problem was that by this time there were a huge number of established clubs and halls everywhere in London. Britain was still coming out of the depression. Initially, there seemed little appetite for either dancing or boxing and there were some internal disputes about how the operation was being run. Morris and some of the other backers were struggling to get a return on their money. They were worried. Not so, Solomons. Jack realised that the country was coming out of recession and knew there was also a stream of good young amateurs coming along to swell and improve the ranks of professional boxers.

With an expanded and solid fish business behind him, Jack offered to buy the other partners out. True to Jack's business reputation his offers were low, but the other men agreed and Jack took over the venue and had total say over how it was run. Within a few months Jack had turned its fortunes around. Some exciting talent was emerging from the amateur scene and Jack not only managed many of these young boxers but he also used his venue to showcase their skills. So he was collecting money managing and promoting as well as through ticket sales.

The Devonshire went from strength to strength and some great nights were to be had there. Its Friday night programmes became extremely popular. Solomons brokered a deal with the BBC to broadcast a top bout from there regularly most weeks. Jack was becoming a wealthy man and a big player in the game. He then set up his own gymnasium in Soho and many of the top British fighters of the day trained there over the years. By the outbreak of war, Solomons had settled in at his gym in Soho and had some offices opposite, from which he ran his business. Just as it was during the First World War, boxing continued but it was curtailed somewhat. In 1941, a large bomb fell very close the Devonshire Hall and it was damaged beyond repair.

Jack still promoted boxing around London during the war years at various venues, but from 1946 most of his promotions

One of Jack Solomons' big promotions: Jack London (left) fighting Bruce Woodcock (right) at Tottenham's White Hart ground in July 1945. A British and Empire title fight, Woodcock won it in front of a crowd of 40,000.

took place at the Harringay Arena in Wood Green, North London. These post-war years cemented his reputation as a great matchmaker and promoter. He got to know America's top boxing promoter, Mike Jacobs, which provided the opportunity for Solomons to bring over some American top boxing talent to face British opponents. In September 1946, the powerful American heavyweight Gus Lesnevich was brought over to fight the British heavyweight champion Bruce Woodcock at the Harringay Arena. It could not have gone any better for Solomons as Lesnevich, who was famed for his granite jaw, was knocked out by Woodcock in the eighth round. Further transatlantic fights followed with the likes of Ike Williams, Archie Moore, Joe Brown, Emile Griffith, Joey Maxim and Sugar Ramos all visiting these shores to fight in Jack Solomon's promotions.

Stars and Scars: The Story of Jewish Boxing in London

Solomons also staged the epic Bruce Woodcock v Freddie Mills battles in 1946 and 1949. To top that, he brought over the best pound for pound fighter in the history of boxing, the great Sugar Ray Robinson, to fight the British middleweight hope Randolph Turpin. Another proud night for Jack, as Turpin beat Robinson to take the world title, only the second defeat for the legendary boxer in eleven years and 130 fights. That fight took place at Earls Court in 1951, but Turpin featured regularly for Solomons at the Harringay venue, including his European and his Commonwealth title wins, both at middleweight, and later his light heavy British and Commonwealth title fight. Randolph Turpin was a brilliant performer for Solomons throughout the late 1940s and 1950s.

Solomons handled all three of the Turpin boxing brothers at one time or another and all of them trained a fair bit at Jack's Soho gym. The gym was in Great Windmill Street, a few steps away from the famous Windmill Theatre and in the middle of London's theatreland. Jack had a quite relaxed approach to how the gym operated. Some Windmill girls would often pop in and watch the boxers work out. Several well-known West End stars would also show up. The place buzzed. Jackie Turpin, the second eldest of the Turpin boys, described the place in his 2005 biography, *Battling Jack, You Gotta Fight Back*:

Solomons' gym, I ain't kidding, everybody congregated there – in the gym, on the stairs, on the landing and in the offices – champions, contenders, retired professionals; boxing fans hoping to see big names; managers and promoters looking for deals; gamblers sniffing around for a good bet; reporters ear-wigging for stories and gossip. Gangsters and hard men would turn up there; Jack Spot, Frankie Frazer; The Kray twins and their brother Charlie with some of their mates. Actors and comedians too like Bud Flanagan out of the Crazy Gang – practically anybody who was interested in doing or talking boxing. Jack Solomons lorded it over the lot of 'em, arguing and shouting, cracking jokes and puffing away on his king-sized cigars. All day long it was like Paddington Station during the rush hour. There were some right dodgy-looking bleeders there, an' all, with big overcoats on and their trilby hats pulled down. It'd be in the middle of the summer and they'd have their hands dug in their pockets and their collars turned right up.

Solomons' grip on British boxing continued throughout most of the 1960s, handling a multitude of boxers of different abilities. His gym in Soho continued to attract West End entertainment stars who would often pop in to watch the boxers going through their paces. A few boxers who did not quite make the grade with Jack ended up in the entertainment business as a result of rubbing shoulders with some of the showbiz names.

The popular TV sitcom *Auf Wiedersehen, Pet* from the 1980s, featured the actor Pat Roach, who played 'Bomber', the big, gentle West Country builder. Pat boxed as a teenager and Jack Solomons managed Pat for about a year after he turned professional in 1965. What probably attracted Jack was Pat's stature. Almost six and a half feet tall, with wide shoulders and barrel-chested, he tipped the scales at around seventeen stone. His very short time with Jack as a boxer was unsuccessful and he was persuaded to take up wrestling. Wrestling in the 1960s was becoming very popular and featured on TV regularly, so maybe working out of the Soho gym around some stage and screen professionals helped Pat make the transition. Pat was actually serious about the sport and excelled at it, becoming British and European heavyweight champion, before moving into acting. Pat appeared in a great many films including some blockbusters in the 1970s before landing his most famous role in the TV series that made stars out of Jimmy Nail, Kevin Whately and Timothy Spall.

Pat was one of Jack Solomons' few failures in management. Jack was unrivalled in promoting and matchmaking. In 1963, probably his most famous promotion took place at Wembley when he matched the then Cassius Clay against 'Our 'Enery'. Cooper's sweetest of left hooks is what lives long in the memory, but Cooper did lose. Clay went on to become the world champion and the world's greatest sporting personality. The re-match that Cooper and Ali fought in 1966 was not a Jack Solomons promotion. He lost out to his great promotions rival Harry Levene for that one. Jack managed to match Brian London with Ali later that same year in a world championship bout, realising his ambition to stage a world heavyweight title fight in this country. His powers waned somewhat toward the end of that decade with more televised boxing events being scheduled. In total, he promoted twenty-six world title fights.

Throughout much of the time Solomons was building his empire Jack heavily relied on **Sam Burns**. He was Jack's right-hand man for a quarter of a century. Sam Burns was born in 1914 and was the son of champion middleweight boxer Sid Burns. Surrounded by sporting folk all his life, he once worked in the tape room of the old *London Evening News* and also wrote on racing and boxing for the *Sporting Life* under the by-lines of 'Bendigo' and 'Straight Left'. Burns was Jack's general manager and between them, from adjoining offices in Soho, they set the standard for British boxing promotions. They staged the great battles of boys' own heroes like Freddie Mills, Bruce Woodcock, Len Harvey and Randolph Turpin at venues like Harringay, White City and Earls Court. Burns eventually went on to manage Terry Downes, the 'dashing, crashing, bashing' middleweight from Paddington who defeated the world champion, Paul Pender, in nine rounds at the old Wembley Pool in July 1961. By this time Burns and Solomons had parted and

Sam Burns helping his fighter, British featherweight champion Bobby Neill, in training.

Burns did most of his later business with the promoters, Jarvis Astaire, Mickey Duff, Harry Levene and Mike Barrett.

Along with Solomons, the other great promoter of those mid-twentieth century years was **Harry Levene.** In fact, Levene established himself as a main player in managing boxers and setting up boxing events long before Solomons. Both Jack and Harry came from East London but Harry's actual boxing experience was limited to a few amateur and a couple of pro fights. However, he had a great love of the sport. He was a very intelligent lad and developed a sound business mind as well as excellent communication skills. Harry was about seven years older than Solomons so his involvement in the game started just before the First World War. Previous to this, Harry worked in journalism as a junior reporter and went over to America to work on the *New York Daily News* for a year or so.

When he got back to England, he started to move more into London's boxing circles. He travelled around the small gyms and clubs in the area looking for talent to manage. Approaching established amateur boxers as well as a few younger professional ones, he gradually built up a roster of reasonable boxers on his books. Harry Levene made his name with Danny Frush. Danny and Harry knew each other from their days at the Brady Street boys' Club. Danny was a good solid amateur and hungry to turn professional.

Danny Frush was a bit of a late starter as a boxer. In his early teens he joined the Merchant Navy and spent several years at sea travelling around the world. He may have had the odd unlicensed fight in a couple of faraway places, but when he settled back in London he turned professional with Harry Levene. His early fight records are a bit vague but it appears he had his first fight in September 1916 in West London with maybe another two or three later that year. By this time, Harry Levene was dabbling with matchmaking as well as managing boxers. When working in New York he made some contacts in the fight game over there. He also knew that more money could be made Stateside and it could be made more quickly.

Frush was about to follow the tried and tested route up the boxing ladder. Normally, in Britain, once a boxer had turned pro, he would be given a few three- or four-round bouts and then move on to six-round matches to get him started. They would, most likely, be on the undercards of minor events in smaller local venues, quite often being first up on a matinee bill. There would then follow at least a year or two of travelling around Britain's various venues, gaining experience before tackling, if good enough, some of the better and more experienced journeymen boxers over longer bouts. Winning these would hopefully pave the way for them to fight area championship bouts before going for national and possibly world titles. What Frush and Levene did, however, was more or less the opposite.

In February 1917, soon after Danny signed up with Levene, Harry and Danny set sail for New York. They hit the ground running. With his established contacts, Harry started setting up matches and after a couple of wins over three rounds for a few dollars, Harry pitched Danny into ten-round matches with a great deal of success. The pair started to make some serious money. Danny was matched with some decent journeymen fighters but they all underestimated him. He possessed a really big punch and used it to win match after match.

Danny settled down well in America and set up home in Cleveland. Unlike Britain, where boxers generally have to go through the area titles and then British and European titles before they would normally get a shot at the world crown, In America if you rose high enough in the rankings you could get your chance after a relative short length of time. And so, in September 1921, Danny got that chance. Danny Frush fought Johnny Kilbane for the world featherweight championship in his adopted home, Cleveland. Not only was Danny fighting on his home patch, he was up against a boxer who, although very experienced, was clearly reaching the end of his career. The match started well for Danny and he was well on top when his opponent started to resort to some dubious tactics. First Danny was caught with a low blow which the ref spotted and warned Kilbane about. In the seventh round, Kilbane again delivered a low punch which sent Danny down. Danny complained but got up and continued. A few moments later, Danny was down again clutching his groin. The ref counted him out. Danny lodged a complaint, but the fight was awarded to the American. Danny said no more until a couple of days later when he saw a private recording of the fight and it more or less confirmed that Kilbane had forcefully delivered his knee into Danny's groin. Another complaint was lodged but the authorities refused to view the recording and the decision remained. Danny stayed on to fight in America for a couple more years before returning to Britain. Harry Levene returned earlier and continued with his operations in London.

By the 1930s, Levene was promoting more and was getting the occasional American over to fight. After the war, Harry greatly expanded his operation and was then the country's leading promoter/manager, arranging fights all over Britain. During sixty years in the game, he managed or promoted dozens of top boxers including Ted Kid Lewis, Jack Kid Berg, Terry Downes, Floyd Patterson, Sugar Ray Robinson, Chris Finnegan, Joe Bugner and many more. After the Second World War, with the rise of the Jack Solomons' promotions, the two parties fell out badly. Both Solomons and Levene had a reputation as hard, uncompromising individuals. For many years Levene couldn't bear to be in the same room as Solomons. It was a sad situation, dominating as they did the first seventy years of twentieth-century boxing promotions. But both men were assured of their place in Boxing's Hall of Fame.

Jack Solomons and Harry Levene were managing and promoting at the height of the fight game in this country in terms of the numbers of boxing matches being staged and the number of paying customers who witnessed them. They were old school London Jewish boxing entrepreneurs and were in their dotage when boxing fundamentally started to change in the 1970s. In the wake of television's involvement in the sport and the new wave of American boxing superstars of the late 1960s and 1970s, boxing was forced to drastically change its modus operandi. Big gala events and big money TV coverage was the new way forward for the sport and boxing needed someone to spearhead Britain's conversion to this new way of promoting the fight game. Step forward, Monek Prager... Who?

In the summer of 1938, Poland was looking west across the border to neighbouring Germany. Fears were escalating for the Polish people, particularly for the large Jewish communities that could be found all over the country. The Prager family lived near Gdansk, the large port on the Baltic Sea. Word had already reached them of what was happening in Germany and when the Germans took control of nearby Sudetenland, the Pragers realised that they had to move to somewhere safer. Like thousands of others they picked London. Shipping between Britain and the Gdansk Port was regular, so there was no problem with the passage. Leaving with them was their young son Monek. They made their way to Aldgate to join the large Jewish community in that part of London.

Monek had just turned nine when he arrived in London, He was a street-wise kid and bright, too. His father was a rabbi and quite strict. From a young age Monek never really got on with his father. Once in Britain, he wanted to integrate quickly into the country's way of life. He picked up the language easily and he joined a local boxing club in 1939. He progressed very well as an amateur and was entered into the 1941 London

Schoolboy championships. He decided at this point that he wanted to box seriously so even at this early age, he knew that boxing was for him. He also decided to anglicise his name so when he received the entrance forms for the championships, he wrote down the name Michael Duff.

Mickey Duff progressed quite well through the amateur boxing ranks and his chances at becoming a decent professional boxer were good, but he was astute enough to realise that, given the risks, it might not be a long and rewarding career. Shortly after he turned professional in 1945, he applied for a manager and a promoter's licence. He did have a good crack at boxing first, so he put any further thoughts of managing or promoting to one side and had his first fight in September.

His relationship with his father worsened when he turned professional and sadly, never improved. They never spoke to each other for over thirty years. Most people would know little of Duff's boxing career as he was mainly known for his managing and promotion work but Mickey was actually a very good boxer. He had a pretty sensational start to his career when he knocked out fellow debutant Sid Beech inside two minutes of the first round. Unlike Solomons and Levene, Mickey was more than an average boxer and had a reasonably lengthy boxing career. He racked up almost fifty recorded fights, although it is possible that several more went unrecorded. He also fought at some of the popular boxing booths that toured with the fairground shows around the country.

Duff only lost eight of his recorded fights, although his record shows he never fought any of the top boxers of the day. All the time though, he was picking up knowledge of the fight game. He started off fighting at some of the smaller venues in and around London and the South before moving up the ranks to fight at more established locations like West Ham Baths and The Mile End Arena. He started to mix with managers and promoters more, and it was at the Mile End Arena in 1951 that he first came across the notorious Ron and Reg Kray. They both fought their debut professional matches there on 31 July that year. Duff had started to manage a bit as well as box and he was at the Mile End arena as a manager of one of the other boxers when their paths first crossed.

By 1953 he had retired from boxing and was looking to increase his management of boxers and matchmaking fights around the London boxing scene. Although he was still learning this side of the business, he was adding some decent up-and-coming boxers to his stable. He had a good eye for exciting new boxers. The young Terry Downes was one. A terrific fighter, tough as teak and fast. He was an excellent amateur champion. Downes became known as the 'Paddington Express' and in May 1957, Mickey Duff, in his role as a matchmaker, paired Downes against a little-known boxer called Dick Tiger who had just settled in Liverpool from his native Nigeria, in West Africa.

As I mentioned at the beginning of this chapter, one of the main prerequisites of matchmaking and promotions is pairing up boxers of roughly equal abilities. Unfortunately for Terry Downes, Mickey had clearly not done his homework on the Tiger because if he had, he would have picked up on the fact that Dick Tiger had boxed at a high standard in his home country. Nigeria was fast becoming a hot bed for boxing talent in Africa and Tiger was a rising star there. By the time he faced Downes, Dick Tiger had fought over thirty matches including a dismantling and subsequent knock-out of the highly rated South Londoner, Johnny Read, in his previous fight. This was only Terry Downes's third professional match and although Downes was an exciting young talent he was still learning the ringcraft needed to become a decent professional. Mickey Duff was his usual confident self and told Terry and his manager Sam Burns, that it would be a straightforward fight for the talented North Londoner.

The contest was staged at Shoreditch Town Hall in May 1958. Any thoughts that Sam and Terry had that it would be a comfortable fight were dispelled in the first round when a withering left-right combination floored Downes. The following round he was put down again. Terry struggled on for another three rounds before the ref stopped the fight due to Terry's cut eye. Terry had been outclassed. Later Terry, who was always good for a quote or two, explaineded to a reporter: 'Very strange that. I was boxing away quite happily when suddenly I thought to myself; 'ello, Dick looks a lot taller than I remember him. Then I realise I'm flat on my back looking up at him!' When asked who he would like to box next, quick as a flash, Downes snapped: 'The fucker that set that fight up for me!'

I don't think Mickey Duff hung around too long that night. It was a while before Duff promoted another Downes fight. Downes himself went on to claim both the British and world middleweight titles under the watchful eye of the experienced Sam Burns. Dick Tiger went on to win the world middleweight title and later, the light heavyweight crown.

By the end of the sixties, with Solomons and Levene's influences beginning to diminish, Duff was handling some of the new breed of British boxers that were coming through. It is rumoured that the Krays, whom he knew from those earlier days, were trying to muscle in on his business and would turn up to events to put pressure on Duff to let them in on his operations. It took a great deal of courage, but Mickey stood his ground with the twins and then barred them from his events. Mickey started promoting some big fight nights at some of London's top boxing venues. York Hall, Wembley and the Royal Albert Hall all featured regular Mickey Duff promotions.

Duff, along with Jarvis Astaire, Benny Schmidt and Mike Barrett, were the main promoters who facilitated the British boxing scene's transition from the piecemeal approach to events that had prevailed for over 200 years to the big gala events that took place in large stadiums and halls throughout the second half of the twentieth century. Duff worked with sixteen world champions and many world-class British fighters and British champions, including Frank Bruno, Joe Calzaghe, John Conteh, Jim Watt and Lloyd Honeyghan. Micky Duff's record in boxing is comparable with that of Jack Solomons and for a long time he and his American counterpart, the flamboyant Don King, dominated world boxing promotions.

Undoubtedly, Solomons and Levene monopolised the professional matchmaking and promotion of top British boxing for half a century and it wasn't until Mickey Duff came along that their grip on the British fight game was broken. Duff is viewed by many as bringing boxing into a new age with bigger promotions and adding more entertainment value to the fight nights that he started to set up. Duff though, was one of four who worked together to make this happen. For the next three decades, Duff formed an alliance with trainer and manager Terry Lawless and fellow promoter, Mike Barrett. It was though, the fourth, Jarvis Astaire, who pushed Duff's promotion into the spotlight, literally.

Jarvis Astaire was born in 1924. His grandparents escaped from Russia the previous century and settled in East London. His birthname was Josephs and he was born in Stepney. He was football and cricket mad as a kid but never boxed. His greatest love though was theatrical entertainment, which he got from his mother, Esther. It stayed with him all his life and the influence and style he brought to boxing reflected that. He realised at an early age that boxing was a sport that could improve by introducing more of an entertainment element and even more importantly, greater media coverage. Initially, Astaire worked with Harry Levine and they staged major fights involving, among others, Mohammed Ali and the hugely popular former world middleweight champion Terry Downes. It was when Downes was due to fight the American champion Willie Pastrano for the world light heavyweight title in late November 1964 that Astaire secured a television breakthrough that he would later describe as the pivotal moment in his career, the one that made him a key player in the entertainment industry for the next 30 years.

Astaire and Levine had been unable to find a London venue for the bout and were forced to book the much smaller King's Hall in Belle Vue, Manchester. Astaire had been trying since 1959 to secure closed-circuit television rights for his shows, only to be rejected. But now his pleas that Downes' thousands of fans would be unable to travel to Manchester led to a relaxation in regulations by the General Post Office, which at the time granted broadcasting licences. In a first for the UK, the fight was therefore broadcast simultaneously to a theatre audience in London. The idea was a huge commercial success and the closed-circuit concept, cornered in the UK by Astaire, became an established format for staging big sporting events.

He was at the forefront of all the big gala promotions that hit the screens from the late 1960s onwards. His was the business brain behind securing the best deals for TV coverage at some of Britain's biggest venues. By the mid-1970s you had the likes of Terry Lawless training and managing boxers and Micky Duff managing boxers and match arranging contests all over the world. Astaire worked with Mike Barrett and Duff on promoting but unlike Duff, he was quite happy to stay in the background. If Solomons and Levene had a grip on boxing in their days then Astaire, Duff, Barrett and Lawless had a stranglehold on British boxing in the latter half of the twentieth century. Some called it a cartel.

Jarvis Astaire once claimed that boxing never represented more than 20% of his British business interests. That could well be right as he managed, or was an agent for, many well-known names away from the British fight scene. He was Mohammed Ali's agent in the UK and for several years represented top Hollywood actor Dustin Hoffman. He also claimed that he was approached to manage the Beatles but he and his wife were not a fan of the music so turned the offer down. He produced a couple of Hollywood films and was a racehorse owner and breeder. Most of his wealth probably came through his property portfolios and he was a major financier. Astaire died in August 2021.

Solomons, Levene, Duff, Wolfe and Berliner were some of the big players in boxing promotions, but they tended to stage the big events in the bigger venues of the day. These venues, although important to the sport, were only the tip of the iceberg when it came to staging fight nights. In London, for each so-called major boxing venue, there were twenty or more much smaller ones that were dotted around the capital. They were equally important to the sport. They provided the rings where huge numbers of young boxers had their first taste of the professional fight game. For each so-called major promoter there were a dozen lower profile promoters who staged the 'bread and butter' bills of boxing.

Jack Greenstock, whom we featured earlier in his series of matches against Ted Lewis, was one such promoter. His achievements against Lewis and his decent boxing career have been duly noted but his work in boxing promotions has barely been recognised. Even by the time he was coming to the end of his boxing career, Jack was arranging boxing matches in some of the lesser-known venues around the capital and further afield. Ilford Ice Rink, Poplar Hippodrome and the Manor Hall, Hackney, hosted some of his promotions.

Harry Greenberg was another Jewish promoter who set up fights in some of the more obscure venues, including Leyton Orient football ground, East India Dock Hall at Poplar and most bizarrely, a wartime boxing event at Queen Mary's hospital at Roehampton in Surrey.

15

COLOURFUL CHARACTERS

Many Jewish boxers led colourful lives outside the ring. Maybe it was because they lay their health, possibly even their lives, on the line every time they climbed inside the ropes that they became outgoing and fun-loving individuals outside of them.

Harry Mason was London born and bred, up to a point anyway. Harry was born in Bethnal Green in 1903 but around the age of nine, his parents moved to Leeds in Yorkshire. You may recall that Cockney Cohen's parents also moved to Leeds. I really don't know what the attraction of Leeds was in those days. I have visited the place a few times and never much enjoyed the experience. Maybe it's because on two occasions I travelled all the way up to Leeds United's Elland Road ground to see my beloved West Ham get stuffed by Don Revie's powerful Leeds teams of the 60s.

At least Harry Mason found a club up there that taught him to box. Very well, as it turned out. Anyway, although the city may have been dour, Harry Mason certainly wasn't. He was a flamboyant character. Not only did Harry Mason learn to box but he also learnt to play the violin as well and with some skill. There was no doubting his boxing ability but despite his talents in the ring, he was not universally liked, especially amongst his boxing colleagues. It appears that Harry was not bothered about winning any popularity contests, he was quite happy winning boxing matches and playing his violin. It was a somewhat strange combinations of skills he had but he used them both to great effect during his long, interesting and impressive life.

During his time in the ring, he always bought his fiddle with him. He used to play it in his dressing room just before lacing up his gloves to go out and fight. It would relax him. I doubt Mohammed Ali was ever serenaded with 'Hava Nagila', 'Shalov Rav' or even 'My Yiddishe Mama' by an opponent before a fight but Harry Mason's opponents along the corridor certainly were!

Harry was a great boxer and a prolific one at that. Starting out on undercards in the Leeds area, by 1921 he had gravitated to fight almost exclusively in London for the next couple of years. At Olympia Kensington he gained the British and European lightweight titles in May 1923 after James 'Nobby' Hall was disqualified for delivering a badly low punch. He retained the title twice more, to win the Lonsdale Belt outright in June 1925. At this time Harry was sharing the same manager as Jack Kid Berg who was the big rising star. They both fought at around the same weight but Harry's reputation as a bit of a 'piss-taker' ensured they never sparred together. Their manager could not risk his star boxers falling out with each other.

The notable boxing journalist, Gilbert Odd made this observation about Mason: 'Mason was undoubtedly a boxer and a very skilled one at that but Mason could incite trouble. I've seen him leaning over the shoulder of his opponent winking at some of the ringside audience, while throwing kidney punches! Often some of the crowd booed but it didn't seem to bother him.'

A lot of commentators thought that Berg could bring Mason down a peg or two so it was unsurprising that there was a call for these two Jewish fighters and stablemates to be matched up in a fight, but their manager resisted the temptation. Berg, when asked about a possible match, replied, 'Harry's not my cup of tea really.'

Harry then moved up a weight to win the welterweight crown in November that year. At that weight there was little chance that Berg and Mason would face each other. By 1927, Mason was fighting regularly all over the world, as far afield as South Africa and Australia. He fought many times in the States as well. It was a glittering life inside the ring and his life outside of it was quite sparkly as well.

His fiddle playing did not go unnoticed and he started to get requests to play in public, especially at boxing events. With one eye on his life after retirement, he started to play as well as box professionally. Harry certainly had a bit of showbiz blood in him and started moving in some of these circles during his later time in the ring. Around 1924, possibly while fighting in America, he met the Hilton twins. Violet and Daisy, who were born in Brighton. They were Britain's first conjoined twins to survive beyond a few months after birth. They were fairly well known in this country and went over to America in 1917, as teenagers, to perform their unique song and dance routines in American vaudeville. Mason got friendly with the girls and got engaged to Violet. As the twins worked more and more in America and Harry started to box around the world, the engagement to Violet did not last more than a year. He did though keep in touch with the girls and it is thought that he may have had a relationship with Daisy as well at some stage.

Harry Mason racked up a mammoth number of fights. He fought 212 times over a seventeen-year career. In February 1937, after one or two indifferent results, Mason was matched up to fight Jack Kid Berg. They had eventually caught up with each other at welterweight. Berg, the former world super-lightweight champion was still very much at the top of his game. Mason was all too aware of Jack's all-action approach to fights, but that did not stop him being floored in the first round. He just managed to recover and boxed on for two further rounds before failing to appear for the fourth round. Harry decided that his time was up and he announced his retirement shortly after. A year or so later with war approaching, he was offered a chance to manage a large hotel in South Africa, which he did for many years. He was, by all accounts, a very congenial host. He died in 1974.

Morris Abraham Cohen was probably the most colourful Jewish character with a boxing background to come out of this country, let alone London. He has an astonishing story to tell. There is just one small problem and that is that a couple of 'facts' about Cohen contradict each other. I will stick to the information that appears to be bone-fide. Even his place and date of birth have been called into question. What we do know is that he was either born in Poland in 1887 or Whitechapel in 1889. From my research I think the former is probably true.

Morris or Moishe Cohen was born to strict orthodox Jewish parents who were heavily involved with the local Synagogue. Morris was a bright young lad but hated school and often played truant, which in turn led him into mischief. He fell in with one of the 'Wild Boys gangs' and started stealing. He would get paid to throw rocks through windows to drum up trade for a local glazier. According to Morris, the going rate was one halfpenny per pane of glass. By the time he was ten he started to indulge in unlicensed boy fights in the back yard of a blacksmiths, before fighting professionally under the name of Cockney Cohen.

As mentioned earlier, there were two boxers that used this ring name around the same time but this 'Cockney' only fought a few fights. He remembers getting paid two shillings (10p) for his first professional fight. In between fights he acted as a 'shill' (bogus customer) for a street corner trader. He then got caught for pickpocketing and as he was only just a teenager, he was sent to the Hayes Industrial School, which was a form of Jewish reform school where boys were taught to learn skills.

He was released on his sixteenth birthday and went back to some of his old activities again, mixing a bit of boxing with some minor criminal activities. He was heading for a long stint in a men's prison. The local Synagogue found out and with the agreement of his parents he was shipped off to Western Canada to keep him out of prison. He was not yet seventeen and after a few years working on farms and with livestock, he ended up helping organise the mainly Chinese workforce that worked on the Canadian Pacific Railroad. Thousands were employed all down the west coast of America. He became friendly with a number of supporters of Doctor Sun Yat-Sen who, back in China, was working towards overthrowing the antiquated and fragmented Chinese government.

During his time in Canada, Cohen had learned to ride and became an excellent shot. He could obviously handle himself and was well regarded by the Chinese. When Doctor Sun visited Canada to rally support in 1914, Cohen was recommended as a bodyguard to the Doctor. Sun was a supporter of Zionism and they forged a long-term friendship and Sun offered him a position on his staff. However, before he could get to China, the First World War broke out.

Morris joined the Royal Canadian Army, made sergeant, and was twice wounded in action, once quite badly. He saw the end of the war from a hospital bed. He returned home a hero and his Chinese friends were waiting. Dr Sun, it seemed, wanted someone he could trust absolutely; a foreigner who would keep away from Chinese internal politics and who would look after his personal safety. So started the next incredible episode of Cohen's life. His army service rounded off his personality and his fighting skills and his organisational acumen was excellent. He was handy with guns and could shoot well using both hands. He became known as Cockney 'Two Gun' Cohen as he would later be seen walking round with a gun in either hand.

Morris not only served as Doctor Sun's bodyguard, he also did undercover work, helped handle some economic negotiations, and smuggled guns for him. Since there was a civil war raging in China, he did a bit of fighting on the side. In August 1922, Morris landed in Shanghai with eight guns in his luggage. He was thirty-three and now a colonel in the Chinese Revolutionary Army. He was also the aide-de-camp to Sun. He set about training Sun's small but dedicated army. Soon, 'Two-Gun Cohen' was known throughout China. Doctor Sun eventually gained the upper hand and formed the first Nationalist Government of China, sweeping aside the various warlords that had ruled over China for centuries. When Sun died, Morris became General Cohen, the highest ever ranking non-Chinese military officer in Chinese military history.

His life was full of amazing events and dark intrigue, dealing with Russian female agent provocateurs, Chinese warlords and Japanese insurgents. He fought against both Chinese communist rebels and Japanese forces. Cohen was eventually captured by the Japanese during the Sino-Japanese war. He was tortured and imprisoned for a couple of years. He was then repatriated to Canada in 1943. He managed to make the odd trip back to China and was still held in some esteem by the Chinese authorities.

In 1947, Cockney was to play one final role in world history. A committed Zionist, Cohen was by now convinced that the Jewish people needed a land of their own. The question of creating a Jewish State by the division of Palestine was a thorny subject and some western powers, as well as Russia, were against it. Cohen worked behind the scenes to get the Chinese to back the plan. Cohen produced a letter from his old friend Doctor Sun that expressed his wish that China would support any Zionist movement. The Chinese delegates at the crucial UN vote, supported the formation of Israel. It was their vote that swung it. The Jewish people had their own country and Cockney 'Two

Morris 'Two Gun' Cohen (centre) during his service with the Canadian Army around 1916.

Guns', the street fighting, tearaway kid from Whitechapel, helped to create it.

Another great personality is the ubiquitous **Lew 'Buster' Cohen**. Buster was a larger-than-life character in more ways than one. His big voice and even bigger frame could be seen several times a week at boxing events during the first half of the twentieth century, he was the resident master of ceremonies at Premierland for almost twenty years. Buster boxed a little in his younger days, but it was evident from his build that his appetite for competitive boxing paled somewhat in comparison to his appetite for food. He also worked out that there was another way to make money inside the ropes than just slinging leather.

Buster was one of the great ring masters and had a wicked wit to go with it. When Premierland closed in 1930, he went on to work at the Devonshire Club in Hackney with Jack Solomons and Sid Hull. He could also be seen compering gentlemen's sporting nights as well as the odd variety show. Sometimes boxing was mixed with variety. Often variety performers could be seen ringside at boxing matches and variety returned the favour. However, not only did boxers have front row seats for shows they also occasionally appeared on stage.

Here is a report in the *Peterborough Standard* from December 1939, welcoming boxing supremos Solomon and Hulls with their prodigy, Eric Boon. Boon had just become British lightweight champion and was a local lad. The evening events at the city's Embassy Theatre were described:

M.C. Buster Cohen introduced the champ. He gave a brief description of his achievements and then Eric went through a training routine of shadow boxing, punch bag and skipping work which was commented upon with great gusto and not a little amusement by Buster. They were then joined on stage by his trainer and also his sparring partner, Harry Silver. Dancing girls then appeared dressed in boxing trunks and singlets and proceeded to make up a sort of boxing arena. Four of them, dressed in red, white, blue and green made up the four posts and similar coloured ropes were held between them to complete the ring. A short sparring match then took place with Buster acting as an impromptu referee. It all finished with a KO which managed to collapse the ring with the boxers, ref and girls all ending up on the floor.

Buster brought a smile to the faces of audiences for over forty years.

Bethnal Green boxer, Harry Mansfield's career was, to all intents and purposes, standard fare. His record alone would tell you little about the man. Quite ordinary in boxing terms. However, if you dig a little bit more into his life, both inside and outside the ropes, you discover that Harry often found himself close to some extraordinary events during his twelve years in the ring.

Harry Mansfield was born Harry Ginsberg in 1888 in Aldgate but moved to Bethnal Green in his teenage years. He actually fought under the name Jack Jones. His early fights took place around London and they were distinctly average. His first twelve fights were all at the Wonderland Arena but in December 1907 he travelled over to Canada for a series of four fights and a couple of exhibition matches. He won three out of the four matches. In December 1908 Mansfield fought the second of his exhibitions. Harry was boxing at middleweight when he took on the 'Galveston Giant', the phenomenal heavyweight Jack Johnson, in an exhibition bout.

The hugely controversial Johnson was well on his way to claiming the world crown and becoming the world's first black heavyweight champion. He was also beginning to fight a few exhibition matches around North America, something he did more regularly in his later career in both the States and Europe. Harry was giving away about two stone and about 6 inches in height when these two mis-matched boxers met for this exhibition bout. The match was supposed to showcase the contender's skills, but Johnson often used these sessions to fight lighter but faster boxers to sharpen up his movement. He did not spare any boxer that stepped into the ring with him.

Mansfield realised at an early stage that this was going to be a bit more than a casual workout and seriously upped his game. Using some great footwork and hand speed he proved more than a match for the great man. Equipping himself so well against Johnson did not go unnoticed and he was asked to box in America. He relished the chance to earn good money and he boxed there for the next three years.

He settled in Philadelphia. After New York, Philly was a real hotspot for American boxing. It was a close-knit boxing community with several professional boxers sharing the same gym for training. Two boxers could be training in the gym together one day and then fighting the next. It was at the gym that Mansfield got to know the black Jack Blackburn. Blackburn was, like Jack Johnson, a flamboyant and controversial figure and was a very good boxer. Harry Mansfield got to know him and his brother and sometime manager, Fred, quite well.

In a period when they were both fighting at middleweight, the two were matched together. Blackburn was by far the superior fighter and the match that took place in December 1908 was a fairly one-sided affair that Blackburn won quite comfortably. Jack could be a volatile man and moved in some bad circles in Philadelphia. The day after his Mansfield fight, there was an argument between Jack and his brother about money and Fred slashed Jack's throat. Fortunately, it was not too deep and Blackburn survived.

Around a month later, Jack, who had been training with Harry, left the gym and was on the street outside when he got into an altercation with a couple. It is unclear what exactly happened but Jack drew a gun and shot and killed Alonzo Polk and also shot and wounded Polk's wife. Mansfield witnessed the aftermath. Blackburn was arrested and convicted of manslaughter and received fifteen years hard labour. This was later reduced to eight years and he walked free in less than six.

By the time Blackburn was released, Harry Mansfield had long since returned to London. Inside the ring, trouble also seemed to follow Harry. In a fight at the Wonderland in 1911, angry at two low blows in the fifth round, his opponent, Dai Thomas, rushed Harry to try and head-butt him and then appeared to bite Harry's left cheek. A riot ensued when a spectator swung a chair at Thomas. The referee, having fled the ring, refused to let the bout continue once order had been restored, despite both boxers being willing to do so. That match was one of the last to be staged at the Wonderland as it was gutted by fire a few weeks later.

Mansfield boxed on. The following year he was matched to fight Bill Curzon in an eliminator fight for the British middleweight title. It was to be the high-water mark of his career. The fight, over fifteen rounds, saw Mansfield turn in one of his better performances. Curzon was a good boxer and a very close-fought match ensued, which ended in a draw. Harry was disappointed that he was not awarded the match and criticised Britain's top referee at the time, Herbert Douglas, who was officiating that night. I don't think that could have gone down to well with the Sporting Club committee members, as he was not offered a return match.

Mansfield's last big fight was against the fellow Jewish boxer and previous world welterweight champion, Harry Lewis. Lewis was American and Mansfield knew Lewis quite well from his days spent fighting in the States. Lewis, like Mansfield, boxed out of Philadelphia when Lewis was in the lightweight division. The fight took place in Liverpool in March 1913 and surprisingly, a twenty-round contest was set up for the match. It was hard-fought by both men and the last few rounds developed into a bit of a slog. The match was called a draw. At the end of the fight the two old Jewish pros from either side of the Atlantic hugged each other in mutual respect. In hindsight, this match was to signal the beginning of the end for both boxers.

Lewis returned to America and it was there, a few days later, that he was involved in a serious road accident that left him badly injured. Lewis tried to box six months later but it was a fight too far. He was badly knocked out in the fifth round. Already suffering from nerve injury from his accident, he developed paralysis down one side and never fought again. Harry Mansfield did have a few more fights but lost most of them and at the outbreak of war, in 1914, he more or less retired, having just one fight in 1917 against his old adversary, Bill Curzon, to help raise money for the war effort

16

MOVING ON

For most young people growing up at the start of the 1960s, the war was either a vague early childhood memory or something only their parents or elder siblings spoke about. It was a decade for moving on. The capital was a vibrant place and Londoners were experiencing a new, liberated way of life.

Over in America, racial tensions still ran high. Martin Luther King's dream that all men being born equal should be a self-evident truth was still some way off. Apart from the short-lived Notting Hill race riots a few years earlier, the integration of the large ethnic groups that arrived in our capital over the previous 100 years had happened relatively peacefully. Unlike America, and some other countries, here in England integration tended to be a peaceful process and generally religious relations were good. For this country, the main struggle for many years, centuries even, concerned class.

The explosion of Jewish boxing in the capital after the turn of the last century had a ripple effect on both the demographics of London and the development of the Jewish lifestyle in British society. In the years following the Second World War, the Jewish communities of the inner city, notably those in the eastern and northern areas close to the City of London, gradually started to move out. The working-class Jewish population of the Victorian and Edwardian era had mainly prospered throughout the first half of the century and by the 1960s many were part of the English middle classes.

By this time there was very little need for young Jewish men to pull on a pair of boxing gloves to help feed their family. Even those less fortunate had the post-war welfare state safety net to fall back on. Life was changing and moving on, and London boxing was no exception. Youth clubs were becoming ever more secular, but boxing was still producing some decent amateur Jewish fighters, although nowhere near the numbers forty or fifty years earlier. Even fewer were turning professional. The small venues scattered all around London gradually started to close in favour of bigger arenas. Hundreds of Jewish boxers had appeared at these smaller spots but by the 1970s venues like Leyton Baths, Pitfield Street Baths, Shoreditch Town Hall, Ilford Ice Rink and Manor Place Baths in Walworth had closed their doors on the sport.

In this new age, it was the bigger arenas like the Empire Pool, Wembley, Earls Court, the Royal Albert Hall and York Hall that were showcasing the big events, and it was TV that was bringing the sport to the masses. The emphasis was on quality, not quantity. Fewer amateur boxers were now progressing into professional careers. Of the up-and-coming young Jewish lads who took up the sport at amateur level, most did not need to carve out a living on the professional circuit. For the majority it was simply an enjoyable hobby sport in which they excelled.

Ralph Gold was a fine London amateur international boxer in the late 1950s and early 1960s, winning he won the London ABA Championships in 1961. The following year he was on track to secure a national title, but he got injured just before his semi-final fight and had to withdraw. He competed for Great Britain for several years, and was very good, but possibly realised that it would take a big step forward to become a competitive professional fighter. Instead, he dropped boxing to enter the business world. With his brother and fellow boxer David, he was to establish a very lucrative business in adult entertainment and the fashion trade. They went into football club ownership as well. Both brothers were directors of Birmingham City FC for a while, and David was a director at West Ham United.

An even better amateur was **Michael Abrams** from Battersea. Mickey was a three-time light flyweight ABA champion in the early 1970s and a British international for many years. He was a Commonwealth Games medallist in 1970 and fought in amateur competitions in America. He got to know actor Dustin Hoffman whilst stateside and remained pals with him for many years. He had a lengthy amateur career but, again, did not turn pro. It was not until the turn of the millennium that another couple of decent Jewish boxers with a connection to London would appear in the rings of London.

Roman Greenberg was born in Moldova in 1982 but emigrated to Israel with his family when he was only six. He started boxing there a few years later. He was obviously a natural talent and as an amateur he won silver medals at both the European and World junior championships. In early 2001 he turned pro, set up home in Finchley, North London and started to train and box there. As a professional he boxed mainly at heavyweight. He trained in Maidenhead and had his first professional fight at Paddington in November that same year. He beat fellow debutant Dave Clark, stopping him in the fifth round. It was to be the start of a run of twenty-seven straight wins. Throughout his career, which took him around the world, he displayed the Star of David proudly and never gave up his Israeli home and citizenship. Roman possessed

Ralph (above) and David (right) Gold. Both boxed at an amateur level out of the East Ham and West Ham Boys Clubs. Ralph progressed a little further in amateur boxing but David had a leaning towards football. The brothers went into business together and were co-directors at Birmingham City FC before David moved back to his West Ham roots, taking control at the club he once lived opposite.

some of the quickest hands of any heavyweight, a fact remarked upon by the great trainer Angelo Dundee when he witnessed Roman perform. In March 2006 he won the International Boxing Organisation (IBO) intercontinental title against Alexander Vasilev in Monte Carlo and defended it later in the year against Alexey Varakin with a knockout victory.

In 2007 Greenberg had beaten the very useful one-time American cruiserweight champion Damon Reid, and he must have had an eye on a tilt at the world heavyweight championship. There was even talk of Greenberg becoming the first Jewish heavyweight world champion since Max Baer eighty years before (this is disputed as Baer was probably only one-quarter Jewish). In 2008 he was pitted against Cedric Boswell, the rising American heavyweight star. It was a tough test, and Greenberg failed it. He was easily outboxed for the first two rounds before the referee stopped the fight. It was a shock and a big setback for Roman and his team. Greenberg returned to London and the very next day flew to Israel. It is reported that he had family problems and other issues in his home country, with his mother diagnosed with cancer shortly before the fight. His promoter Robert Waterman later said: 'In retrospect, none of us should have let him go through with that fight. It was he who wanted it. Possibly I wasn't the best promoter or manager at the time. I take some responsibility for it.'

Whatever the reason, he never fought again. But Greenberg didn't hit the skids – he found work in anti-terrorist security.

I will mention one last London Jewish boxer. Some 230 years after the great Mendoza first set foot in the ring – albeit a 'ring' that was probably made up of surrounding spectators gathered on a bit of waste ground – **Tony Milch**, who was born in Edgware,

North London, fought his debut bout at the Camden Centre in July 2013, in a proper roped ring in a comfortable indoor arena. Milch convincingly beat his Bulgarian opponent, the serial loser Danny Donchev, in four rounds. It is doubtful that Tony harboured any thoughts that he would be the next Daniel Mendoza, but after reaching his fourteenth fight with a 100 per cent win record, he may have convinced himself that a title might just come his way.

To get his foot firmly on the title ladder, Milch was lined up to fight Matt McCarthy for the vacant Southern Area super-welterweight title. On paper they were exceptionally well matched, but boxing takes place on canvas, not paper, and the master on that night was McCarthy, who delivered the knockout blow to Tony's ambitions by stopping him in the fifth round at York Hall in October 2017. That was followed by a further loss, and although he narrowly defeated Danny Little, a very average boxer, on points in November 2018, Tony thought long and hard about his future.

Eighteen months later Milch set up the 'Gloves and Doves' programme, which seeks to bring Arab and Israeli boxers together in the spirit of coexistence. Supported by the 'boxing Rabbi' Yuri Forman, the former American champion, its boxing events were due to start in 2020. Covid took its toll, but plans are still there to realise Tony Milch's dream that an aggressive sport such as boxing can be used to encourage peace.

From Mendoza to Milch, 230 years of London Jewish boxing has witnessed some astonishing events. Although Jewish boxers no longer dominate the London fight scene, their legacy is there for all to see. We arrive at the end of this story with a reference to something I first mentioned right at the start: the importance of Jews to sport and the perceived notion that their involvement was marginal. Remember the two young ladies playing tennis? Minorities win famous tennis victory.' Jewish boxing helped to make sure comments like that disappeared from print.

There are still a couple of Jewish entrepreneurs who manage and promote in the boxing game, but these days, with the amount of money in football, several high-profile Jewish businessmen in London have become big players in professional football. It is safe to say that Jewish boxers and promoters played no small part in breaking down the barriers that prevailed in those early days, which made it possible for the likes of Alan Sugar, Daniel Levy, Eric Hall, Barry Silkman and David and Ralph Gold to play prominent roles in football's development in more recent years. London's David Triesman, meanwhile, became the first independent Chairman of the Football Association.

APPENDICES

Roll of Honour – List of London Jewish Champion Boxers (1780–2010)

Area, English/National, British Empire, European and World titles. The following boxers featured in the book held one or more of these senior professional championship titles during their career.

Daniel Mendoza

Young Barney Aaron

Dick Burge

Ted Kid Lewis

Harry Reeve

Harry Mizler

Jack Bloomfield

Johnny Brown

Mike Honeyman

Sam Kellar

Lew Lazar

Al Phillips

Samuel Elias (Dutch Sam)

Jewey Smith

Sid Burns

Ernie Veitch

Jewey Cook

Jem Smith

Jack Scales

Matt Wells

Jack Kid Berg

Young Joseph

Benny Caplan

Harry Mason

Kid Froggy (Jack Hyams)

Al Foreman

Dave Finn

Joe Shear

Young Dutch Sam Elias

Greenberg

Dave Kellar

Harry Solomon

The London Boxing Venues

In the years during which bare-knuckle boxing was the dominant force in boxing, there were very few purpose-built or adapted venues. In the very early days bare-knuckle fights often hastily took place whenever or wherever a suitable place could be found. Once the gloved version of the sport began to take over and the popularity grew, then more appropriate places for staging the sport began to appear.

Jem Smith was the one boxer, more than most, that epitomised the transition from non-gloved to the gloved version. In his early years, during the 1870s he could be found fighting unregulated matches in cobblestoned London courtyards and public houses in front of a few rough and ready spectators. By 1896 he was fighting championship bouts at London's leading venue the Sporting Club at Covent Garden in front of hundreds of evening-suited, cigar smoking patrons.

During the first half of the twentieth century, many hundreds of venues started to appear that staged boxing matches around London. For some it was just the odd event every now and again and the venue was shared with other activities. Many venues though featured boxing regularly, maybe three or four times a week. Here is a list of some of the popular venues in the capital that featured boxing prominently and where London Jewish boxers could regularly be seen fighting.

East London Boxing Venues
Arena – Mile End
Blue Anchor (Pub) – Shoreditch
Cambridge Athletic Club – Bethnal Green
Devonshire Club – Hackney
Drill Hall – Bethnal Green
Drill Hall – Bow
Drill Hall – Walthamstow
East Ham Baths

Excelsior Theatre – Bethnal Green
Goodwin Gymnasium – Hackney
Ilford Ice Rink
Hippodrome – Poplar
Judean Club
Kings Hall (Baths) – Hackney
Leyton Baths
Manor Hall – Hackney
Osbourne Social Club – Stepney
Palais De Dance – East Ham
Paragon Music Hall – Mile End
Pavilion Theatre – Whitechapel
Peoples Palace – Mile End
Pitfield Street/Hoxton Baths – Hoxton
Poplar Hippodrome
Premierland
Romford Road Baths
Shoreditch Town Hall
Shoreditch Athletic Club (Club Room)
West Ham Baths
Whitechapel Pavilion Arena/Theatre
Wonderland
York Hall

City and North London Boxing Venues
Alexander Palace – Crouch End
Alexander Theatre – Stoke Newington
Alcazar – Edmonton
Caledonian Road Baths – Islington
Collins Music Hall – Islington
Cosmopolitan Sporting Club – Marylebone
Empire Pool – Wembley
Holborn Empire

Holborn Stadium
Hornsey Town Hall
Sadler's Wells Theatre
Seymour Hall – Marylebone
Tee to Tum Club – Stamford Hill
Vale Hall – Kilburn
Wembley Town Hall
Wembley Stadium/Arena
West End School of Arms – Marylebone

West End and West London Boxing Venues
National Sporting Club – Covent Garden
Bob Habbijams West End School of Arms, Newman St – Soho
Cambridge Theatre – Charing Cross
Earls Court/Olympia
Empire School of Arms – Marylebone
Fulham Baths
Hammersmith Stadium
Holland Park Rink
Lime Grove Baths – Shepherds Bush
New Adelphi Theatre – Strand
Paddington Baths
Queensbury Club – Soho
Royal Albert Hall – Kensington
St George's Hall – Westminster
Vale Hall – Kilburn
Walham Green Baths – Fulham
White City Stadium
West London Stadium – Marylebone

South London Boxing Venues
Bollingbroke Club – Clapham
Beresford Street Drill Hall – Woolwich

Bermondsey School of Arms
Canterbury Theatre of Varieties – Lambeth
Crystal Palace – Sydenham
Drill Hall – Woolwich
Kings Hall – Southwark
Manor Place Baths
Plumstead Baths
Ring – Blackfriars
Streatham Ice Rink
South London Palace – Lambeth

A–Z Professional London Jewish Boxers' Records, Gloved

Thousands of London Jewish boxers have competed in both the amateur and professional codes of the sport over the last two and a half centuries. Too many to mention and in the cases of the very early bare-knuckle exponents of the sport, many fights had incomplete recorded information or were never recorded at the time at all.

The following is a list of London Jewish boxers that boxed using gloves under Marquess of Queensbury rules from 1880 to 2010, from a period when records are more accurate. I have only included those boxers that I have found reliable records on and that fought in excess of twenty-five professionally recorded fights during their career.

Name		Years Active	Won	Lost	Draw/ ND
Joe	(A)Brahams	1935–1939	21	10	9
Harry	Aarons	1919–1927	28	30	0
Harry	Abrahams	1900–1918	12	18	2
Bert	Adams	1898–1913	111	68	2
Jack Kid	Berg	1924–1945	157	26	9

Name		Years Active	Won	Lost	Draw/ND
Jack	Bloomfield*	1918–1924	28	6	2
Joe	Bloomfield*	1920–1930	58	36	12
Harry (Kid)	Brooks	1910–1927	65	36	6
Harry	Brooks*	1922–1939	83	64	16
Kid	Brooks	1925–1934	12	15	2
Young Joe	Brooks* (Bayardo)	1909–1924	110	49	8
Nat (Young)	Brooks*	1909–1929	104	48	23
Johnny	Brown*	1919–1928	62	29	4
Young Johnny	Brown*	1920–1932	65	25	5
Sid	Burns	1909–1921	67	25	6
Cockney	Cohen	1901–1912	49	18	14
Sid	Cohen	1909–1924	12	16	2
Young Johnny	Cohen	1909–1921	72	28	12
Alf	Conn	1925–1938	13	29	6
Dave	Conn*	1911–1919	40	7	1
Joe	Conn*	1911–1925	69	32	6
Jewey	Cook	1894–1912	64	22	13
Harry (Young)	Daniels	1908–1911	27	8	8
Jack	Daniels	1906–1922	69	50	14
Micky	Duff	1945–1948	33	9	4
Dave	Finn	1930–1946	91	64	16
Al	Foreman	1920–1934	111	22	12
Jack	Fox	1935–1942	14	13	0
Nat	Franks	1927–1939	74	35	8
Danny	Frush	1917–1928	67	17	5
Jack	Gold	1910–1922	46	48	15
Dick	Golding	1901–1909	30	25	3

Name		Years Active	Won	Lost	Draw/ND
Alf	Goodwin*	1906–1922	41	26	12
Joe	Goodwin*	1900–1912	78	28	14
Johnny (young)	Gordon	1924–1936	3	20	4
Roman	Greenberg	2000–2008	27	1	0
Harry	Greenfield	1891–1910	18	29	2
Jack Kid (Young)	Greenstock	1910–1926	31	25	7
Jack	Guyon	1893–1912	90	50	9
Fred	Halsband	1909–1921	77	28	8
Mike	Honeyman	1914–1926	95	40	19
Bill	Housego*	1920–1931	23	23	5
Fred	Housego*	1910–1929	78	38	14
Jack	Hyams (Kid Froggy)	1924–1943	107	47	14
Tommy	Hyams	1923–1940	105	66	23
Freddie	Jacks	1910–1928	81	91	16
Albert	Jacobs	1902–1911	36	16	9
Alf	Jacobs (Marylebone)	1908–1913	22	10	4
Alf	Jacobs (Mile End)	1902–1914	30	36	3
Alf	Jacobs (Spitalfields)	1896–1919	17	8	1
Jack	Jones	1905–1917	36	33	15
Aschel (Young)	Joseph	1903–1914	94	23	21
Dave	Kellar* (Keller)	1933–1938	29	17	7
Sam	Kellar* (Keller)	1902–1919	80	38	25
Bob	Kendrick	1902–1917	43	28	17

Name		Years Active	Won	Lost	Draw/ ND
Nat	Keyser	1899–1909	20	36	6
Harry	Lazar *	1938–1950	84	25	4
Lew	Lazar*	1951–1958	48	8	4
Jimmy	Lester	1934–1942	51	28	7
Kid	Levene	1904–1914	18	27	10
Con	Lewis	1928–1935	27	20	10
Jack	Lewis	1902–1911	26	21	0
Ted Kid	Lewis (see notes p 269)	1909–1929	232	46	21
Mark	Leznick	1924–1929	31	13	8
Joe (young)	Lipman	1910–1920	12	13	2
Phil	Loloski (y)	1925–1934	24	11	3
Alec (x)	Lyons	1935–1939	26	4	3
Alf	Mansfield	1910–1920	61	56	25
Harry	Mansfield	1909–1917	21	10	4
Jack (Private)	Marks	1909–1918	50	28	9
Harry	Mason	1920–1937	144	53	15
Harry	Mizler*	1933–1944	63	16	2
Moe	Mizler*	1926–1932	30	16	6
Ike	Moss	1899–1905	12	14	1
Moe	Moss	1928–1943	98	49	27
Harry	Moyse	1908–1915	6	18	1
Jack	Negal	1928–1932	21	3	3
Young	(Josephs) Nipper	1904–1916	72	46	27
Al	Phillips	1938–1951	73	14	3
Lew	Pinkus	1926–1932	35	60	13
Harry	Reeve	1910–1934	84	52	20
Phil	Richards	1922–1935	87	50	16
Joe	Rood	1946–1953	21	15	3

Name		Years Active	Won	Lost	Draw/ ND
Jack	Scales	1896–1911	43	29	6
Dave	Sharkey	1945–1950	24	21	4
Joe	Shear	1909–1920	45	17	12
Harry	Silver	1936–1949	61	16	8
Alf	Simmons	1919–1933	83	55	14
Sam	Simmons	1910–1915	36	7	5
Jewey	Smith	1908–1915	34	23	4
Sid	Smith	1907–1919	78	17	5
Ernie	Vietch*	1895–1907	50	26	7
Jack	Vietch*	1907–1910	23	19	3
Gus	Warman (Worman)	1924–1934	22	29	8
Matt	Wells	1909–1922	31	19	2
Charlie	Wise	1936–1947	36	14	2
Jack	Wise	1896–1911	19	17	5
Jimmy	Young	1926–1938	19	24	7

Some 'no decision' (ND) results may not be included and some may have been recorded as drawn matches rather than no decisions.

* Denotes boxers who were related.

NOTES

1 *Pride and Pugilism*

1 Prior to the introduction of the Broughton Rules, boxing's first set of recognised guidelines, boxing was an unsafe 'free-for-all' affair between two men, generally for a wager or purse: a prize-fight. The very earliest prize-fights merely stipulated that biting and gouging were not allowed, nor hitting or grabbing below the waist. Other than that, most other things were allowed. It was often a mix of boxing and wrestling. Unlike modern boxing, there were no specifically timed rounds. In this form of boxing, a round was classed as such if a boxer was knocked down or yielded. The referee would then allow 30 seconds for that boxer to recover and resume or else he was counted out. Rounds therefore could last any amount of time from a few seconds to even an hour or more. It was more often the former, so that is why some bare-knuckle prize-fights could be recorded as lasting more than fifty rounds and several hours. The Broughton Rules, followed by the London Prize Ring Rules and lastly the Marquess of Queensbury Rules combined to create greater safety in the ring, give greater structure to the sport and ensure more evenly contested and disciplined bouts of boxing.

2 The argument that broke out between Bill Richardson and Ben Bendoff was probably about gambling debts owed by Richardson. Prior to the events of 1865, it is on record that Richardson owed Bendoff £500, a debt he ran up after a lengthy card session. After a few weeks of trying to collect the debt, Bendoff finally gave up and 'sold on' the iou to Richardson's brother-in-law for £75. Bendoff had a reputation for being a very good card player and made a bit of money from it. After his last fight he used this ability as his main source of income.

2 *Street Life*

1 One of the most referenced books about the Rookeries is the second edition of Reverend Thomas Beames' *The Rookeries of London* (1852). Within, he describes six main rookeries: St. Giles, Saffron Hill, Jacob's Island, Ratcliffe Highway, Berwick Street District of St James, and Pye Street of Westminster. You can add to this list the Old Nichol and Spitalfields rookeries that came into existence after Beames' book was published. There were plenty of other areas however, that perfectly fit the description of a 'rookery', although Beames had named the most notorious and most publicized up to that point. What links them all and sets them apart from the increasing number of 'slums' is the criminal element within each distinct area. Each had defined boundaries and each seemed to have their own speciality in crime.

3 *Welcome to the Club*

1 From around the mid seventeenth century, smallish groups of immigrants came to London, mainly from Europe. Four main groups, the Protestant French and Belgian Huguenots, The Irish Catholics (weavers), the Sephardic Jews from Spain and Portugal, and a smaller group of Ashkenazi Jews from Germany and Poland, settled in the areas of Spitalfields, Aldgate and

Whitechapel immediately to the East of the City of London. Although the odd flashpoint occasionally occurred between the groups themselves, generally these people, together with the local population, lived peacefully together. The Huguenots and the Sephardic Jews in particular settled well and prospered.

At the time Queen Victoria ascended to the throne in 1837, Britain was already the world's most dominant power. The world trade boom and the Industrial Revolution, which was spearheaded by this country, cemented Britain's place at the top table of the commercial world. The British Empire was continually expanding. It was no surprise then, that people from all around the world that were either destitute, persecuted or war refugees, were looking for a way out of their plight and Britain, particularly London, was seen to be the place to go. By far the highest number were Central European and Russian Jews who between 1850 and 1905 arrived mainly in London. It is estimated that between 1880 and 1910 two million Russian Jews migrated from western Russia and its associated territories. Huge numbers ended up in Britain or America. Immigration to London during the 19th century can be split down into these approximate numbers:

Asian Lascars/Indian Subcontinent	12,000
Germans	15,000
Dutch	3,000
French	3,000
Italians	8,000
Africa and Afro/Caribbean	5,000
Chinese	8,000
Irish	70,000
Eastern European (Ashkenazi Jews)	30,000
Russian Jews	110,000
Others	18,000
Total	**282,000**

By the turn of 20th century, it was clear that these huge numbers of immigrants flooding into the capital and some other major British cities had to be curtailed for a number of reasons and so in 1905 the government of the day introduced the Aliens Act and later further restriction of movements into the country was implemented through the 1914 Aliens Restriction Act. In the late 1930s the situation for German, Polish and Austrian Jews was looking bleak and restrictions were relaxed to allow another influx of Jewish immigrants into the country. A large number ended up in London, especially the ones that had relations here. Almost as many settled in Leeds and Manchester.

2 The earliest organised boys' clubs were set up by the Church of England. The charismatic Reverend A. Osborn Jay founded his club for older teenagers and young men around 1860 as a way to reduce crime and violence on the London streets. He set up a fully functioning boxing gymnasium where these young men could channel any aggression into a more controlled activity. Other well-known boys' clubs were Oxford house and the Webbe Institute, but again these originally had strong ties with the Church of England. With the growing population of the Irish and Jewish communities, clubs were starting to be set up to accommodate young people from these backgrounds. Clubs such as St John Bosco and the Stepney Institute in East London and the Westminster Club were the predominantly Catholic equivalent to the Brady Boys' Club, Oxford and St George's and the JLB Jewish clubs. More secular clubs started to appear around the turn of the century and they included clubs that were much more focused on sports activities, of which boxing was a major element. Repton club in Bethnal Green started life as a youth club but developed into the world's greatest amateur boxing club. So, too, the West Ham Boys club in Plaistow, which turned out lots of great boxers. Eton Manor in Hackney

was a tremendous multi-sports youth club that produced superb amateur boxing champions of all faiths. Further south and west in the capital, clubs such as Lynn AC and the Caius House Youth and Community Club in Camberwell and Battersea were set up in the early 1880s, and quickly developed their boxing sections. They are still successful today. Fitzroy Lodge in Lambeth has welcomed boxers of all faiths and colour since 1910.

4 *The Amateur Scene*

1 During the Nazi purge of Jews from Berlin, Max Schmeling personally saved the lives of two Jewish children by hiding them in his apartment. It was not the first time that Schmeling defied the Nazi regime. It is said that Hitler let it be known through the Reich Ministry of Sports that he was very displeased at Schmeling's relationship with Joe Jacobs, his Jewish fight promoter, and wanted it terminated, but Schmeling refused to bow even to Hitler. During the war, Schmeling was drafted into the parachute regiment. The German parachute units had gained a reputation for enduring high casualty rates. It is thought that Hitler specifically requested Schmeling's move to the paratroopers. In May 1941, he was wounded in his right knee by shrapnel during the first day of the Battle of Crete. After recovering, he was dismissed from active service after being deemed medically unfit for duty because of his injury. He later visited American POW camps in Germany and occasionally tried to help improve conditions for the prisoners.

5 *Star Quality*

1 Woolf Bendoff was a very interesting character. There appears to be very little documentation of his life and as far as his career is concerned there are only around twenty fights that have been accurately recorded. Bendoff is thought to have had

as many as 100 fights. The vast majority of his bouts were bare-knuckle matches but there are a few gloved matches that he fought towards the end of his time. His loss to Jack Scales was most certainly a gloved fight. Bendoff could have been born in America or London. In some quarters he is said to have been Jewish-American, but it seems clear that he was actually born in Spitalfields to Jewish parents around 1868. He was well travelled and he has been described as both the British and African heavyweight champion and world middleweight champion, but these fights appeared to take place in the mid-1880s in some strange venues and could never be fully ratified. He was a big, rough and ready, indeed violent man, but his boxing abilities were very limited. He lost a lot more than he won. He also lost a couple of courtroom battles. He was convicted and jailed for attempted murder in Liverpool in 1892. He served seven years. He was involved in an illegal pawnbroking operation for which he received a prison sentence. He is credited with fighting for the greatest purse ever put up under prize ring rules, although the amounts reported for this do vary. It is thought to have been in excess of £30,000, which for an 1896 fight was an astronomical sum.

2 Ted Kid Lewis fought Johnny Basham, the excellent Welshman, three times between June 1920 and October 1921 and managed to win each time. All three fights were great matches fought in the prestigious surroundings of The Royal Albert Hall and Kensington Olympia. The two met once more over eight years later in December 1929. By then, both boxers were in the twilight of their careers. This fourth and final match was not contested under the lights of any such prestigious venue. This time Johnny Basham faced his old nemesis at the Pitfield Road baths in Hoxton. Lewis won yet again via a knockout in the third round. After Johnny recovered, both men embraced each other, their mutual respect plain to see. A little later they both

left the baths by the side door, stepping into the cold London night air and into retirement together.

Ted Kid Lewis professional championship titles

June 13th 1913-1915	British and European featherweight champion (retained twice)
August 31st 1915-1916	World welterweight champion (retained 8 times)
June 25th 1917-1919	World welterweight champion (retained 8 times)
September 1st 1919	World middleweight champion
March 11th 1920	British middleweight champion
June 9th 1920	British/British Empire and European welterweight champion (retained once)
June 27th 1921	British middleweight champion (retained once)
October 14th 1921	European middleweight champion
November 17th 1921	British light heavyweight champion
June 19th 1922	British Empire middleweight champion
July 3rd 1924	British/British Empire and European welterweight champion

Lewis was inducted into the Ring Boxing Hall of Fame in 1964, the Jewish Hall of Fame in 1983 and the International Boxing Hall of Fame in 1992.

3 The topic of conversation at Harry Mizler's wedding in 1939 was his fights against Hans Drescher. Mizler fought two tough matches against the German-born Dane in late 1938, which resulted in a close win and a draw for the German. The press was predicting a third match later in the next year but with the growing war threat, this never happened.

7 *Brothers in Arms*

1 All five victims of Jack the Ripper lived or worked in the predominantly Jewish quarter of London, between Whitechapel and Bishopsgate. There were some who suggested that Jack the Ripper was an Anti-Semitic psychopath who killed women in the hope that they were Jewish. Only Katherine Eddowes, the Ripper's fourth victim, who was butchered in Mitre Square near Aldgate, may possibly have had some Jewish heritage. Eddowes was of dark complexion and had black hair and was the most Jewish looking of the women he killed. It was the fact that a bloodied piece of Eddowes' clothing was found in a nearby doorway and chalked on its wall was the words: 'The Juwes are the men that will be blamed for nothing,' that led some to believe that it was a religious hate crime. The theory has since been dismissed. In fact, Eddowes does have a connection to boxing. Eddowes' mother worked at the renowned Peacock Inn in Wolverhampton. It was the Midlands foremost 'Fighting Pub' that staged high-profile bare-knuckle boxing during the 1850s and 1860s. William Perry, the 'Tipton Slasher' and the English heavyweight champion, fought there a couple of times. Eddowes was born in Wolverhampton and her uncle, Thomas Eddowes, also boxed at the pub under the name of 'The Snob'. A Snob was a shoemaker, which was Tom's trade. Eddowes witnessed his match against Ned Wilson before she moved down to London to start her life on the streets with fatal consequences.

2 When Mosley's 1936 march through the East End was first announced, the Jewish Board of Deputies advised strongly against London Jews counter protesting. The Jewish population in 1936 was far different from that of 50 years before, and the plea fell on deaf ears. Mosley had recruited Ted Kid Lewis to help train his para-military style black shirts a couple of years earlier. A strange episode for Lewis but at that point

Mosley was preaching national unity, working class rights and individual freedom rather than anti-Jewish rhetoric. His strong anti-Semitism surfaced a little later and it was at this point that Lewis had a rather strong physical falling out with Mosley and a couple of his men. I am sure Lewis must have looked back on a couple of photos of him sharing a stage with Mosley with acute embarrassment.

3 Three months prior to the Cable Street stand-off, the Spanish Civil War started, to bring more fascism to Europe. Jews though, were about to fight back. What started in a small corner of London was the catalyst for British Jews to rally against fascism. The International Brigade was around 35,000 strong and they were from all over the world, including 5,000 Jews. It is estimated that just under 3,000 British, mostly men, enlisted in the International Brigade between 1936 and 1939, including the boxer Phil Richards (Caplan) and Harry Gross, the young communist leader. About 550 came from London and of these nearly 300 were of Jewish faith.

4 The 43 Group was formed in 1946 at the Maccabi House (sports club) in Hampstead, North London. Daniel Sonabend's book *We Fight Fascists: The 43 Group and their Forgotten Battle for Post-War Britain*, sheds more light on the movement, as does *The 43 Group: Battling with Mosley's Blackshirts*, written by Morris Beckman, a founding member of the group. The 62 Group, as the name suggests, was formed in 1962, originally as the 1962 Committee and headed by Harry Bidney. Bidney was a Soho night club manager and worked with Gerry Gable, who later founded the magazine *Searchlight,* which worked (and still works) to expose racism and anti-Semitism in society. Jo Bloom wrote the novel *Ridley Road* in 2014, the 63 Group being the backdrop, which was the basis of a later TV programme.

8 *The Journeyman*

1 Len Wickwar (11 March 1911-1 June 1980) was a boxer from Leicestershire who fought between 1928 and 1947, mostly as a lightweight. His record is both astonishing and now considered impossible to beat. He fought more genuinely recorded professional fights than any other boxer in the history of the sport. He contested 473 matches (it may have been nearer 500) and completed well over 4,000 rounds of boxing during his nineteen-year career. He never contested a senior title but became the ultimate journeyman fighter, although only two of his fights took place abroad.

10 *The Man in the Middle*

1 By 1925, Teddy Sheppard had fought eight previous fights against some very good boxers, including Jack Kid Berg, and just a few weeks before this fight Teddy had gone fifteen attritional rounds with the 'Millwall Mauler', the ultra-tough Ernie Jarvis. Teddy had lost each one. He was clearly boxing out of his depth. That day he was taking increasing punishment from the early rounds and in hindsight his physical condition was probably not what it should have been when fighting that afternoon.

11 *Entertainment Value*

1 Andrew Jephtha fought against the welterweight champion Curly Watson for what was supposed to be an English, British and Empire and European title fight. Jephtha knocked out Curly in the fourth round. The Wonderland had held a British title fight before and had also held a couple of world title fights. This result though, was disputed by the governing authorities on what was thought to be a bit of a technicality, and they only ratified the Empire title part. Jephtha's manager was still arguing the point when, four months later, Jephtha

defended his titles against Joe White and lost. The argument was dropped, so Jephtha was never recognised as a British champion.

2 Since its inception in 1929, the role of the Board has changed immeasurably. In its early years the BBBofC was concerned primarily with the procedural side of the sport such as the recognition of championships. However, within a few years it expanded its remit. It started by raising medical protection standards. This was soon followed by arbitration and disciplinary procedures, revision, upgrading and the application of the Rules and Regulations. Appointment of referees and timekeepers, the licensing of people involved in the sport and representation of the interests of British boxing internationally make up the bulk of the remainder of the board's work.

12 *Shadow Boxing*

1 Isaac Bogard appears to have become a reformed character. Bogard enlisted to fight in the First World War. 263049 Pte. I. Bogard, SW Borderers, from Stratford East (London) was awarded the Military Medal. He was gazetted in the 22 February 1918 edition. I take it that this means he was awarded it for actions in Nov/Dec 1917, possibly Cambrai with the 2nd, 10th, 11th or 12th Battalion. (*London Gazette/* National Archives). In the late 1920s he ended up working for the former head of the Flying Squad, Fred 'Nutty' Sharpe, who had become a bookmaker in Wandsworth after leaving the Met and liked to employ former villains.

13 *Blood Brothers*

1 John Herbert Douglas, originally from Clapton in London, was a very senior referee who handled high-profile matches, particularly at the NSC. His refereeing career was immense.

Between 1890 and his premature death 1927 (drowned at sea) he presided over more than 3,000 bouts. He was previously an ABA boxing champion and became a very wealthy timber importer during the late nineteenth century. His son Johnny was also an ABA champion and the Olympic middleweight boxing champion at the 1908 Olympic Games.

BIBLIOGRAPHY

General Reference
ABA: Its History (H.G.H.C) Amateur Boxing Association.
   Records (1965)
Ancestry UK
Bishopsgate Institute
BoxRec.com
Boxing News
British Newspaper archives
Brown (Eckman) family history
Centre for Jewish History (New York)
Etaples Base Camp Diaries, National Archives, WO-95-4027-5
frommonologues.com – Music Hall Lyrics Collection
Goodson family history
Jewish Chronicle archives
Jewish East End of London, photo gallery & commentary (Philip
   Walker www.jewisheastend.com)
Jewishpress.com
Lazarus family history
Lolosky family History
London and Manchester Jewish Museum
London Metropolitan archives
Museum of Docklands

National Library of Israel
New York Times
Pegasusarchive.com (The Parachute Regiment)
Royal Albert Hall archives
Spitalfields Life
The International Brigade Memorial Trust
US Library of Congress

Books

Bullman, J., Hegarty, B., Hill, N., *The Secret History of our Streets* (London: BBC Books, 2012)

Cruickshank, Dan, *Spitalfields* (London: Windmill Books, 2016)

Dee, David, *The Hefty Hebrew – Boxing and Jewish-British Identity1890-1960* (De Montfort University Press, 2012)

Deghy, Guy, *Noble and Manly: The History of the National Sporting Club* (London: Hutchinson, 1956)

Fox, Terry, *Battling Jack; You Gotta Fight Back* (Edinburgh: Mainstream publishing, 2005)

Forbes, Lady Angela, *Memories and Base Details* (London, Hutchinson, 1921)

Gale, Tony, *Up to Scratch* (London: Queen Anne Press, 1998)

Green J, *A Social History of the Jewish East End of London* (Lampeter: Edwin Mellen, 1991)

Greenman, Leon, *An Englishman in Auschwitz* (Elstree: Vallentine Mitchell, 2001)

Harding, Arthur, *East End Underworld: Chapters in the Life of Arthur Harding* (London: Routledge and Kegan Paul, 1981)

Harding, Jack, *Jack Kid Berg, The Whitechapel Windmill* (London: Robson Books, 1987)

Henning, Fred W., *Some Recollections of the Prize Ring* (London: Henning & Co publishing, 1888)

Kitchen, Paula, *Britain's Jews in the First World War* (Stroud: Amberley, 2019)

Lee, Raymond, *Premierland, Whitechapel – 1911 to 1930* (publisher unknown)

Rubenhold, Hallee, *The Five – Untold Lives of Women killed by Jack the Ripper* (London: Penguin, 2019)

Wheldon, Wynn, *The Fighting Jew: The Life and Times of Daniel Mendoza* (Stroud: Amberley Publishing, 2019)

ACKNOWLEDGEMENTS

Grateful thanks to Adam Corsini and Staff (London Jewish Museum), Alan Parson, Bess Walker, Brenda Jones, Dr Cyril Sherer, Ray Lee, and Vic Brett.

ILLUSTRATIONS CREDITS

p. 199. Pinterest

p. 203. © Alamy Images

p. 212. Unknown source

p. 221. © Alamy Images

p. 225. © Victor D Cooper Collection

p. 242. © Jewish Lives Project (London Jewish Museum)

p. 251a.© Alamy Images

p. 251b.© Alamy Images

Plate Section

1. *New York Times*
2. *Apollo* magazine (*Shot in the Dark* studio still)
3. Gustave Doré Collection
4. Pinterest
5. © Jewisheastend.com (Bess Walker)
6. Jewish Museum archives
7. © Alamy images
8. Courtesy of Docklands Museum
9. By kind permission of London Jewish Museum
10. Unknown source
11. Pinterest (Cable Street UK)
12. Lolosky family history
13. Unknown source
14. Author's collection
15. © National Portrait Gallery
16. BBC Archives (Genome project)
17. *The Glasgow Herald*
18. Wikicommons
19. Wikicommons
20. By kind permission of Ray Lee (Premierland)
21. Royal Albert Hall Archives
22. By kind permission Roman Road magazine
23. Independent R's fanzine

24. Unknown source
25. © Alamy Images
26. © Alamy Images
27. © Alamy Images
28. © Alamy Images
29. © Alamy Images
30. © Wellcome Collection (Progress Studio)
31. © Jewisheastend.com (Bess Walker)
32. Wikicommons

INDEX